THE

GENESIS

QUESTION

SCIENTIFIC ADVANCES
AND THE ACCURACY OF GENESIS

SECOND EXPANDED EDITION

HUGH ROSS

NAVPRESS®

BRINGING TRUTH TO LIFE

OUR GUARANTEE TO YOU

We believe so strongly in the message of our books that we are making this quality guarantee to you. If for any reason you are disappointed with the content of this book, return the title page to us with your name and address and we will refund to you the list price of the book. To help us serve you better, please briefly describe why you were disappointed. Mail your refund request to: NavPress, P.O. Box 35002, Colorado Springs, CO 80935.

The Navigators is an international Christian organization. Our mission is to reach, disciple, and equip people to know Christ and to make Him known through successive generations. We envision multitudes of diverse people in the United States and every other nation who have a passionate love for Christ, live a lifestyle of sharing Christ's love, and multiply spiritual laborers among those without Christ.

NavPress is the publishing ministry of The Navigators. NavPress publications help believers learn biblical truth and apply what they learn to their lives and ministries. Our mission is to stimulate spiritual formation among our readers.

Library of Congress Catalog Card Number: 2001030627
ISBN 1-57683-230-9

Cover photo by D2 Designworks

Some of the anecdotal illustrations in this book are true and are included with the permission of the persons involved. All other illustrations are composites of real situations, and any resemblance to people living or dead is coincidental.

Unless otherwise identified, all Scripture quotations in this publication are taken from the *HOLY BIBLE: NEW INTERNATIONAL VERSION* ® (NIV®). Copyright ©1973, 1978, 1984 by International Bible Society. Used by permission of Zondervan Publishing House. All rights reserved. Another version used is the *King James Version* (KJV).

Ross, Hugh (Hugh Norman), 1945-
  The Genesis question : scientific advances and the accuracy of Genesis / Hugh Ross.—
2nd expanded ed.
    p. cm.
  Includes bibliographical references and index.
  ISBN 1-57683-230-9 (pbk.)
  1. Bible. O.T. Genesis I–XI—Criticism, interpretation, etc. 2. Bible. O.T. Genesis
I–XI—Evidences, authority, etc. 3. Bible and science. I Title.
  BS1235.2 .R68 2001
222'.1106—dc21   2001030627

Printed in the United States of America

3 4 5 6 7 8 9 10 11 12 13 14 15 / 09 08 07 06 05 04

FOR A FREE CATALOG OF NAVPRESS BOOKS & BIBLE STUDIES,
CALL 1-800-366-7788 (USA) or 1-416-499-4615 (CANADA)

CONTENTS

Preface to the Second Edition

Since the publication of *The Genesis Question,* first edition, scientists have made many more discoveries substantially strengthening the evidence for the accuracy of the first eleven chapters of Genesis. This new edition describes these new discoveries, for example the discovery and dating of early plant species, fossils indicating the special creation of whales, the recovery of mitochondrial DNA from two more Neandertal skeletons, biochemical pathways for explaining long pre-Flood life spans, and dates and locations for the origin of wheat and goat domestication. Also included are new discoveries that add to the evidence for a theistic explanation for life's origin and for supernatural speciation. In response to readers' requests, several more biblical evidences for the location and conditions of Eden and for a universal local Flood have been included.

Several dozen suggestions offered by readers of the first edition were incorporated to make my theological points clearer and more specific and to make the text more understandable for lay readers. My prayer is that readers will see in this expanded edition even more of God's glory, power, and wisdom in His revelation of cosmic and human history.

ACKNOWLEDGMENTS

I began working on this book twenty-five years ago, before the publication of any of my other books. It has special significance to me because my investigation of the Bible and of the possibility that God had something to do with it started in Genesis. The opening verse grabbed my attention and never let go. It pulled me to the next and the next and the next, and I'm still studying, still amazed at the precision with which the Bible anticipates scientific discovery.

When I live with a book in my head, Kathy, my wife, lives with that book too. So I'd like to express my thanks to her first. She helped me think it through, organize it, and choose its words.

Janet Kobobel Grant, Kenneth Samples, and other members of the publications team at Reasons To Believe, put in many hours reading, checking, and evaluating the manuscript. I owe much to their research and suggestions. Bob Stuart, Greg Rice, and Steve Sarigianis helped with the figures. Marj Harman, a Reasons To Believe volunteer apologist, helped me find some elusive references. Thanks to Tani Trost and Sandra Frantz for their work in proofreading the text and in updating the indexes.

My review team, including research scientists Sam Conner and David Rogstad, and theologians Craig Keener, Mick Ukleja, and John Rea, contributed significantly to the book's academic integrity. They, Tim Boyle and editor Eric Stanford, also suggested rewordings to make the book clearer and more understandable.

Finally, I would like to express my thanks to the NavPress team. Their support and encouragement through two years of the writing, editorial, and marketing process went far beyond the call of duty. I enjoy working with a publishing enterprise that puts ministry first.

CHAPTER ONE

A PERSONAL JOURNEY

The Holy Bible, the best-selling book of all time worldwide, makes a compelling claim for itself: divine inspiration.[1] Given the high respect this book has been accorded over many centuries, this claim would seem dangerous to ignore. Yet the Bible is ignored more and more in popular culture, which has moved on to more "sophisticated" conceptions of spirituality and revelation.

The justification I hear more often than any other for leaving the Bible behind is that "everyone knows" it is antiquated and full of scientific nonsense, if not blatant contradictions. Amazingly, when I ask people to cite examples, many cannot bring to mind even one. Apparently, they base their opinion on hearsay and reflect a widespread misconception.

Among those who do answer my question, one Bible portion draws more vigorous attack than all others combined: the first few chapters of Genesis. That attack opens a tremendous door of opportunity for me — and for every other believer who knows even a little about the scientific discoveries of the past few decades. Instead of offering an excuse for unbelief and rejection, these chapters offer some of the most persuasive proofs ever assembled for the supernatural authorship and authority of the Bible.

The language of these chapters is amazingly clear and specific. The words repeatedly associate spiritual events with physical events, and physical events are, in a word, testable.

I would say they literally beg to be tested. However, as if that implied invitation to test weren't enough, the apostle Paul exhorted his readers to "test everything,"[2] to see what holds water and what does not, and to keep only what does. In the case of Genesis 1–11, the content is largely scientific (as well as historical and spiritual, of course), and so some of the appropriate tests will come from the relevant disciplines of science.

Scientific Testing

Genesis 1–11 speaks of the history of the universe, Earth, life on Earth, and of humanity's origin and early development. With the help of many remarkable advances in astronomy, physics, geophysics, chemistry, paleontology, biochemistry, and anthropology, the words of the first eleven chapters can be subjected, point by point, to rigorous investigation. They can be verified or refuted with greater precision and to a greater depth than previous generations might have imagined possible.

Of course, not all biblical miracles can be subjected to scientific testing. But those that cannot be tested are not automatically invalidated. Rather, if the Genesis 1–11 miracles can be validated, they indicate the reality and availability of the power and the love attested to by these nontestable miracles: the virgin's pregnancy, Lazarus's resurrection, and the water's transformation into wine, for example. While Mary, Lazarus, and the wine drunk at the wedding feast are not available for scientific analysis, the universe, Earth, Earth's fossils, and living creatures certainly are, and they can be subjected to the degree of scientific scrutiny needed to confirm or deny the creation, Flood, and post-Flood events reported in Genesis 1–2 and 6–11.

My Own Discovery

The scientific content of Genesis 1–11 holds special significance for me because it revolutionized my thinking and, thus, changed my life's direction.[3-4] Until I reached my late teens, my singular passion was science, astronomy in particular. My life's purpose was to learn more about the universe; nothing beyond that really interested me. By the time I turned sixteen, I had studied enough cosmology to become convinced that of all the origins models ever proposed, the big-bang model best fit the observational data. Soon after my sixteenth birthday, the implications of that model began to dawn on me.

Without consciously doing so, I took a huge philosophical and spiritual step—actually, a series of steps. I understood that the big bang meant an expanding, "exploding" universe. I agreed with Einstein that an exploding universe can be traced back to an explosion, a beginning. If the universe had a beginning, it must have a Beginner. The big-bang theory implied that a Creator exists. That much seemed clear, but the rest of the picture seemed less clear. Who was this Creator, or God? What was God like? Had God communicated to humanity through some means other than the creation itself?

Millions of people through the ages have lived and died by their "holy books." But if all the holy books came from the same source and said pretty much the same thing, as my teachers suggested, why did the followers of each book criticize, condemn, and even kill the followers of the others? I began to suspect that all religions were humanly crafted fronts for people's psychological desire to dominate others.

In the physics of the universe I saw harmony and consistency, perfection, freedom from contradiction, a pervading beauty, and an elegance of design. If God had spoken to humanity through a book or books, I reasoned, God's communication would manifest the same qualities as did the cosmos He created. Science had convinced me that the God of the universe was neither capricious nor careless. People, on the other hand, even the most "objective" scientists I had met or read, were prone to at least some weaknesses and inconsistency and to making some errors, particularly the kind of "errors" arising from limited knowledge and understanding. And, when it came to predicting the future, human imperfection and imprecision seemed abundantly (and forgivably) obvious.

On these premises I began—and ended—my investigation of the world's sacred writings. While I found words of interest and beauty and truth in each one, each reflected the limited (now known to be erroneous) scientific knowledge of its time and place—each one except one: the Bible. This particular book stood apart, and dramatically so.

From the first page I could see distinctions. The quantity and detail of scientific content far exceeded what I found in the other books. To my surprise, the scientific method was as clearly evident in Genesis 1 as it is in modern research. Most impressive of all, the four initial conditions and the sequence of major creation events—not just one or two, but more than a dozen—all matched the established scientific record. As I pondered how this accuracy could have been achieved, even if the book were written much more recently than scholars estimated, I calculated the odds that the writer could have guessed the initial conditions and correctly sequenced the events (ignoring for the moment the questions about how the writer could have known what they were), and I discovered that the odds are utterly remote. Only one conclusion made sense to me, the conclusion that the Creator of the universe had something to do with the words of Genesis 1.

When I turned the page, I discovered more of the same documentary-type communication. By the time I came to the Flood chapters, I realized I could not dismiss this book easily, at least not yet. I decided to spend an hour a day (or more), in addition to my homework time, studying the Bible until I reached the end or found a provable error.

Eighteen months later I arrived in Revelation 22. During those months I had read every page and failed to discover anything I could honestly label an error or contradiction. Some parts I had trouble understanding, but that didn't bother me. I understood enough, just as I understood enough of physics and astronomy to trust what I was learning in my university courses. I was so astonished by the Bible's consistent and frequent prediction of future scientific discoveries that I decided to attempt a probability calculation. My scratch paper scribbles showed me the numbers, based on conservative estimates for a small sampling of biblical predictions: the Bible matched the best-established laws of physics in its degree of trustworthiness. I knew how implicitly I trusted the laws of physics for my survival. How could I not trust this book's message and the One who sent it with such supernatural precision through human messengers?

With some delays and more than a little wrestling with personal pride, I did make a transfer of trust, inviting God, the Creator of the vast cosmos, to be my God, the Master of my destiny, through Jesus Christ, His Son.[4]

CHAPTER TWO

REASONS FOR RESISTANCE

While scientific developments of the nineteenth century seemed to nearly smother faith in God, advances of the twentieth century breathed new vitality into that faith. Evidences of a cosmic beginning in the finite past (as in thirteen to seventeen billion years ago, a very recent beginning in comparison with the eternal universe of prior naturalistic science) accumulated, and the standard naturalistic origin-of-life model, which relied on a nearly infinitely old cosmos, lost its footing. Meanwhile, as researchers for the first time measured the far reaches of the solar system, the Milky Way, and the cosmos, they uncovered a growing list of "designed-for-life" indicators. They found a number of physical characteristics that had to be very narrowly defined for any kind of life to possibly exist. These discoveries spawned a new scientific proposition: the anthropic principle, the observation that all the physical features of the universe, including the characteristics of the solar system, are "just right" to suit the needs of life, specifically human life.[1-4]

Science historian Frederick Burnham commented that for scientists belief in God is more "respectable" today than at any time in the last hundred years.[5] At the same time, however, our society has been called "post-Christian." Belief in the Bible as God's Word and in the deity of Jesus Christ seems less "respectable," certainly in academic circles.

Case Closed?

Reasons for resistance to Christianity abound. Intellectual barriers receive the most frequent mention. They are the most socially acceptable ones, though often they serve as a smoke screen to hide the deeper ones: pride, bitterness, lust, fear, and so on.

As I speak to university audiences and to business and professional people across North America, and as I hear from survey teams taking the spiritual pulse of urban and suburban neighborhoods, I find that most of these intellectual barriers (or excuses for dismissing Christianity) come from misconceptions about Genesis 1–11. Time and again I hear this question, expressed or implied: "Why should I give serious attention to the message of a book that contradicts, right from the start, the established facts of science?"

The supposed contradictions have been widely popularized by such well-known personalities as Isaac Asimov and Steve Allen. Asimov, author of today's best-selling commentary on the Bible,[6] says Genesis 1 teaches that the sun, moon, and stars were created after light, after plants, and after the water cycle.[7] He interprets Genesis 2 as more nonsense, placing the creation of plants and animals between the creation of man and the creation of woman. Thus, he justifies his labeling of Genesis 1 and 2 as "folktales."[8] Steve Allen, in his popular critique of the Bible, ridicules the Flood account, saying that if Earth became "one giant ball of water," rain must have come down at the rate of thirteen feet per hour.[9] He goes on to "show" that the Bible gives contradictory figures for the duration of the Flood.[10] He concludes that "acceptance of it [the Genesis Flood] on its own terms is simply impossible."[11] Given the widespread appeal of these celebrities *and* given people's ignorance of the Bible and of exegetical rules, an open-minded perspective may be hard to come by.

This case-closed attitude has become increasingly widespread since the Age of Enlightenment (mid-eighteenth to late nineteenth centuries). During that era and since, science surged forward, challenging virtually every cherished notion in its path, including long-unquestioned biblical interpretations. Many theologians and Bible scholars reacted defensively. When faced with supposed external and internal inconsistencies, they simply backed away from the biblical texts—or from science—rather than launch a painstaking investigation of the scientific "facts" and of the biblical statements.

In this century we see how wide and deep the split has grown: liberal Christians and nonChristians, who for the most part embrace scientific discovery, view Genesis 1–11 as a collection of legends, at best, or of unreliable, contradictory, even laughable tales, at worst. Within that part of the church which did not give up on the reliability and integrity of Genesis, two groups emerged.

The first upheld the findings of modern science but viewed Genesis as devoid of scientific content and intent. The second declared that the "scientific unreliability" of Genesis is simply a mirage produced by unreliable, ever-changing science.

German theologian Franz Delitzsch described the schism ninety-five years ago, and few would dispute the relevance of his words to this day:

> All attempts to harmonize our biblical story of the creation
> of the world with the results of natural science have been
> useless and must always be so.[12]

Fundamentalist Christians, adhering to what is termed creation science, loudly promote the scientific accuracy of the Bible, but they sift or reinterpret science through the tiny mesh of their ideological filter. Not much real science gets through. Whether they admit it openly (as I have heard many do) or not, most, if not all, of their leaders agree with Delitzsch: "secular" science and the book of Genesis clash irreconcilably.

Entrenchment of this schism has been ensured by various complex sociocultural developments. My abbreviated list includes four: biblical illiteracy, the pressure to make "progress," too much Bible science, and the isolation of specialization.

Bible Illiteracy

Most Americans and other Westerners claim to have read all or part of the Bible. However, when asked to identify even four books of the Bible or four of Jesus' disciples or four of the Ten Commandments, fewer than half even attempt to respond and fewer than one in ten respond correctly. People seem reluctant to admit to anyone, even themselves, their ignorance of the Bible.

Ironically, biblical illiteracy is most pronounced among the best educated, even among those who publicly comment on the Bible. More than once on university campuses in America and abroad, I have heard professors assert before scholarly audiences that the Bible teaches a flat Earth geocentrism (placing the Earth at the center of our solar system or the universe), male superiority, or the acceptability of genocide. These are but a few of the bizarre claims revealing what can only be a "hearsay" or eisegetical response to the text.

Pressure to Make "Progress"

Theology once held sway as the "mother of all the sciences," a title that would seem incongruous to most people alive today. While the natural sciences continue to explore new worlds both on and beyond our planet, no additions have been made to the Canon, the sixty-six books of the Bible, since the first century A.D.

Yet in academic environments, theology faculty and graduate students typically face the same "publish or perish" pressure as do the faculty and researchers in fields where the database is doubling every few years. While it makes sense for scientists to be iconoclasts, to break new ground, making significant revisions or additions to old interpretations of the natural realm based on an abundance of new information, the same does not necessarily hold for other scholars, such as logicians, historians, theologians, and Bible scholars. Bible scholars must make a difficult choice: invest years working to increase the database by whatever amount may be possible through painstaking historical or linguistic research, or break new ground by proposing new perspectives, new interpretations.

Theologians and Bible scholars may rightfully argue in a few cases that previous generations of scholars were misinformed or naive in their interpretations of Scripture. The more popular approach these days, however, is to argue that the Bible writers themselves were misinformed and naive.

Too Much Bible Science

That so many Christians today believe the Bible is largely devoid of scientific content is, at least in part, a reaction to the last two hundred years of dialogue between science and theology in which Christian theology appears to have been bested repeatedly by secular science. The Bible, unlike any other book, is intended to be read and understood by people living in eras spanning at least 3,500 years. This places some serious constraints on the quantity and kind of science it can contain.

For the Bible to adopt the scientific paradigms or language of any age would compromise the ability of the text to speak to earlier or later generations. But, because the Bible does have the capacity to communicate to all generations of humanity, many Bible interpreters are tempted to read into the text far too much of the science of their time. For example, I have received more than ten unsolicited manuscripts from individuals who are convinced that Genesis 1, properly understood, gives a detailed exposition of the origin and structure of various families of fundamental particles even though no word in the text even hints of particles.

The Isolation of Specialization

The word *university* denotes an institution dedicated to uniting (as in integrating) knowledge from all disciplines of scholarship. How far we have strayed from that original purpose! Integration still receives more lip service than funding. The pressure to specialize that has propelled us far into new frontiers of knowledge also has left us at loose ends. The separation is great within the sciences, the arts, and the humanities, and even greater between one area and another.

Perhaps no gap is wider than the one dividing scientists from theologians. The two groups seem to have little if any awareness that their studies actually overlap. Both groups seem to despise any suggestion that their work intersects. The United States National Academy of Sciences recently issued the following statement:

> Religion and science are separate and mutually exclusive realms of human thought whose presentation in the same context leads to misunderstanding of both scientific theory and religious belief.[13]

For their part, most theologians (since the trial of Galileo) have preferred isolation, hiding behind such oft-repeated comments as this: The intention of the Bible is to teach us how to go to heaven, not how the heavens go.[14-15]

Many, perhaps most, scientists regard religion as "emotional nonsense." They react to attempts at integration as a "throwback to a prescientific model of reality."[16] Michael Ruse, well-known zoologist and philosopher of science, emphatically asserts this view.[17]

Do you hear what I hear? This condescending, mocking attitude among some well respected scientists, and anticipated by nonscientists even when it does not exist, widens the chasm and ensures the isolation.

Nonintellectual Obstacles

As I mentioned earlier, intellectual questions about Genesis are understandable, even expected. If they are genuine, the person who raises them will show a willingness to listen and explore possible answers.

However, not everyone who raises questions really wants a response. Some seem more interested in arguing. Some just walk away. Why?

How a person interprets the first eleven chapters of Genesis may be determined by how that person responds to some other part of the Bible. For example, if a person has been badly hurt or mistreated by someone bearing the "Christian" or "biblical" label, objectivity probably has been lost. If a person objects to biblical teachings (rightly or wrongly interpreted) on moral issues, objectivity probably has been lost.

Other fears come from misunderstanding the biblical definition of faith. The prevailing view exalts "blind" faith and rejects the principle that facts are the crucial foundation for meaningful faith. The misapplied mandate to "walk by faith, not by sight"[18] frequently causes problems. Perhaps a deeper fear, more difficult to express, is that connecting faith to scientific facts subordinates the Bible to human endeavors or places Scripture at risk of contradiction by new discoveries that could overturn previously developed interpretations.

Herein lies a paradox. People who seem most concerned with defending biblical inerrancy may be the most resistant to any information, not derived from the Bible, that might help illuminate its meaning. Logically, taking Scripture seriously means being passionately concerned about interpreting it correctly and thus welcoming any evidence that exposes erroneous understandings of the biblical text.[19] Unfortunately, many zealous Bible students and teachers confuse their favorite interpretations of the Bible with the Bible itself.

Removing the Mistrust

Clearly, many hindrances stand in the way of any study or discussion of the scientific and spiritual content of Genesis 1–11. By identifying some of the obstacles at the outset, I hope to help readers acknowledge them and make the choice to suspend them, at least for as much time as it takes to read the chapters that follow. For in these chapters I present what I have found in the latest scientific research to eliminate obstacles altogether.

Let's open the Book!

CHAPTER THREE

CREATION OF THE COSMOS

"In the beginning God created the heavens and the earth" (Genesis 1:1). With this simple yet profound declaration, the biblical account of God's interaction with the human race begins. Hundreds, perhaps thousands, of pages of commentary have been devoted to this one statement alone.[1] Its explosive impact bursts upon the reader like the creative blast we modern physicists have come to call the "big bang."

The Beginning
The assertion of a *beginning* immediately catches our attention. For centuries the philosophical pendulum has swung back and forth on the questions of the eternality of matter, energy, space, and time. Immanuel Kant was neither the first nor the last but perhaps the most convincing proponent of an infinitely old universe model.[2] Later, his concept donned scientific garb as the "steady state" model.[3-5] Later still, scientists revived the Hindu doctrine of a universe that oscillates for infinite time through cycles of birth, death, and rebirth.[6-7] The Bible says in unequivocal terms that the "heavens and the earth" began, that they exist for finite time only,[8] and that God exists and acts inside, outside, and before the universe's space-and-time boundaries.[9] He alone is everywhere present and always existing.

The Hebrew verb for "created" is *bara*. This verb, or predicate, appears in the Bible with only one subject: God. Its usage suggests a kind of creating that only God, and no one else, can do. Hebrew linguists define it as "bringing into existence something new, something that did not exist before."[10] While it can refer to creation *ex nihilo* (that is, out of nothing), its usage is less restrictive.

(See discussion of the five different kinds of nothing, page 62.) Its emphasis rests on the newness, or uniqueness, of what has been brought forth. Hebrews 11:3 offers this amplification: the universe we can see, detect, and measure was made from that which we cannot see, detect, or measure.

The Heavens and the Earth

Hebrew differs significantly from English in many respects, including the size of its vocabulary. While English words number in the millions, biblical Hebrew encompasses only slightly more than three thousand words.[11] To understand the meaning of *shamayim* and *'erets* ("heavens" and "earth") requires more than knowing the definition of each term. *'Erets* has six different meanings: the soil; the territory or land possessed by an individual, family, tribe, or nation; a city state; the territories of all peoples and nations; the underworld; or all the land and water, as well as the foundations that support them (what we now know as the planet Earth).[12] *Shamayim*, a plural form (hence, "heavens"), has three meanings: the part of Earth's atmosphere where rain clouds form, that is, the troposphere; the abode of the stars and galaxies; and the spirit realm from which God rules.[13] (New Testament writers and both ancient and modern rabbis sometimes used the ordinals "first," "second," and "third" to identify which of these "heavens" they meant.)[14]

Hashamayim we ha'erets ("heavens" plural and "earth" singular with the definite articles and the conjunction) carries a distinct meaning, just as the English words "under" and "statement" or "dragon" and "fly" put together as compound nouns take on specific meanings. *Hashamayim we ha'erets* consistently refers to the totality of the physical universe: all of the matter and energy and whatever else it contains.[15-16] All of the stars, galaxies, planets, dust, gas, fundamental particles, background radiation, black holes, physical space-time dimensions, and voids of the universe—however mysterious to the ancient writer—would be included in this term.

According to Genesis 1:1, the entire universe came into existence, brand new, a finite time ago, by the creative action of God. This statement reverberates throughout the pages of Scripture.[17] No other "holy book" makes such a claim on its own. The concept appears elsewhere only in those books that borrow from the Bible, such as the Koran and the Mormon writings.

The importance of this unique doctrine cannot be overstated. Not only does it set biblical revelation apart from other so-called revelation, but it provides evidence for the supernatural accuracy of Genesis.

New scientific support for a hot big-bang creation event, for the validity of the space-time theorem of general relativity, and for ten-dimensional string theory verifies the Bible's claim for a beginning. In the final decade of the twentieth century, astronomers and physicists have established that all of the matter and energy in the universe, and all of the space-time dimensions within which the matter and energy are distributed, had a beginning in finite time,[18-19] just as the Bible declares.

A Crucial Shift

The frame of reference, or point of view, for the creation account suddenly shifts in Genesis 1:2, from the heavenlies that make up the entire physical universe to the surface of planet Earth. For whatever reasons, perhaps because it comes so abruptly, most readers—even scholarly commentators—miss the shift. I am convinced that my absorption in science prepared me to see it. In fact, I was struck with amazement that this ancient document actually is structured like a modern research report.

The same steps scientists use to analyze and interpret natural phenomena appeared on that first page of the Bible. At the time I was unaware, as many people still are, that the step-by-step process we now know as the scientific method owes its formulation to men and women well versed in the Scriptures. (See Appendix A: Biblical Origins of the Scientific Method.) They recognized a pattern in Bible texts describing physical sequences of events. In each case the passage identifies the reference frame (or viewpoint) from which events are described, the initial conditions, a chronology, a statement of final conditions, and some conclusions about what transpired. The Bible repeatedly exhorts readers to consider such contextual elements as essential to correct interpretation[20] and warns us against the dangers of overlooking them.[21]

The Scientific Method

Although the wording and number of steps delineated may vary slightly from one introductory science text to another, the basic components of the scientific method include these seven:

1. Identify the frame(s) of reference or point(s) of view.
2. Determine the initial conditions.
3. Perform an experiment or observe the phenomenon, noting what takes place when, where, and in what order.
4. Note the final conditions.
5. Form a hypothesis about the how and the why of the phenomenon.
6. Test the hypothesis with further experiments or observations.
7. Revise the hypothesis accordingly.

These steps apply just as strategically to biblical interpretation as they do to the study of natural phenomena. They do not guarantee objectivity and accuracy, but they certainly help minimize the effects of oversight, personal bias, and presuppositions. However, we must at all times remember that we remain limited in our knowledge and understanding, so our interpretations will continually fall short of perfection. Thus, we must always be willing to adjust and fine-tune. Conclusions can never become rigidly fixed.

For this reason the scientific method is best practiced repetitively. After completing steps one through seven, we must be prepared to take step eight, which is to go back to step one and see whether, in light of steps two through seven, we need to change or adjust our identification of the frame(s) of reference. Step nine would be to see if, based on steps three through eight, changes or adjustments in our determination of the initial conditions are in order. Steps ten, eleven, twelve, and so on, would proceed in a similar manner.

The success of modern Western science may be attributed, in large measure, to the rigorous application of the scientific method. It keeps us moving closer and closer to the correct, complete understanding about nature. If we were to apply it just as rigorously to biblical interpretation, it would have the same effect. It would move us closer and closer to "rightly dividing the word of truth," to unity rather than conflict in establishing sound doctrine. In the case of the Genesis creation and Flood accounts, applying the scientific method—derived substantially from these very portions of Scripture—offers our only hope for consistent interpretation, that is, interpretation free of both internal and external contradiction.

From the Heavens to Earth's Surface

Notice the shift of perspective in Genesis 1:2:

> Now the earth was formless and empty, darkness was over the surface of the deep, and the Spirit of God was hovering over the waters.

The observer's vantage point is clearly stated: "the surface of the deep . . . over the waters." Yet the vast majority of Genesis commentaries mistakenly proceed as if it were still high in the heavens somewhere in the starry realm above Earth. This one oversight accounts for more misunderstanding, more attacks on the credibility of Genesis, than all other interpretive errors combined. The problem glares from the page at anyone slightly aware of how nature works. If the storyteller's viewpoint lies in the starry realm above, plants (created on Day Three) appear before the sun even exists (Day Four).

Initial Conditions

One of Earth's initial conditions is surface darkness. The first creation day tells us that the darkness was pervasive. A look ahead to the third creation day indicates that the waters initially covered the entire surface of the planet. The psalmist certainly picked up the latter point (see Psalm 104:6):

> You [God] covered it [the earth] with the deep as with a garment; the waters stood above the mountains.

No continents rose above the water, and the whole of Earth's watery surface remained in darkness. No light reached through.

Water is one of the most abundant molecules in the universe, so in this sense the watery nature of Earth is no surprise. What is exceptional, however, is the vast quantity of permanent surface liquid water. As we shall soon see, unless the physics and chemistry of Earth's surface is very carefully fine-tuned, the kinds, quantity, and distribution of water needed for diverse life will not be available.

Genesis 1:2 mentions two more initial conditions, *tohu wabohu*, translated "formless and empty," "without form and void," or "unformed and unfilled." Given that the creation account focuses centrally on God's preparing Earth for life and filling Earth with life, the reference to "unformed" for life and "empty" of life makes perfect sense. Context holds the key to interpretation of these words.

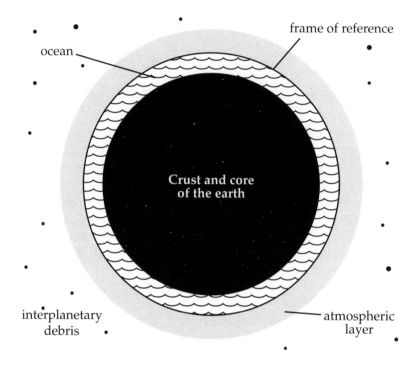

Figure 3.1: The Frame of Reference for Genesis 1:3-31
The events of the six Genesis creation days are described from the point of view of the surface of the ocean, underneath the cloud layer, as the second verse of Genesis 1 clearly states.

A Gap?

Some scholars interpret the *tohu wabohu* of verse 2 as implying a huge time gap in creation.[22-23] They translate the Hebrew verb *haya* in the first part of the verse as "became" instead of "was." Thus, they imply that Earth did not *begin* formless and empty. It *became* formless and empty.

One rationale for this translation arises from the observation that *tohu wabohu* usually carries a negative or pejorative connotation elsewhere in the Bible. A second and perhaps more compelling rationale comes from the desire to reconcile the voluminous scientific evidence for Earth's antiquity with the modern interpretation of the six creation days as six consecutive twenty-four-hour periods. As noted in chapter eight, literal definitions of the Hebrew word for day, *yôm*, would permit either six roughly twelve-hour periods, six twenty-four-hour periods, or six long time periods or ages for the creation days of Genesis 1.

The "gap theory" proposes that the beautiful universe and Earth God created "in the beginning" somehow became ruined (the most popular interpretations blame Satan and the rebel angels, or demons) and was later repaired by God as described in the six-day account. According to this theory, astronomers, geophysicists, paleontologists, and anthropologists are measuring the ancient, ruined creation, whereas the Bible addresses the recent, repaired creation.

This theory, popularized by C. I. Scofield's study Bible published at the beginning of the twentieth century,[24] still holds sway among some Bible interpreters.[25] However, it falters on several significant points, both biblical and scientific:

1. The Bible teaches that God alone, not Satan or any other created being, has the power to create and to destroy what God creates.[26]
2. Astronomers, physicists, and geologists have established that the physical laws governing the heavens and the Earth have not changed since the universe was created about 15.5 billion years ago.[27-28]
3. Genesis 1–3 makes no indication of any change in the physical laws. Thermodynamics, electromagnetism, and gravity, for example, are implied throughout.[29]
4. The Hebrew verb *haya*, used in the beginning of Genesis 1:2, is not followed by the Hebrew preposition *la*. Only the combination of *haya* + *la* would render the translation "to become." An example of this combination is found in Genesis 2:7, "Man became a living being."
5. The phrase *tohu wabohu* appears in only two other passages of Scripture: Isaiah 34:11 and Jeremiah 4:23. In both instances the context points to future actions by sinful humans. No compelling reason exists to put a pejorative spin on *tohu wabohu* in all contexts.[30]
6. Choosing six twenty-four-hour days as the "correct" literal interpretation for the Genesis creation days, as opposed to six long time periods, places dozens of Bible passages in contradiction with one another.[31]

7. The gap theory's resolution of the major contradictions between the scientific record and the twenty-four-hour-creation-days interpretation is one of silence only. According to this theory, the Bible bears no testimony to natural history, and the record of nature bears no testimony to biblical history. Thus, it makes a mockery of those Scripture passages commanding us to "test everything" and to look to the creation for evidence of God's existence and character.[32]

Additional serious flaws with the gap theory are discussed at length by the theologian and philosopher of science Bernard Ramm in his book *The Christian View of Science and Scripture*.[33]

Initial Conditions Confirmed

We don't need the gap theory to explain the "formless and empty" state of early Earth. Science confirms that indeed those terms well describe what Earth was like in its earliest years. And some of the evidence for this comes from observations of how other planets are being formed.

Technological advances in the late 1970s gave astronomers their first opportunity to observe the "disks" around young stellar objects (YSOs). More than one hundred YSOs have been studied thus far, and each one is surrounded by an extensive shell of gas and dust.[34] This discovery proves consistent with new theoretical studies demonstrating that young bachelor stars (stars that are without nearby partner stars and that were formed later than ten billion years after the cosmic creation event) should be surrounded by "circumstellar disks," or flattened shells of gas and dust debris.[35-36] These and other theoretical studies and new observations show that a large fraction of these disks eventually will condense into planetary systems.[37-43] Indeed, such planetary systems are being discovered at a rapid rate. Since the beginning of 1994, when researchers first acquired the means to detect such systems beyond our solar system, more than ten have been discovered.[44-46]

The theory and observations both confirm that all planets start with opaque atmospheres. Thick layers of such gases as hydrogen, helium, methane, and ammonia surround them. (Giant, cold planets, such as Jupiter and Saturn, perpetually retain their primordial, opaque atmospheres.) This gas cloud, combined with a dense shroud of interplanetary dust and debris, guarantees that no sunlight (or starlight) can reach the surface of a primordial planet such as early Earth.

Land masses, or islands and continents, arise gradually as a result of vulcanism (volcanic activity) and plate tectonics (movement of large crustal sections relative to one another). Plate tectonics and vulcanism wrinkle Earth's surface, and erosion smooths it. Neither the wrinkling nor the smoothing activity remains constant. Vulcanism and plate tectonics are driven primarily by heat release (from the decay of radioisotopes in Earth's crust), which has decreased fivefold since Earth began.[47] The erosion rate changes as the land masses increase and Earth's rotation rate decreases (rotation has slowed as a consequence of tidal interactions between the earth and the sun and the moon by a factor of about three during the past four billion years).[48-49]

As a net result, tectonics and vulcanism superseded erosion until continental land masses rose above the ocean to cover about 30 percent of Earth's surface. Since then, the smoothing forces have roughly balanced the wrinkling forces. Research has confirmed both theoretically and observationally (via studies of Earth's oldest rocks) that indeed water initially covered all of Earth's crust.[49-51]

The "formless" and "empty" conditions of Earth would be expected, given the initial opaque atmosphere and interplanetary debris. Without light, photosynthesis could not occur. The large pieces of interplanetary debris crashing onto Earth's surface at that time would generate catastrophes no life could survive. We can easily understand why no evidence of life on Earth dates earlier than four billion years ago.[52-53]

The description of these conditions dramatically—and accurately—sets the stage for the chronology of divinely engineered transformation and creation events that follows in Genesis 1:3-27, the "days" of creation.

CHAPTER FOUR

CREATION EVENTS: DAYS ONE AND TWO

G enesis 1:2 gives a hint, at least, that God's work of creating life on Earth may have begun before the first events recorded in the following six days of creation. The last clause of that verse tells us that "the Spirit of God was hovering over the waters." The Hebrew word for "hovering" is *rahap*.[1] It appears only one other time in the Bible, in Deuteronomy 32:11. In that passage it refers to a female eagle that is stirring up her nest and "hovering over her young." The image of the eagle's activity has led some linguists to infer that the Spirit's "hovering" over the waters refers to life's origination in Earth's ocean—even before light for photosynthesis shone through.[2] This interpretation may be valid, but the basis for drawing a firm conclusion seems insufficient.

Earth's geology testifies that marine life did indeed arise before all other life-forms. The oldest fossils found to date show us unicellular, marine-like organisms in clearly identified marine sediments.[3] Whether or not Earth's first life-forms depended on photosynthesis, researchers cannot yet say with certainty. The fossil record extends back only 3.5 billion years,[3] and the most ancient fossils do appear to represent life that relies on photosynthesis. However, carbon-13 to carbon-12 ratios in ancient apatite grains indicate that life dates back as far as 3.86 billion years.[4-5] Atmospheric models based on the quantities of oxides in ancient rocks and the analysis of photo-dissociation of water vapor (sunlight decomposing water vapor into hydrogen and oxygen gases) demonstrate that oxygen sufficient for photosynthesis first appeared between 4.1 and 4 billion years ago.[6] The existence of life-forms today that can survive without light, such as those found in and around deep ocean vents, provides at least some possible support for the notion that Earth's first life could have been nonphotosynthetic.

Information Gaps

Genesis 1 reports only a handful of creation events. These dozen or so "miracles," or divine interventions, by no means tell the whole creation story. God gives us just the briefest highlights of His creative activity on Earth. Elihu said in his discourse with Job that God's creative works are beyond human fathoming, measuring, or counting.[7] What God does unfold for us is a selected summary of the most significant stages in preparing Earth for the human race, for the fulfillment of God's plans and purposes.

The events recorded in Genesis reflect God's perspective on what is most important for all human generations to know. We moderns bemoan the lack of specific information about dinosaurs and bipedal primates, among other things, but because these creatures went extinct before Adam and Eve came on the scene, and because they are not Adam and Eve's progenitors (see chapter fourteen), their mention (or lack of mention) makes no significant difference to the story's development.

The brevity of Genesis 1 can be viewed as an expression of God's wisdom and mercy. He wants us to be certain that He wrote the story, but He gives us the privilege—and the thrill—of filling in the details. He does not seek to bury us under a mountain of data that might distract us from His main themes: communicating His plan for our redemption and securing forever all that is good against the presence, and even the possibility, of evil.

Only a few generations of humanity have had the desire and the capability to comprehend more detail than we have been given in the Genesis text, and even now such interest remains limited to a minority of individuals in a few parts of the world. May we be content to embrace the challenges He has laid before us. After all, we have yet to identify and name all living organisms!

Day One: Light Comes

The appearance of light takes center stage on the first creation day. The Hebrew verb used in God's opening statement for the day, "Let there be light," is *haya*, meaning "to exist; to be; to happen; or to come to pass."[8] The verbs *bara*, *asa*, and *yasar*, meaning "create," "make," and "form," respectively, are not used, and this word choice makes sense. God created physical light, that is, electromagnetic radiation, "in the beginning," when He brought the cosmos into existence. The matter and energy of the cosmos included light. Indeed, light is the dominant form of energy for both the primordial and present-day universe.

Remembering Earth's initial conditions and that the frame of reference for this passage is Earth's surface, we can comprehend what happened on Day One: light penetrated Earth's dark shroud for the first time. God cleared away some of the debris that had previously kept light from coming through. Earth's atmosphere changed, too, from opaque to translucent—not transparent, yet, but clear enough to permit light's passage.

The clearing of the debris we can easily understand. Through time, gravity (more specifically, gravitational accretion) pulls much of the dust and weightier material from the circumstellar disk into the star (in this case, our sun) and planets.

The change in Earth's atmosphere presents a serious challenge to our understanding. The rule of thumb in planetary formation is that the greater a planet's surface gravity and the greater a planet's distance from its star, the heavier and thicker its atmosphere. Yet Earth departs from that rule. Theoretically, Earth should have an atmosphere heavier and thicker than that of Venus, but in fact it has a far lighter and much thinner atmosphere.

The Moon Miracle

The solution to this mystery apparently lies with Earth's moon. Most moons in our solar system are formed from the same solar disk material that generated the planets. As such, they are relatively small compared to their planets. A few moons orbiting the outer planets are foreign bodies that have been captured. Earth's moon, however, is the exception. It orbits a planet that is close to the sun, and it is huge compared to its planet.

The moon is younger than Earth. According to the Apollo lunar rock samples, it is only 4.25 billion years old, compared to Earth's 4.59 billion years. The same lunar rocks gathered by Apollo astronauts tell us that the moon's crust is chemically distinct from Earth's. Its distinct chemical makeup and its younger age establish that the moon and Earth did *not* form together.

Astronomers have seen and measured the moon's slow and steady spiraling away from Earth[9] and the slowing of Earth's rotation.[10-11] Their calculations suggest that the moon was in contact or near contact with Earth about 4.25 billion years ago. This implies some kind of collision or near collision at that time.

Only one collision scenario fits all the observed Earth-moon parameters and dynamics: a body at least the size of Mars (nine times the mass of the moon and one-ninth the mass of Earth), possibly twice as large, made a nearly head-on hit and was absorbed, for the most part, into Earth's core.[12-16] Such a collision would have blasted almost all of Earth's original atmosphere into outer space. The shell, or cloud of debris, arising from the collision would orbit Earth and eventually coalesce to form our moon.

This remarkable event, if it occurred as the evidence indicates, delivered Earth from a life-suffocating atmosphere and produced a replacement atmosphere thin enough and of the right chemical composition to permit the passage of light to Earth's surface. It increased the mass and density of Earth enough to retain (by gravity) a large quantity of water vapor (molecular weight, 18) for billions of years, but not so high as to keep life-threatening quantities of ammonia (molecular weight, 17) and methane (molecular weight, 16). It so elevated the iron content of Earth's crust as to permit a huge abundance of ocean life (the quantity of iron, a critical nutrient, determines the abundance and diversity of marine algae, which form the base of the food chain for all ocean life), which in turn permits advanced land life.[17-18] It played a significant role in salting Earth's crust with a huge abundance of radioisotopes, the heat from which drives most of Earth's exceptionally high rates of tectonics and vulcanism.[19] (Heavy elements from the body colliding with Earth were largely transferred to Earth whereas the light elements were either dissipated to the interplanetary medium or transferred to the cloud that would eventually form the moon.) It gradually slowed Earth's rotation rate so that a wide variety of lower life-forms could survive long enough to sustain the existence of advanced life-forms, which required still slower rotation rates. It stabilized the tilt of Earth's rotation axis, protecting the planet from life-extinguishing climatic extremes.[20-23]

In summary, this amazing collision, for which we have an abundance of circumstantial evidence, appears to have been perfectly timed and designed to transform Earth from a "formless and empty" place into a site where life could survive and thrive. In fact, the number of conditions that must be fine-tuned—and the degree of fine-tuning needed for each of these conditions—for life to possibly survive that is manifested in this single event argues powerfully on its own for a divine Creator. Even if the universe contains as many as 10 billion trillion (10^{22}) planets, we would not expect even one, by natural processes alone, to end up with the surface gravity, surface temperature, atmospheric composition, atmospheric pressure, crustal iron abundance, tectonics, vulcanism, rotation rate, rate of decline in rotation rate, and stable rotation axis tilt necessary for the support of life.[24-25] To those who express the desire to see a miracle, we can assure them they are looking at one whenever they gaze up at the moon.

Distinguishing Day and Night

With sunlight now penetrating the interplanetary medium and Earth's atmosphere, an observer on the planet's surface could detect, for the first time, the cycle of day and night. Not until this time, though Earth had been rotating since its beginning, do "day" and "night" become discernible (Genesis 1:5). When all of Earth's surface was permanently dark, no easy means existed for marking time. Now a fixed period of light would follow a fixed period of darkness.

The much-thinned atmosphere would generate greater temperature modulations so that life would not face a single unrelenting temperature. Air and ground temperatures would now vary smoothly and continuously from daytime highs to nighttime lows.

All of these changes were significant for life, but none was more crucial than the possibility of photosynthesis. Light from the sun became available to plants for efficiently transforming large quantities of water and carbon dioxide into food: sugars, starches, and fats.

Day Two: Water Cycle Begins

No less significant for life's survival than light is a stable water cycle. By the time significant land masses would arise (Day Three), Earth would require a cycle of condensation and precipitation—abundant, but not too abundant. A system in which snow, ice, and liquid water freely melt and evaporate from Earth's surface, and just as freely condense to fall back on it as snow and liquid water, would be ideal. Advanced life can survive only if the evaporation and precipitation average between 25 and 60 liquid water inches per year, and only if snow and rain condense in the right proportions.

For advanced life to be well supported by an abundance of lower life-forms and a diversity of species, the rainfall must vary from one geographical area to another. The range must fall between about 2 inches and 600 inches per year—not just for a few millennia, but for a few billion years.

RUNAWAY CLIMATE CHANGES

A car parked in the sun provides a helpful example of the greenhouse effect. Visible light from the sun passes through the car's windows, is absorbed by the interior, and is reradiated at infrared wavelengths. But the windows, being less transparent at infrared wavelengths, trap the infrared radiation inside the car. Thus, heat accumulates inside the car.

Carbon dioxide and water vapor in the atmosphere work like the car's windows. Earth's early atmosphere contained more carbon dioxide and water vapor than our current atmosphere does, but the first plants extracted this carbon dioxide and water and released oxygen. Hence, the increase in the sun's luminosity was balanced at Earth's surface by the decrease in the greenhouse effect of Earth's atmosphere caused by the plants' consumption of carbon dioxide and water. However, if the sun's luminosity were to increase even slightly more rapidly than it does, as it would if the sun were slightly more massive, the extra warmth would evaporate water more efficiently. This extra water vapor would trap more heat. This extra heat would evaporate yet more water, which, in turn, would trap more heat. Eventually, all of Earth's ice and liquid water would be transformed into water vapor.

If the sun's luminosity were to increase a little more slowly, as would be the case if the sun were very slightly less massive, runaway freezing would result. With a slower increase in heat, more snow and ice would form on Earth's surface. Since snow and ice reflect better than other surface materials, Earth would absorb less solar energy. Thus, the surface temperature would drop. In turn, more snow and ice would form, reflecting away even more heat. Eventually, all of Earth's water would turn to snow and ice.

A water cycle that meets such exacting requirements demands intricate balancing of multiple factors: the physical characteristics of the sun and Earth; atmospheric composition, temperature, and pressure; wind velocities; and the changing values of all these atmospheric characteristics at various distances out from Earth's surface. As precise as these environmental factors had to be to allow transformation of Earth's atmosphere from opaque to translucent, they had to be even more precise to permit a stable, life-supporting water cycle.

The sun's stability holds enormous significance. As stars go, our sun burns its fuel at an unusually constant and reliable rate. However, even though the sun has entered its most stable burning phase, its luminosity changes. As nuclear burning slowly expands outward from the sun's core, the sun's brightness increases. The sun shines about 35 percent more brightly today than it did on Earth's first life-forms.[26-27]

This steady increase in solar luminosity perfectly suits the gradual introduction of life-forms, layer upon layer, in a sequence from primitive to advanced. However, the start date for the first life-form and the rate of introduction of subsequent life-forms must be carefully timed. The primordial Earth is highly susceptible to irreversible glaciation. Because carbon dioxide clouds are highly reflective, oceans typically tend to freeze much more quickly than greenhouse gases like water vapor and carbon dioxide can accumulate in the atmosphere.[28] Certain kinds and abundances of life must be introduced in synchrony with the sun's increasing luminosity, or the greenhouse effect operating in Earth's atmosphere can destroy life by trapping either too much heat or too little.

The synchronism is delicate, to say the least. If the sun's luminosity and Earth's biomass and biodiversity fall out of sync by even a slight amount, the result would be either a runaway greenhouse (heating) effect or a runaway freeze. (See "Runaway Climate Changes," page 32.) Either would permanently destroy virtually all life-forms on the planet.

Recent research has uncovered what could represent a deadly imbalance in the water cycle and, at the same time, the remarkable phenomenon that compensates for it. Complex life processes result in an ongoing conversion of water (as well as carbon dioxide and other substances) into sugars, starches, fats, and proteins. A significant fraction of these bioproducts are then transformed by weather catastrophes, volcanoes, and tectonics into deep underground deposits of coal, oil, gas, kerogen, limestone, and marble.[29] In addition, a small amount of water escapes Earth through gravitational dissipation. In other words, Earth's gravitational pull is not quite strong enough to hold onto all of Earth's atmospheric water indefinitely. However, an independent phenomenon largely unknown until the 1980s and unproven until the late 1990s replaces the lost water (and carbon dioxide) in just the right quantity—a changing quantity, at that—to maintain the balance life demands. This phenomenon is an ongoing influx of water-rich extraterrestrial material. Comets of all sizes—regular, small, mini, and micro—which rain down on Earth's upper atmosphere, are the dominant contributors.[30-34]

Because the influx rate of cometary material cannot be directly influenced by the rates of tectonic, volcanic, and chemical activity or by the quantity and kinds of biological activity, the maintenance of a balance among all these processes seems all the more remarkable. Consider that the cometary influx rate must have been accurately compensating throughout the past four billion years for the 35-percent increase in the sun's brightness, the 80-percent decreases in both vulcanism and tectonic activity, changes in weather catastrophes, and the variations in both biomass and biodiversity. May such miraculous wonders never cease!

On Day Two, "God made the expanse and separated the water under the expanse from the water above it" (Genesis 1:7). God called the expanse "sky" (verse 8). The Hebrew words for "expanse" and "sky" are *raqia* and *shamayim*. Both refer to the visible "dome" above us, though the latter is used more specifically for the portion of Earth's atmosphere where clouds form and move.[35-36] The Hebrew verb *asa* (meaning "make," "manufacture," "fabricate," or "construct")[37-38] implies that God Himself designed and "built" Earth's atmosphere. This seems perfectly plausible given the phenomenal degree of fine-tuning outlined earlier and about which we still have more to learn.

God's "separation" of the water accurately describes the formation of the troposphere, the atmospheric layer just above the ocean where clouds form and humidity resides, as distinct from the stratosphere, mesosphere, and ionosphere lying above. This interpretation receives confirmation in Psalm 148 (a psalm reflecting on Genesis 1), which distinguishes the "highest heavens" from the "waters above the skies" and declares that God "set them in place." The psalm begins and ends appropriately with this refrain: "Praise the LORD."

CHAPTER FIVE

CREATION EVENTS: DAYS THREE AND FOUR

With light coming through the still permanently overcast sky, with day distinguishable from night, with poisonous atmospheric gases almost gone and protective gases building up, and with a gentle water cycle established, the stage is set for the introduction of land life. All Earth needs is a place to put it, and that is what God arranged on Day Three.

Dry Land Emerges

"Let the water under the sky be gathered to one place, and let dry ground appear" (Genesis 1:9; see also Psalm 33:7). Solid ground already existed, of course, as the ocean floor, but the time had finally arrived when the forces that raise portions of Earth's crust and lower others brought land, a large body of it, above the waters to stay and to dry out.

As chapters three and four explained, plate tectonics and volcanic activity cause the wrinkling of a planet's surface. Compared with other planets, Earth experiences an extremely high level of both kinds of activity. These levels not only maintain the conditions necessary for life support but also lead eventually to the emergence of land masses above sea level, masses large enough and high enough to resist Earth's powerful erosion forces and remain above sea level for very long periods of time.

The Genesis text refers to the gathering of surface water "to one place." Psalm 33:7 amplifies this breakthrough event:

He gathers the waters of the sea into jars; he puts the deep into storehouses.[1]

The Genesis wording suggests that continental land began as a conglomerate, one mass in one locale, with the ocean surrounding it. Psalm 33 speaks of multiple oceans, Earth as we know it today. What does geology tell us? Not as much as we would like to know. But it does tell us that for the first four billion years of Earth's history, the landmass grew from 0 percent of the planetary surface to 29 percent. What that original landmass looked like and exactly where it was located remains a mystery. However, we do know that for the past quarter-billion years, pieces of a single supercontinent (called "pangea" in most textbooks) have been splitting away and moving in different directions at particular rates of speed (typically about one-half-inch per year) to form Earth's seven present continents.

Psalm 104 explicitly states that though the entire surface of Earth was once covered with water,[2] the time came when God sent the water to its preassigned locations.[3] The psalm concludes with a proclamation that continents will persist throughout Earth's history. Never again will the oceans completely cover the whole surface of Earth.[4]

This poetic piece accurately depicts the geophysical dynamics of Earth. Though plate tectonics and vulcanism continue to subside, the ongoing "spin down," or slowing, of the earth's rotation rate simultaneously reduces the impact of wind and water erosion. We can safely predict that erosion will never gain enough of an advantage over tectonics and vulcanism to wear down the continents completely.

The proportion of Earth's surface area covered by land compared to oceans plays a crucial role in the development of life. In fact, this ratio determines the amount of biodiversity and biocomplexity possible on the planet. Remarkably, and yet not surprisingly given the awesome wonder of the universe's and Earth's existence, the current ratio of 29 percent land surface to 71 percent water surface has been theoretically and observationally demonstrated to provide the maximum possible diversity and complexity of life. With some help from the moon, this ratio and the placement of the continents also yield tides strong enough to enrich the seashores and continental shelves with nutrients while cleansing them of pollutants, but not so strong as to devastate them. In other words, our calculations show that Earth's ratio of continents to oceans and the placement of the continents allow for the greatest possible biomass of advanced species of life.

Later on Day Three: Production of Plants

"Let the land produce vegetation: seed-bearing plants and trees on the land that bear fruit with seed in it, according to their various kinds" (Genesis 1:11). The newly formed dry land now brings forth vegetation.

The words "seed," "trees," and "fruit" have much more specific meaning in English than in Hebrew, and this difference has led to some misunderstanding and unwarranted criticism of the text. The Hebrew nouns used here, *zera'*, *'es*, and *peri*, mean, respectively, "semen" or "the embryos of *any* plant species,"[5] "*any* large plant containing woody fiber,"[6] and "the food and/or embryos produced by *any* living thing."[7] *Zera'* and *peri* could refer to any plant species that has ever existed. The *'es* certainly includes all large plants containing cellulose and could possibly refer to all larger-than-microscopic plants whose fibers provide a measure of stiffness. Thus, these terms do include the relatively primitive plant species scientists have identified as the first land vegetation.

The text does not say that all land vegetation appeared at this time, but emphasizes, rather, that God chose this time for dry land to abound with vegetation. The Hebrew verb *dasha'*, or "produce," has broad meaning. It can be interpreted to mean that plants arose through natural processes, but it also can be interpreted, just as accurately, to mean that plants arose directly from divine miraculous intervention. Any combination or type of divine intervention and natural process would certainly be acceptable, from a linguistic point of view. In other words, this particular text cannot be used to state definitively to what extent God may or may not have employed natural processes in the development of plant life on Earth. This is an issue science is attempting to comprehend.

A recent discovery establishes that even large trees date very early in the fossil record. An international team of paleobotanists determined that an extinct plant, Archaeopteris, had vegetative features similar to living conifers.[8] Though it produced spores that were released like those of modern-day ferns rather than seeds that were retained, the spores are consistent with the *zera* of Genesis 1:11-12.

The team not only dated their fossil find as ancient, namely 370 million years old, but that Archaeopteris was quite likely a dominant species worldwide throughout the Devonian and post-Devonian eras. This, too, is consistent with Genesis 1:11-12.

Another recent research study places the first angiosperms or flowering plants much earlier than previously supposed. Flowering plants now are thought to arise as early as about 290 million years ago.[9-10]

The Miracle of Life

Scientists continue to debate the issue of how life originated. More and more questions and problems arise on the naturalistic side while evidence accumulates on the supernaturalistic. The following list summarizes some of the latest developments in that debate:

1. All non-theistic origin of life scenarios require kerogen tars and carbonaceous molecules to self assemble in some kind of primordial soup or mineral substrate into living organisms. However, when living organisms die, they decay into the same kerogen tars and carbonaceous molecules. By carefully measuring the ratio of carbon-13 to carbon-12 in such tars and carbonaceous material, physical chemists can ascertain whether these substances are prebiotic or postbiotic in nature. Their conclusion: it is all postbiotic.[11] Thus, a prebiotic primordial soup or mineral substrate never existed upon the earth.
2. The time scale during which life arose is very brief, less than five million years. Life has been abundant on Earth throughout the past 3.86 billion years.[12-13] Between 3.5 and 3.86 billion years ago, dozens of life-exterminating bombardment events took place (for example, collisions with enormous asteroids).[14-15] Apparently, life originated and reoriginated as many as fifty times within the 360-million-year time span. Given the abundance of life during this era, several of the origins of life must have occurred in time windows briefer than five million years. If life arose through natural processes alone in such brief time spans, it should be easy to construct in a laboratory. However, as yet, biochemists cannot manufacture (from

scratch) a single DNA or RNA molecule or any of the more complex proteins, let alone a complete, functioning organism.[16-19]

3. The vast complexity of even the simplest life-form argues against random or natural self-assembly. If all the chemical bonds of Earth's simplest living creature were broken, the chance of its reassembly, even under ideal environmental and chemical conditions and even if no components were allowed to escape and no foreign substances were permitted to intrude, is less than one in $10^{100,000,000,000}$,[20] a number so large it would fill nearly a thousand sets of *Encyclopedia Britannica* with zeros if anyone were to write it out in standard notation. Even if most of the sequence positions for the atoms are not critical, the odds by the most conservative of calculations are still less than one in $10^{3,000}$ for assemblies attempted continuously over ten billion years.[21] More rigorous calculations are presented in textbooks written by atheists[22] and agnostics,[23] as well as by theistic scientists.[24]

4. The simplest chemical step for the origin of life, the gathering of amino acids that are *all* left-handed and nucleotide sugars that are *all* right-handed (a phenomenon known as "homochirality"), cannot be achieved under inorganic conditions.[25-27]

5. The various nucleotides essential for building RNA and DNA molecules require radically different environmental conditions for their assembly.[28] Cytosine and uracil need near boiling water temperatures, while adenine and guanine need freezing water temperatures. Thus, it seems highly unlikely that under natural conditions all four building blocks would come together in adequate concentrations at the same site.

6. At the time of life's origin Earth's surface was relatively hot, probably between 80 and 90°C (176-194°F), with little temperature variation.[29] That is, Earth's surface was without any cold spots. At these warm temperatures RNA nucleotide sequences decouple. Moreover, new experimental results demonstrate that all of the RNA nucleotides themselves degrade at warm temperatures. They can last only from 19 days to 12 years.[29] The most

optimistic naturalist hypotheses demand that they hold together for millions of years. Even at water's freezing point, cytosine decomposes in less than 17,000 years.[29] Outside the cell there is no environment providing sufficient stability and protection for RNA molecules and their nucleotide bases. This means RNA molecules cannot survive without cells while cells cannot survive without RNA. Both must be constructed simultaneously.

7. Life transported from some distant "exotic" location in the cosmos to Earth would arrive dead, in fact, so broken down that none of life's building blocks (DNA, RNA, or proteins) would survive. Stellar radiation pressure strong enough to move microbes across the long reaches of interstellar space would kill the microbes in a matter of days.[30-31] If the microbes were embedded in sizable dust grains, their chemical properties might be protected from the effects of most interstellar radiation, but only supergiant stars generate enough radiation pressure to move such dust grains, and life is impossible anywhere in the vicinity of a supergiant star.[32]

8. Life involves more than the assembly of all the molecular machines an organism requires. Each machine must have the capacity to survive some random destruction of the components making up its inner workings. Multiple forms of radiation essential to life[33] occasionally disturb the positions and the types of amino acids and nucleotides comprising proteins, DNA, and RNA molecules. Life assembly, thus, becomes all the more challenging. Certain "backups," or redundancy, must be available at the right times in the right locations for molecules to survive and continue their essential functions. The task is roughly analogous to writing a computer program that can still perform even when 1 percent of its code is randomly shuffled or destroyed.

9. The energy released from the decay of the radiometric isotopes of uranium, thorium, and potassium sets up a reaction whereby ocean water feeds a continuous stream of oxygen into the earth's atmosphere.[34] This streaming was much greater a few billion years ago than it is now. It is sufficient to guarantee the complete shutdown of

chemical reactions that possibly could cause prebiotic molecules to assemble into biotic molecules.

10. Without oxygen in the atmosphere, no ozone shield will ever form. Without an ozone shield solar ultraviolet radiation will penetrate unimpeded to the earth's surface. Such radiation will shut down the chemical reactions that are essential for the assembly of prebiotics into organisms. Either way, a naturalistic explanation for life's origins is doomed. The existence of oxygen will shut down the required chemical reactions. The lack of oxygen will also shut down the required chemical reactions.

Plants appear to have a limited capacity for speciation (production of new species) through natural processes. Botanists have actually observed a few plants develop new "species."[35-36] However, in these cases the word "species" may be a misnomer. Boundaries between plant species are much less distinct than boundaries between animal species. No plant species radically different from already existing species has arisen under human observation. The rapid rate at which plant species go extinct, both today and during the fossil era,[37-38] implies that supernatural rather than natural processes are responsible for the major changes in plant species evident throughout plant history.

Day Four: Lights in the Sky

For many millions of years after light first pierced the dark shroud surrounding Earth, the sky would continue to resemble the heavy overcast of a stormy day. Certain atmospheric constituents, along with air temperature, pressure, and humidity, would have prevented any break in the cloud cover. Volcanic activity also may have contributed to this permanently overcast condition. The carbon dioxide level was substantially higher than the current level, contributing to high humidity. Fossil evidence affirms the existence of such conditions. Through time, changes in these various environmental factors—stabilization of air temperature and pressure, consumption of carbon dioxide by plants, and decrease in volcanic activity—would have brought about another major transformation of the atmosphere, this time from translucent to transparent. At least for some moments, probably only a few at first, the clouds would break.

A significant factor was the slowing down of Earth's rotation rate.

A slower rotating Earth means calmer wind velocities (much calmer—Jupiter with a ten-hour rotation rate has average wind velocities exceeding a thousand miles per hour). Calmer wind velocities mean significantly less efficient sea-salt aerosol production. (Sea-salt aerosols are produced as winds whip up ocean waves.) Since a new discovery establishes that sea-salt aerosols make up by far the largest fraction of cloud nuclei,[39] Earth's cloud cover would thin dramatically as its rotation rate slows down.

Plants had some help in removing carbon dioxide and water vapor from Earth's atmosphere. Carbon dioxide easily reacts with atmospheric water to form carbonic acid. This carbonic acid quickly falls to the surface, where it reacts with the crustal rocks (from the third creation day onward) to form carbonates. If it were not for some mitigating factors, these carbonates would have leached enough carbon dioxide and water from the atmosphere to turn this planet into a permanently frozen, arid wasteland. This scenario does, in fact, describe what happened on Mars.

Earth escaped this carbonate doomsday because of its strategic level of plate tectonics and vulcanism. Plate collisions drove surface carbonates deep underground. Pressure, heat, and chemical components deep in the crust broke down the carbonates into carbon dioxide, water, and minerals. Subsequently, volcanoes recycled these trapped residuals, or most of them, back up to the surface.

As chapters three and four explained, the driving force behind Earth's level of plate tectonics and vulcanism is the release of heat from slow-decaying radioisotopes in the crust.[40] The spectacular collision that resulted in the formation of our moon helps explain how Earth acquired some of its enormous abundance of long-lasting, heat-releasing radioisotopes. Strategically for life, this heat release diminishes through time, simultaneously slowing down the processes it drives. Today, Earth's tectonic and volcanic activity has dropped to one-fifth their original level.[40]

This drop, of course, favors life. Too many and too powerful earthquakes and volcanic eruptions would be catastrophic to life. Too few, on the other hand, would render the planet too cold and dry for life.

Advanced species show the least tolerance for earthquakes and volcanoes; primitive species, the greatest tolerance. We can reasonably surmise that God created primitive life on Earth at the first opportune moment and created human beings near the last (and, thus, the most) opportune moment. He exquisitely designed the sun, Earth, and moon to maximize the proliferation and duration of life on Earth. In so doing, God endowed humans with abundant biological resources (for example, several feet of topsoil, a trillion barrels of oil, hundreds of billions of tons of coal, quadrillions of cubic feet of natural gas, billions of tons of limestone and marble, millions of diverse species of life, and so forth).

One result of all these changes—from all these forces working in balance—Genesis records in chapter one, verse 14:

> "Let there be lights in the expanse of the sky to separate the day from the night, and let them serve as signs to mark seasons and days and years."

On Creation Day Four, the sun, the moon, and the stars became distinctly visible from Earth's surface for the first time.

Verse 16 may confuse readers who do not recognize it as a parenthetical note, a brief review:

> God made two great lights—the greater light to govern the day and the lesser light to govern the night. He also made the stars.

The Hebrew verb *'asa,* translated "made," appears in the appropriate form for completed action. (There are no verb tenses in the Hebrew language to parallel verb tenses in English, but three Hebrew verb forms are used to denote action already completed, action not yet completed, and commands.) Verse 16 does not specify when in the past the sun, moon, and stars were made. However, the wording of verses 17 and 18 does provide a hint:

> God set them in the expanse of the sky to give light on the earth, to govern the day and the night, and to separate light from darkness.

Notice the echo of wording from Day One (verses 3-5). This verse tells us *why* God created the sun, moon, and stars and suggests that the sun was in place to fulfill its role on the first creation day. The *shamayim wa'eres* (heavens and earth) in verse 1 places the making of the sun and the stars before the first creation day. The moon, however, could possibly have been made during the first creation day.

THIRD-DAY DIVINE LIGHT SOURCE?

Because the verb translated "made" in verse 16 does not by itself specify when, within or before the first four creation days, God actually makes the sun and stars, some Bible interpreters insist on placing the birth of the sun and stars on the fourth creation day.[41-45] As to how the third creation day plants survived without the light of the sun, these interpreters speculate that God sustained the plants during the third creation day with the light of His shekinah glory (the same light that emblazoned Moses' face on Mt. Sinai[46]).

One of the problems with a fourth creation day birth of the sun, however, is that a lot more than the sun's light is necessary to sustain plant life on Earth. Most critically, the gravity of the sun is essential to maintain the life-essential positions and orbits of the earth, moon, planets, asteroids, and comets. It also critically influences the earth's rotation period. Such gravity implies that the "divine light source" sustaining the third creation day plants must manifest both the identical mass and position, relative to Earth, of the sun. Moreover, the light needed for plant survival must exhibit the same spectral response and effective temperature as the sun's.

For all practical purposes, the hypothesized divine light source would be indistinguishable from the sun. This leads to two further problems. The first is how could life on Earth possibly survive the removal of the first sun and its replacement by the second sun? The second is how one can possibly force fit a two-sun interpretation into the various creation accounts of the Bible?

Thankfully, Genesis 1:1 relieves us of such concerns. It places the making of the sun before the six creation days.

Ozone Balances

While the transformation of the atmosphere from translucent (light-diffusing) to transparent (light-transmitting) requires intricate design and implementation, to accomplish this change without exposing land life to too little or too much ultraviolet radiation demands even more. As the plants introduced on the third creation day were consuming carbon dioxide through photosynthesis, they were also expelling oxygen. After a period ranging from thousands to millions of years, enough oxygen had diffused into the upper stratosphere to permit, under certain precise conditions, formation of a thin and delicate layer of ozone.

This ozone layer offers essential life protection. It absorbs ultraviolet radiation from the sun that would otherwise damage and destroy advanced land life. Only recently have scientists recognized the importance and fragility of this ozone shield. Their fear now is that the nitrous oxides, fluorocarbons, and particulates expelled by human activity may have already damaged the shield and may even threaten its temporary destruction. Measurements do indicate a thinning of Earth's stratospheric ozone layer.[47-51] More of the sun's ultraviolet rays are coming through to damage our skin and our crops. We are fighting skin cancer with sunscreen, and we are still searching for ways to protect food crops, especially the grains vital to our nutrition and health.[52-53]

Researchers also recognize that too thick a stratospheric ozone layer would present problems just as severe. If too little ultraviolet radiation gets through to Earth's surface, plant growth is inhibited and certain vitamins will not form in certain animal species. In other words, unless the stratospheric ozone layer is just right, neither too thin nor too thick, Earth's biomass, biodiversity, and biovitality will be impaired.

Some very recent studies indicate the delicacy of ozone quantities in the troposphere (the first six miles, or nine kilometers, above Earth's surface) and the mesosphere (from fifteen to fifty miles, or twenty-four to eighty kilometers, above Earth) as well as in the stratosphere (between six and fifteen miles, or nine to twenty-four kilometers, above Earth). Tropospheric ozone (about 10 percent of the total) appears to be augmented, rather than depleted, by human activity. However, this augmentation wields a deadly impact. Fossil-fuel burning and agricultural burning have so increased ozone in regions over the north midlatitudes and the continental tropics as to increase the incidence of respiratory failure in humans and other large animals, reduce crop yields, and wipe out certain ozone-sensitive plant species.[54]

However, the right quantity of tropospheric ozone serves an important purpose. This ozone cleanses the atmosphere of certain kinds of biochemical smog (mainly from trees) and industrial smog.[55] Ozone may be considered the troposphere's detergent.

Mesospheric ozone (about 1 percent of the total) also fulfills a strategic role. Its capacity for ultraviolet absorption helps govern the chemistry and circulation of gases in that layer.[56-57] Mesospheric chemistry and gas circulation largely determine which gases are retained and which are lost by Earth's atmosphere, a determination vitally important to life's long-term survival. Again, the ozone quantity must be carefully balanced between too much and too little.

The existence and integration of the rare and perfect conditions necessary for development of our delicate, life-essential ozone shields (nowhere else in the solar system or beyond can we find any) constitute a set of miracles. (I use the word *miracle* here to mean something in the natural realm manifesting supernatural design and occurring with supernatural timing and placement.) The stability and extent of these shields, including the stability and extent of their recently discovered interlayer transport mechanisms, [58-59] throughout hundreds of millions of years are yet another set of miracles.

CHAPTER SIX

CREATION EVENTS: DAYS FIVE AND SIX

The stage is now perfectly set for another dramatic scene to unfold. With light and breathable air, dry land and oceans, an abundance and a diversity of plants, a water cycle and ozone shields to help them flourish, and discernible sky lights to govern biological clocks, Earth is ready for a new wonder: advanced animal life.

Day Five: Lower Vertebrates

In Genesis 1:20, God declares, "Let the water teem with living creatures, and let birds fly above the earth across the expanse of the sky." The Hebrew nouns for the different animals mentioned in this verse are *sheres*, *nephesh*, and *op*. *Sheres* refers to swarms of small or minute animals. This same word appears frequently in the Pentateuch (the first five books of the Old Testament) with reference to all the smaller animals that are neither birds nor mammals. When used for land creatures, it usually includes insects, amphibians, and reptiles. When used for water creatures (fresh or salt), it usually includes mollusks, crustaceans, fish, and amphibians.

This Genesis passage mentions only the water-dwelling *sheres* and does not specify which kinds of *sheres* appeared in the water on this fifth day. Water-dwelling *sheres* are the most primitive creatures that require the visibility of the heavenly bodies to regulate their biological clocks.

Clearly, many species of *sheres*, even whole phyla, receive no mention. However, I see this brevity as an understandable feature of the text, for its focus seems narrowed on the most important preparations for the introduction of humankind.

What About the Dinosaurs?

Even individuals who feel no particular fondness for reptiles describe an almost irresistible fascination with dinosaurs. These large (and a few small) reptile species appear to have dominated Earth's land and sea life from 250 million to 65 million years ago. Their creation probably belongs to the fifth creation day.

Perhaps because of their sheer enormity and the longevity of dinosaur species, the largest land animals God ever made, people have difficulty imagining that the biblical creation chronology would give them no special mention. However, we must take into account not only the theme of the text but also our own historical context.

DINOSAURS IN JOB'S STORY?

Some Christians assert that the Bible does speak of dinosaurs. They see the "behemoth" and "leviathan" of Job 40 and 41 as references to such fearsome creatures as triceratops, tyrannosaurus, or possibly some other dinosaur species. One problem with their interpretation of Job 40 and 41, which they would call "literal," is that no creatures on Earth, alive or extinct, fit the literal descriptions. No dinosaur, for example, ever breathed fire or smoke or had bones of iron and brass.

The writer of these descriptions left many clues that they are to be taken figuratively. The comparative words *as* and *like* appear in this passage fifteen times in the *New International Version* and seventeen times in the *New American Standard Bible*. The point of the passage is to convey the impression that these creatures struck terror in the hearts of human beings who may have encountered them.

A look at the Hebrew gives further insight. The Hebrew word for "behemoth" appears in its singular form, *behema*, as part of the description of certain land mammals created on the sixth Creation day. Because dinosaurs were reptiles, not mammals, "behemoth" probably would not be used in reference to them.

There are two animals present on Earth today that strike terror and cause mayhem matching the descriptions in Job 40 and 41: the hippopotamus and the crocodile. Indeed, in some parts of Africa these two species account for more human deaths than all other large animals combined.

The theme of the account, as I have stated before, is the preparation of Earth for Adam and Eve and their progeny. From a historical perspective, only a few people ever to hear or read this story—people living mostly in Western cultures since the nineteenth century—would possess any awareness of or interest in dinosaurs' existence.

If we consider God's purpose—to communicate a memorable report—short enough to be written on a single page of His creative work for all people of all time, the dinosaurs' importance dims.

The popular claim that human footprints crossed over trails of dinosaur footprints in the Paluxy River bed in Texas has been overturned.[1] No credible evidence whatever suggests the coexistence of primates and the great dinosaurs.

Day Five: "Soulish" Animals

Genesis 1:20-21 goes on to introduce some animal species radically different from any previously mentioned. These creatures are identified by the Hebrew noun *nephesh*. It has the following definitions: soulish creature; person; mind; land creature with the breath of life; creature capable of expressing yearnings, emotions, passions, and will; and self-aware creature.[2] The word *nephesh* appears many times in the Bible. Occasionally, as in Leviticus 11:46, the context connotes the broad definition, land creature with the breath of life, meant to include nearly all "living" animals—reptiles, amphibians, insects, birds, and mammals. Most of the time, the narrower definition, soulish creature or creature capable of expressing yearnings, emotions, passions, and will, is implied. More than physical bodies with nervous, digestive, respiratory, circulatory, and reproductive systems, as marvelous and intricate as those systems may be, these creatures manifest attributes of mind, will, and emotions—what the ancient Hebrews and others would call "soulish" attributes.

Anyone who has had much contact with birds and mammals realizes that such creatures are uniquely endowed with the capacity to form relationships—with each other and with humans. They have unique ways of expressing their understanding, their choices, and their feelings. Unlike other animals, birds and mammals can be trained to perform tasks that are irrelevant to their survival. They respond to human authority and personality. They show delight and sadness, anger and fear, among other feelings. They form emotional bonds with humans.

Here, for only the second time in the Genesis account (verse 21), the verb *bara'* is used. In this passage both *bara'* and another Hebrew verb, *'asa*, appear. Without reading more into this word choice than may be warranted, I see at least a suggestion that God manufactured (*'asa*) some aspect of the *nephesh* from existing resources, and, additionally, created something brand new, something that did not exist previously. I see *'asa* as applying to construction of the body, and *bara'* as applying to creation of the soul.

The soulishness of the birds and mammals places them at a level distinct from other animal species. A bird or mammal would be much more valuable to humans, at least in some respects, than the other plants and animals on Earth. These creatures also have greater needs, and God expects us to treat them with as much respect and consideration as their well-being requires and deserves.

As the only creatures with the capacity to form relationships with humans, birds and mammals can be influenced (in ways that other creatures cannot) by human sin. For example, a pet dog treated with gentleness and kindness and showered with affection will tend to be friendly and affectionate, whereas a dog that constantly has been mistreated and abused by its owner will tend to be mean and vicious. By comparison, human abuse or affection bestowed upon a cockroach does little to affect that cockroach's behavior. Because the behavior patterns of birds and mammals can be altered by sin, at times they alone, of all Earth's animals, are designated to receive with humans the consequences of God's wrath against profound wickedness.

Sea Mammals' Timing

Genesis 1 has been discredited by some paleontologists for placing the introduction of sea mammals (Day Five) before the introduction of land mammals (Day Six). A careful reading of the text, however, removes the basis for their criticism. The fifth creation day mentions the sea mammals generically; however, the sixth creation day narrows in on only three specialized kinds of land mammals. When the other land mammals are introduced we cannot say from the text. Scientific research will have to give us that information. The sixth creation day introduces just three recently created categories of land mammals (before introducing humans).

Recent discoveries reveal that the first sea mammals date much earlier than paleontologists had once thought. Fossils of four extinct species of whales—Pakicetus, Nalacetus, Ambulocetus, and Indocetus—have been dated at 52 million, 52 million, 50 million, and 48 million years ago, respectively.[3] These dates eliminate any credible challenge to the placement of the first sea mammals on the fifth creation day.

The dates also effectively eliminate a naturalistic explanation for a newly found change in these whales' morphology. Phosphate isotopes in the teeth of these fossilized whales tell of a rapid transition from freshwater ingestion to saltwater ingestion. Geologists and anatomists from the United States and India discovered that Pakicetus and Nalacetus drank only freshwater. Ambulocetus drank freshwater at least through its formative years, probably all its life, and Indocetus drank saltwater only.[3]

In just two to four million years—or less—whales' physiology changed radically. The transition from freshwater ingestion to saltwater ingestion requires completely different internal organs. The number and rapidity of "just right" mutations required to accomplish such a transition defies the limits set by molecular clocks (biomolecules for which mutation rates can be determined relatively easily). Proponents of punctuated equilibria, the increasingly popular alternative to gradualism (traditional Darwinism), suggest that dramatic genetic changes occurred in sudden jumps propelled by severe environmental stress. The period from 48 to 52 million years ago, however, appears to have been remarkably tranquil, far less stressful than such a scenario demands.

Transitional Forms: Proof of Evolutionism?

For several decades now, evolutionists (those seeking a naturalistic explanation for the changes in life-forms over Earth's history) have pointed to "transitional forms" in the fossil record for proof that their explanation for life's history is correct.[4-5] The fact that the bone structures of certain large land-dwelling mammals, the mesonychids,[6] ancient freshwater-drinking whales, ancient saltwater-drinking whales, and modern whales exhibit an apparent progression persuades them that modern whales naturally evolved from land-dwelling mammals. Evolutionists often cite this progression as their best demonstration of Darwinian evolution. (A recent discovery of ancient whale ankles, however, establishes that the ankles of all whale species are so distinct from those of mesonychids and artiodactyls, the only other suggested ancestor of whales, as to seriously call into question the descent of whales from land-dwelling mammals.[7])

Ironically, the evolutionists' "best example" in reality is their worst. No animal is a less efficient evolver than the whales. No animal has a higher probability for rapid extinction than the whales. Many factors severely limit their capacity for natural-process changes and greatly enhance their probability for rapid extinction.

The ten most significant are:

1. relatively small population levels
2. long generation spans (the time between birth and the ability to give birth)
3. low numbers of progeny produced per adult
4. high complexity of morphology and biochemistry
5. enormous body sizes
6. specialized food supplies
7. relatively advanced cultural and social structures
8. high metabolic rates
9. relatively small habitat size (for some species)
10. relatively low ecological diversity

These factors limit not only whales' capacity to change through natural selection and mutations but even their ability to adapt to environmental changes. A fundamental problem biologists observe (for well understood biochemical reasons) is that deleterious mutations vastly outnumber beneficial mutations anywhere from 10,000 to 1 up to 10,000,000 to 1. Thus, it takes, for example, a very large population, a short generation time, and a small body size for a species to survive long enough to change through beneficial mutations before the onslaught of deleterious mutations and environmental stresses and changes (for example, declining rotation rate, increasing solar luminosity, changing chemical composition of the atmosphere, changing biodeposits, supernova eruptions, asteroid and comet collisions, solar flaring, climate cycles, etc.) drive the species into extinction.

Crude mathematical models place the balance between a species capable of significant evolutionary advance and one doomed to eventual extinction at approximately a population size of one quadrillion individuals, a generation time of three months, and a body size of one centimeter. These conclusions are confirmed by field observations. Biologists directly observe significant evolutionary advance only for those species exceeding a quadrillion individuals with body sizes and generation times less than one centimeter and three months respectively. (Significant evolutionary advance is well confirmed by direct field observations for several virus and bacteria species; it is debated for ant and termite species; while it is not seen at all for species numbering less than a quadrillion individuals, with body sizes larger than one centimeter, and generation times greater than three months.)

As a consequence of the ten characteristics listed above, whales lack even the remotest possibility for significant evolutionary advance. Moreover, the ten characteristics imply that deleterious mutations and environmental changes and stresses will tend to drive any given whale species to extinction relatively rapidly.

The same conclusions can be drawn for the so-called descent of horses. The same factors affecting whales also severely restrict horses' capacity to survive internal and external changes. Indeed, ecologists have observed several extinctions of horse and whale species during human history, but never a measurable change within a species, much less the appearance of a new one.

Genesis offers this explanation: God created the first sea mammals on the fifth creation day. As the fossil record documents, sea mammals have persisted on Earth from that epoch until now, though not without interruption. Multiple extinctions of sea mammals imply that God repeatedly replaced extinct species with new ones. (See chapter eight for further discussion of this issue.) In most cases the new species were different from the previous ones because God was changing Earth's dynamics (rotation rate and tidal forces), geology, biodeposits, and biology, step by step, in preparation for His ultimate creation on Earth—the human race.

Psalm 104 supports this pattern of natural extinction and miraculous speciation. In the 27th and 28th verses the psalmist declares that all of Earth's creatures wait upon God for their good provision. In the 29th verse the psalmist points out that inevitably Earth's creatures die off. But, in the 30th verse we have the statement that God recreates.

The many "transitional" forms of whales and horses suggest that God performed more than just a few creative acts here and there, letting natural evolution fill in the rest. Rather, God was involved and active in creating all the whale and horse species, the first, the last, and the "transitional" forms.

Day Six: Specialized Land Mammals

The sixth day begins with God's making (*'asa*) three specific kinds of land mammals: "livestock, creatures that move along the ground, and wild animals." This list does not purport to include all the land mammals God made. Rather, it focuses on three varieties of land mammals that would cohabit with and provide support for the human beings to come later.

The three Hebrew nouns used for these creatures are *behema*, *remes*, and *chayya*, respectively. Depending on the context, these three Hebrew nouns can take on broad or narrow definitions. For example, though *remes* refers variously in Hebrew literature and the Bible to mammals and reptiles, just reptiles, or just mammals, the opening phrase of Genesis 1:25 makes clear that these are mammals. All the *behema*, *remes*, and *chayya* are *nephesh*. Both *behema* and *chayya* refer to long-legged land quadrupeds. The former group encompasses those that easily can be tamed or domesticated for agricultural purposes, and the latter, those that are difficult to tame but have the potential to become excellent pets. *Remes* refers to short-legged land mammals, such as rodents, hares, and armadillos.

The *King James* translation of *remes* as "everything that creepeth upon the earth" has led some readers to wrongly conclude that this verse speaks of insects, and this notion that God created insects on the final creation day has led to ridicule and rejection of the text. But, as even a cursory investigation of the context and original language makes clear, these are "creeping" mammals, not bugs. Insects, in fact, receive no mention in the Genesis creation account.

Day Six: A Reflection of God's Image

"'Let us make man in our image. . . .' So God created man in his own image, in the image of God he created him; male and female he created them" (verses 26-27). The use of "our" reflects that God is plural, while the use of "his" and "he" affirms that God is singular. The basis for this paradoxical use of pronouns is the Hebrew word for God in Genesis 1: *Elohim*. As accurately as we can translate it into English, it means "the uniplural God." In other words, God can somehow be simultaneously singular and plural. Here we get our first glimpse of what we later discover to be the Trinity, God's triunity as Father, Son, and Holy Spirit.

The only Hebrew noun used for mankind in Genesis 1 is *'adam*. This noun, used frequently in Hebrew literature, refers exclusively to the first individual human or to the first human couple and their descendants.

In the report of God's creation of *'adam*, we see the third and final usage of *bara* in Genesis 1. Just as in the case of the *nephesh*, a second verb, *asa*, is used. Again, something about *'adam* is completely new, and something about him is not. Because creatures with body and soul already existed, the spiritual dimension of this one creature set him apart from all others.

Only the human, God's final work of the creation days, bears "the image of God." This distinction applies to no other creature.

For the moment, let's investigate the spirit component of *'adam*. From the rest of Genesis and all of Scripture, as well as from a study of human culture through the ages, we see that the human spirit includes the following characteristics, among others:

1. awareness of a moral code "written" or impressed within a conscience
2. concerns about death and about life after death
3. propensity to worship and desire to communicate with a higher being
4. consciousness of self
5. drive to discover and capacity to recognize truth and absolutes

These traits find expression or conscious repression in every human being, regardless of time and place and intellect. They can even be seen, to some extent, in infants and in people with severe mental or emotional impairment. These qualities help define human uniqueness, and any creature who lacks them cannot be considered *'adam*.

The fact that human beings are the only animals that are body, soul, and spirit does not imply in any way that humans are made up of three distinguishable, separate parts. While the soul and spirit of a human are functionally distinct, they are not substantively distinct. While the Bible does acknowledge the possibility of a human existing apart from his or her physical body, it clearly eliminates the possibility of a soulless human or a spiritless human.

Human History Begins

Biblical genealogies serve as one indicator of how recently humans appeared. However, they provide only a loose measure. The problem lies in the flexible usage of the Hebrew words for father and son, *'ab* and *ben*. *'Ab* also refers to grandfather, great-grandfather, great-great-grandfather, and so on. Similarly, *ben* may mean grandson, great-grandson, great-great-grandson, and so on. In the book of

Daniel, Belshazzar's mother refers to Nebuchadnezzar as Belshazzar's father when, in fact, two other kings came between them and they were not biologically related.[8] Such flexibility in the usage of *'ab* and *ben* explains the apparent discrepancies between parallel genealogies (see, for example, 1 Chronicles 3, Matthew 1, and Luke 3). Even the apparently detailed genealogy in Genesis 11 omits at least one name. The parallel record in Luke 3 lists Cainan, and Genesis 11 does not.[9]

The challenge in deriving a date for the creation of Adam and Eve is to ascertain, or even estimate, the completeness or incompleteness of the biblical genealogies. Comparative analysis of overlapping genealogies throughout the Bible suggests that they may range anywhere from about 90 percent complete at best to about 10 percent complete at worst. Using genealogical data alone, we can place the date for the creation of Adam and Eve very roughly between about seven thousand and about sixty thousand years ago. The date might be stretched a little further back but cannot justifiably be stretched far enough to accommodate the early bipedal primate species (circa five hundred thousand to four million years back[10]).

More reasons than this matter of timing can be given for excluding early primates from consideration as "humans," members of *'adam*'s race, spiritual beings as well as soulish. Evidence of man's spiritual dimension would include relics of worship, such as idols, altars, and temples. From a biblical perspective, painting, musical ability, burial of the dead, and use of tools could represent evidence of soulishness, not spirituality. Birds and primates, even elephants, have been observed to engage in such activities, which reflect mind and emotion, not spirit.

Although bipedal, tool-using, large-brained primates roamed Earth for hundreds of thousands (perhaps a million) years,[11-13] religious relics date back only about eight thousand to twenty-four thousand years.[14-15] Thus, the anthropological date for the first spirit creatures agrees with the biblical date. (For further discussion on this issue, see chapter fourteen.)

Though most anthropologists still insist that the bipedal primates were "human," the conflict lies more in semantics than in research data. Support for their views that modern humans descended from these primate species is rapidly eroding. Evidence now indicates that all bipedal primates went extinct, with the possible exception of Neandertal, before the advent of human beings.[16-18] As for Neandertal, the possibility of a biological link with humanity has been conclusively ruled out.[19-20] (See chapter fourteen for more details.)

Creation by Trial and Error?

For many secularists, God's replacement of, say, extinct species of whales, horses, and bipedal primates by other such species seems to run counter to the character and attributes of the God of the Bible. For them, an all-powerful, all-loving Creator should need to create life only at one time. Progressive creation appears to connote a bumbling, stupid, wasteful, or cruel Creator.

What these secularists fail to appreciate is that God created the universe and all life in the universe not just for the benefit of humanity but for the benefit of His angelic and future creations as well. The Bible reveals that Satan and his followers, or demons, introduced evil before Adam and Eve rebelled in Eden. We can infer from Romans 8 and Revelation 20–22 that God created the universe for the purpose of conquering all evil once and for all.[21] (This does not necessarily imply that there was evil before the creation of the universe, only that God was cognizant of its coming.) These same chapters help us understand that gravity, electromagnetism, thermodynamics, and consequently a universe characterized by three large, expanding dimensions of space and an additional finite dimension of time[22] all play a part in evil's conquest. These necessary factors require that the physical conditions of the universe and Earth change dramatically over time. For example, the sun even during its most stable burning phase brightens by about 8 percent per billion years, and Earth's rotation rate lengthens by about four hours per day per billion years. These factors also imply that Earth, the solar system, and the universe must fit within a narrowly constrained set of characteristics for physical life to survive.[23-25]

These conditions lead to some deductions. For humanity to be provided with an abundance of limestone, marble, ozone, oxygen, water, topsoil, coal, oil, gas, salt, phosphate, gypsum, and so on, millions of generations of life would need to predate us. Because the physical realm changes with respect to time, God apparently created different species at different times to suit the changing environment. For instance, only the most primitive and tiny forms of life could survive the eight-hour-per-day rotation period of early Earth. Because highly advanced life requires a more delicately balanced set of characteristics for survival than primitive life, such life forms are much more vulnerable to extinction. But when such species went extinct, God created new ones, sometimes the same, and more often different (according to environmental and ecological conditions and divine timing) to replace them. (See chapter eight.)

The step-by-step approach to bipedal primate creation that we can see in the recent fossil record may reasonably reflect God's understanding of the difficulty other life forms would encounter in adapting to sinful humans. The ecocrises we see in so many places of the world provide abundant testimony to that difficulty. Given this context, we can see that the bipedal primates predating Adam and Eve reflect care rather than waste. Their presence and activities helped prepare the other animals to adapt for future shock—the arrival of human beings.

We can reflect on many more reasons than these few for God's step-by-step creation. Some are discussed in one of my previous books.[25]

Man's Assignment

In Genesis 1:28, God commands the first humans to fill Earth and to "rule over" Earth and all it contains. In other words, humans bear responsibility—with God's help, of course—to manage Earth's resources, living and nonliving. God clearly expects humankind to exercise wise, cautious, ecologically sound management. The Scriptures from Genesis 3 to Revelation tell the story of humanity's failure to meet God's management standards. Thankfully, I can say that they bring us the good news, the gospel, along with the bad.

CHAPTER SEVEN

THE SOURCE CONTROVERSY

Genesis 1 succinctly and eloquently narrates the beginning of "the heavens and the earth." It explains what came into existence, how it came, and in what order. It specifies what scientists have recently verified as Earth's initial conditions. It describes the sequential steps, in correct chronological order, by which God prepared Earth for human habitation. Then it describes the final miracle of the creation week, the creation of humankind, male and female, in the image of God.

This flawless summary of an enormous body of natural-historical information comes to us in just a few dozen sentences. Moses, the probable author,[1-3] penned this account more than thirty-four centuries ago. Somehow he managed to get it right—the right initial conditions, the right events accurately described and correctly sequenced, and the right final conditions—to align with the still-accumulating evidence from multiple scientific disciplines equipped with space-age technological tools.

Ironically, pluralistic opinion today lumps this Genesis account with the host of creation myths from around the world. In fact, because it may not be the oldest *written* account of creation, many scholars assume it represents a "borrowed" and embellished version of the original creation myth, the Sumerian or Akkadian story first recorded in the time of Hammurabi the Great (circa 1750 B.C.), the *Enuma Elish*.

Identifying the Source

Among all the world's creation accounts, the *Enuma Elish*,[4] an epic poem found in the library of Ashurbanipal (circa 640 B.C.) at Nineveh, bears the greatest similarity to the biblical story (as does the very similar *Atra-hasis Epic* of the Sumerians[5]). It describes creation as a sequence of discrete events beginning from a watery chaos. First comes light, then the creation of land, the appointment of various celestial bodies for signs, seasons, and days, and the creation of beasts and creeping things.

In the light of modern science and in comparison with other creation stories, the *Enuma Elish* stands apart. The Germanic *Elder Edda* describes a land of extreme cold (the north) separated by a huge chasm from the land of fire (the south). As ice pours into the chasm from the north, fire from the south turns the ice to mist. Frost maidens and a giant, Ymir, condense from the mist; sparks from the fire form the stars; Ymir is killed by his grandson, who then creates the earth, clouds, and sea from various parts of Ymir's corpse. Ymir's grandson creates humans from the trees, and a gigantic ash tree supports the universe.[6]

The Iroquois tell of an ancient "chief" who pushed a pregnant woman through a hole in the sky onto the back of a giant tortoise that was swimming by on the surface of some water. Birds dived into the water, picked up some mud, and deposited it on the tortoise's back. This mud became Earth's surface. The woman gave birth to twins whose offspring populated Earth.[7]

According to one African account, Mbere, the creator, made man "before anything at all was made."[8] Human beings are the first thing God creates rather than the last.

The Germanic and Iroquois stories reflect the wondrous imaginative capacities of the human mind. The African story reflects the importance of human life. These stories were told and retold to wide-eyed children for generations, but no one with even rudimentary awareness of the physical realm would say they belong to that realm.

As remarkable as the *Enuma Elish* may be in some of its apparent reality connections, that ancient story also departs from fact (or testability) at several points, including these:

1. It places the creation of man before the creation of the animals, large and small.
2. It tells of both a saltwater ocean and a freshwater ocean coexisting (that is, in contact with one another) prior to the creation of land.

3. The material comprising celestial bodies, land, and human bodies comes from one source: the corpses and blood of gods killed in combat with each other.[9-11]

A pattern emerges from a comparison of the various accounts. That pattern suggests that all creation accounts share a common source in spiritual reality and a common source in physical actuality. The spiritual nature of humans convinces us that our life has meaning and purpose and drives us to explain our origin and destiny. The Creator of all spiritual life gave to the first humans an account of our origin and destiny, a way to understand our meaning and purpose. That story was passed from Adam and Eve to their progeny. Many generations later it began to take written form. That God-inspired story emanating from the ancient region of Mesopotamia became increasingly distorted with time and distance from that source. According to the book of Exodus, God corrected all those distortions in a direct discourse with Moses.[12]

Distinctives of the Genesis Account

While Abraham shared the same geography with Hammurabi, he predated him by two or three centuries. Therefore, it seems safe to say that the original creation story, an oral account given long before a written one, seems more likely identifiable by its distinctive characteristics rather than by the date of the earliest-known written document.

As the *Enuma Elish* and other creation stories stand side by side with Genesis 1, striking differences appear. Rather than groping its way through a primeval mist and wandering down corridors of fanciful absurdity and bloody conflicts among demigods, the biblical accounts outline physical events in an ordered, matter-of-fact sequence.

The gods of other creation accounts bear little if any resemblance to the God of the biblical account. He is simultaneously singular and plural, and exists discretely apart from His creation. He possesses unlimited power and goodness, mind and heart. He is a personal being, not just a force or an idea. He is the deity who controls all nature, who is in no way confined or limited by nature, though He is in some sense personally present throughout it. He is not a deified part of nature or even the deification of nature. He manifests none of the moral weaknesses seen in all humanity. Though evil exists both in the physical realm and in the spiritual realm, the evil is not *in* God, as pantheistic and monistic religions assert.

The creating done by the God of the Bible differs fundamentally from any creating of which human beings are capable. This God creates material and spiritual substance out of nothing (see "What Is Nothing?" below). No other account yet uncovered even vaguely suggests that the Creator brought into existence all matter, energy, space, and time.

WHAT IS NOTHING?

Physicists, unlike philosophers, use five different definitions of nothing in their models of creation. The accuracy of the declaration that God created the cosmos out of "nothing" depends on which definition of nothing the statement implies. These are the five: (1) lack of matter; (2) lack of matter and energy; (3) lack of matter, energy, and the four large expanding space-time dimensions of the universe;[13] (4) lack of matter, energy, and all ten space-time dimensions of the universe;[14] and (5) lack of any entity, being, existence, dimensionality, activity, or substance whatever. The Bible says God created the universe we detect and measure from that which no human can detect and measure.[15] In other words, the universe came from nothing as defined in number four above.

Unlike other creation stories, the biblical creation account bears no hint of political motive. The *Enuma Elish* unabashedly advances the cause of Babylonian supremacy over Mesopotamia.[16] Similar racist, elitist, or economic agendas can be detected in many nonbiblical creation accounts. Some seem blatant, others subtle. The biblical Adam, however, is simply "man"; and Eve, "the mother of all humans"; and their dwelling place, "a garden in the East."

The overarching distinctive of the biblical creation account lies in its clear, simple factuality. Unlike any other account, it lies open to testing against established science and history. Though widely publicized misinterpretations of Genesis 1 clash with accepted facts (see chapters ten and eleven), no problems remain when straightforward biblical rules of interpretation are applied. This openness to testing—testing for validity, testing for human limitations and biases—commands attention. The Genesis account of creation cannot be flippantly dismissed as irrelevant. If the probability of its "supernature" can be sustained, then we must indeed face its spiritual implications.

CHAPTER EIGHT

REST: DAY SEVEN

With creation of the human species, male and female, Earth's only spirit beings, designed "in the image of God," the activity of God's creative week ends. Genesis 1 reaches its jubilant climax. But the week isn't over yet. There's one more day (Genesis 2:2-3):

> By the seventh day God had finished the work he had been
> doing; so on the seventh day he rested from all his work.
> And God blessed the seventh day and made it holy,
> because on it he rested from all the work of creating that
> he had done.

Does the word "rest" imply that God grew weary? A look into the Hebrew text sheds light, but even a moment's reflection on the English can help. The Hebrew word for "rested" is *shabat*. It carries a meaning mentioned in some biblical footnotes as "ceased." Anyone who has studied music will recognize that this meaning also applies to the English "rest." When musicians come to a certain symbol in their musical score, they rest or cease from sounding their instrument for as long as the symbol indicates. Their cessation has nothing to do with weariness (though they may be glad for a breather).

God blessed that day and made it holy, setting it apart as a day to rest, or cease, from His work of creating. He also set up a rest day (twenty-four hours) for humans[1] and a rest "day" (one year) for tilled land,[2] knowing what would be best for each.

The Seventh Day Continues

Each of the six creation days closes with the same refrain: "There was evening, and there was morning," then the day's number. The statement suggests that each day had a start time (to begin with evening makes sense, since the creation days began in darkness and ended in light) and an end time. However, the refrain is not attached to the seventh day. Its closure is missing.

Given the consistency of this element in the account of the first six days, its absence from the account of the seventh day can be taken as a meaningful hint: the day has not ended. This interpretation receives confirmation in other portions of Scripture. Psalm 95:7-11, John 5:16-18, and Hebrews 4:1-11, each passage the work of a different writer, declaring that the seventh creation day began after the creation of Adam and Eve, continues through the present, and extends into the future. Revelation 21 reveals that the seventh day will eventually come to an end (after evil is conquered) as God resumes His creative endeavors in the making of a new heaven and earth, a new cosmos with new physical laws, appropriate, as always, to the fulfillment of His divine purposes and plans.[3]

The scientific record, as well as Scripture, affirms the continuance of the seventh day, the cessation of divine creative activity. According to the fossil record, new life-forms proliferated through the millions of years before modern man arrived on the scene. Though frequent extinctions occurred, the introduction rate for new species matched or outstripped the extinction rate. Then came the humans.

In the years of human history, the extinction rate has increased significantly—some environmentalists would say frighteningly—because of human activity.[4-7] Removing the human factor still leaves an extinction rate of at least one species per year.[7] The introduction rate, however, immediately plummeted to a virtual zero. According to biologists Paul and Anne Ehrlich, "The production of a new animal species in nature has yet to be documented."[8]

Botanists argue for ongoing speciation. Field observers have documented some distinguishable differentiation.[9-10] Whether all of these new plants deserve distinct "species" labels remains a debatable question. Many scientists see most of the new plants merely as new breeds, or strains, of the old, rather than as new species. Whatever the case, no one denies the glaring, even frightening, imbalance of extinction and speciation.

Physical conditions on Earth before Adam and Eve, during the era of species proliferation, compared to now, have not changed dramatically. Research indicates that natural evolutionary processes, the observable microevolution, occurs at roughly the same rate today as it did before humans. Science offers no explanation, as yet, for the sudden change in the speciation rate, but the Bible offers one: the difference comes from the change in God's level of creative activity. Before Adam and Eve, it was high. After Adam and Eve, it dropped to zero.

A Clue to the Meaning of "Day"

If the seventh "day" continues, as Scripture indicates, we have a significant clue for interpreting the word *yôm*, or "day," for each of the six creation intervals as a time span longer than twenty-four hours. Interpretation of this word became a controversial issue only in the last few hundred years, as the Bible was translated into English and widely distributed. Many Bible readers were, and still are, unaware of the differences between Hebrew and English, and inaccurate conclusions result.

In English the word *day* enjoys flexible usage. We refer to the day of the dinosaurs and the day of the Romans, and no one misunderstands our meaning. But we recognize this usage as figurative, acknowledging just two literal definitions: a twenty-four-hour period, from midnight to midnight, and the daylight hours (roughly twelve, but varying from one latitude and season to another). English offers us many more word choices if we want to denote a longer time period—*epoch*, *era*, and *age*, among others.

Hebrew, however, with its tiny vocabulary (more than a thousand times smaller than English), must manifest more flexibility. Most words have several meanings that can all be considered "literal," even though these definitions may vary much more widely than English speakers find comfortable. The word *yôm*, for instance, literally means a twenty-four-hour period, the daylight hours, or any long (but definite) period of time.[11-12] In biblical Hebrew (as opposed to post-Mosaic and post-Davidic Hebrew), no other word besides *yôm* carries the meaning of a long period of time.[13-15]

Likewise, many English Bible readers failed to note that twenty-four-hour days in biblical Hebrew are bracketed by evening to evening, less frequently by morning to morning, but not by evening was and morning was. Moreover, the Hebrew words for evening and morning (*'ereb* and *boqer*) also carry the literal definitions "ending of the day" and "beginning of day" respectively. The repeated use of "evening was and morning was" for the first six creation days indicates that they are not twenty-four-hour days but rather time periods with definite start-and-stop epochs.

The King James English wording, "And the evening and the morning were the first day" (and "the second" and "the third," and so on) replaced the two verbs and two subject complements present in each of the respective original Hebrew sentences with just one verb and one subject complement. This error led some English readers to conclude that the only "literal" interpretation of "day" was the twenty-four-hour interpretation.[16] Thus, they saw the creation chronology as a series of events packed into six consecutive twenty-four-hour days.

Later, when geologists, physicists, and astronomers advanced compelling evidence for the antiquity of Earth and the cosmos,[17] battle lines formed. From many a pulpit, churchgoers heard they must choose between the "sure Word of God" and the "uncertain findings of science," between the "pure motives of godly Bible scholars" and the "questionable motives of godless scientists." All this rancor arose from a simple misunderstanding.

Few, if any, other issues today generate as much animosity between Christians and secularists as does this doctrine of a recent, 144-hour creation week. The idea that the beginning of the universe, Earth, and life on Earth dates back only a few thousand years makes a mockery of all the sciences and infuriates scientists. Some, who might be open to considering alternatives to the naturalistic, gradualistic, nontheistic evolutionary scenario cling tenaciously to that theory for fear of giving way, or even seeming to give way, to this preposterous notion.

The creation-date controversy has grown into a huge stumbling block for unbelievers. Unfortunately, though the block is made of paper, it succeeds as a distraction.

Removing the Block

As long as people confuse the *doctrine* of creation with the *date* of creation, the block will be hard to move. The early church fathers understood the distinction, but many twentieth-century fundamentalists and evangelicals struggle with it.

Ante-Nicene scholars devoted some two thousand pages of

commentary to the "hexameron," that part of Genesis 1 describing the six days of creation. No other portion of the Bible received nearly as much of their attention. Yet in all their pages of commentary only about two pages total addressed the meaning of "day" or the time frame for creation.[18] Their comments on the subject remained tentative, with the majority favoring the "long day" (typically a thousand year period) interpretation—apart from the influence of science. Not one explicitly endorsed the twenty-four-hour interpretation. But all believed that God was intimately involved in the creative process, and that this doctrine makes a difference in how we respond to God and His Word.

"It Was Good"

The statement "it was good" appears seven times in Genesis 1: once in God's evaluation of the first day's work, twice in evaluation of the third, once for each of the fourth, fifth, and sixth days, and once again in the concluding remarks. Some scholars and skeptics have raised a fuss—an unnecessary fuss—over its absence from the verses describing Day Two.

God did call His second creation day's work "good" as He looked back over the whole week (verse 31). His evaluation applies to the entire creation, the events of the second day included. Notice that the sixth-day declaration, "it was good," follows God's creation of land mammals, not His creation of Adam and Eve. Does this give us a basis for concluding that He had a negative evaluation of humans? No one could reasonably argue the point, for God makes clear in verses 27-30 and in all of the chapter that follows that He takes delight in all He has made. From a strictly rhetorical perspective, the "it was so" attached to Day Two conveys the essence of "it was good," if we consider whose commands became "so."

From a modern scientific perspective, the omission of the "it was good" for the second creation day may simply imply that God's action during the first creation day went a long way toward bringing about the events of the second day. If that is the case, the "goodness" of the first creation day applies to both days.

"And It Was So"

The statement "and it was so" appears six times in Genesis 1: once in the account of the second creation day, twice in the account of the third, once each in the accounts of the fourth and sixth days, and once again in the chapter's summation. Its placement seems more a matter of artistic license than of interpretive significance. From a theological perspective, it emphasizes the point that when God speaks or decides what will be done, it will be done. We can count it as a certainty. From a scientific perspective, it may simply denote the completion of some aspects of creation while other aspects continue to undergo preparation or transformation. In both cases, the statement expresses an affirmation of God's authority and power.

CHAPTER NINE

A SPIRITUAL PERSPECTIVE ON CREATION
GENESIS 2

Why is the creation story repeated, and why is the second version so different from the first? Does the Bible really claim that Adam named *all* the animals? Was Eve actually made from one of Adam's ribs? Who came first, Adam or the animals? Where was the Garden of Eden and what was it like? Could Adam and Eve have lived forever in the garden if they had not sinned?

These are but a few of the many questions evoked by Genesis 2. They differ substantially from the questions raised by Genesis 1. Why? Because the content has a different theme and a different frame of reference. The questions arising from Genesis 1 focus more on physical creation issues—the what, the where, the how, and the in-what-order of creation. Genesis 2 zeros in on the why of creation. So the questions arising from it tend to address theological and philosophical concerns, most of which I touch on in the paragraphs that follow.

Shift of Purpose
Although physical creation events receive brief mention in Genesis 2, this part of the creation story centers on our progenitors—who they were (thus, who we are) in relation to God and the rest of creation, including each other, and their responsibilities. While Genesis 1 includes a summary statement of humanity's assignments on Earth, Genesis 2 makes only passing reference to the physical creation events, and it does not purport to assign them a sequence or explain them. The cross-references serve a rhetorical function: they bring a sense of cohesiveness to the two passages.

In other words, Genesis 1 presents the major physical creation events in a time-ordered sequence but gives just an abridged list of humanity's responsibilities. In Genesis 2 God lays out humanity's major responsibilities in a step-by-step sequence but provides a mere abbreviated list of physical creation acts. Neither more nor less can be inferred from the differences between the two chapters.

Filling the Earth

In Genesis 1:28 God issued this clear, direct command to Adam and Eve:

> "Be fruitful and increase in number; fill the earth and sub-due it. Rule over the fish of the sea and the birds of the air and over every living creature that moves on the ground."

God gave them authority and responsibility to manage all the biological resources of planet Earth. To carry out their assignment, they would need helpers and they would need to spread out. They and their progeny would have to search out the number and geographic distribution of the various species of life; determine the size, habitat, characteristics, and needs of each species; and discern the various ways each species enhances the well-being of other species, including humans. They also needed to determine the kinds and quantities of various resources required and discern how these resources could best be managed for the benefit of all life. No wonder God commanded them to be fruitful and multiply. This job is big!

But is it too big? Though the numbers I'm about to give you may seem incredible, they can be checked on any pocket calculator (see pages 102 to 103). If Adam and Eve and their progeny had reproduced at the rate of just one child every four years during the "middle years" (equivalent to the childbearing portion of today's average life span) of their long lives, they could have produced as many as 17 billion offspring and still have had many years to enjoy their children, grandchildren, great-grandchildren, and so on, before their 900th anniversary. They did not, however, complete their assignment (for reasons to be discussed later).

Vegetarian Diet

In Genesis 1:29 we read that God gave Adam and Eve some dietary guidelines. They needed help identifying what was healthy for humans to eat at that time and what was not:

"I give you every seed-bearing plant on the face of the
whole earth and every tree that has fruit with seed in it.
They will be yours for food."

Some readers interpret this statement merely as an indication
that all food resources derive from plants. However, Genesis 9:3
suggests that it was, indeed, a specific instruction about what to eat:

"Everything that lives and moves will be food for you. Just
as I gave you the green plants, I now give you everything
[both plants and animals]."

Vegetarianism perfectly suits the potential longevity of the first
humans. Animal tissue contains between ten and ten thousand times
the concentration of heavy elements that plant material contains. This
difference sounds drastic, but it poses an insignificant health risk for
people living only 120 years or less (the limit God imposed at the time
of the Flood). However, the difference is by no means trivial for people
living nearly a thousand years.

God also set diet guidelines for birds and mammals (Genesis 1:30):

"And to all the beasts of the earth and all the birds of the
air and all the creatures that move on the ground—everything that has the breath of life in it—I give every green
plant for food."

He did not alter these guidelines when He widened human
dietary limits (Genesis 9:2-3), so it seems fair to assume that these
represent clues for the sake of management rather than restrictions.

The distinction between God's gift to people, "every seed-bearing plant . . . and every tree that has fruit with seed in it," and His
gift to animals, "every green plant," may be significant. Both animals and humans ingest some non-green plants—mushrooms, for
example—but green plants are the foundation of the food chain.
Perhaps to assist Adam and Eve in their management of the planet's
resources, God helped them understand that all of the life entrusted
to their care depends ultimately on green plants for survival.

Setting the Garden Scene

Whereas the physical creation account of Genesis 1 encompasses the
whole planet, the opening portion of Genesis 2 sets the scene for God's

preparation of a special home for Adam and Eve, the Garden of Eden. He contrasted the past situation of Earth with the richness and beauty He held in store in this one garden. The words are arranged for sensory impact, not for time sequence. The text simply reminds us of a time and place devoid of "shrubs," "plants," "rain," and "man" (Genesis 2:5). The text does not imply that shrubs predate plants or that plants predate rain.

The description "streams came up from the earth and watered the whole surface of the ground" (Genesis 2:6) probably refers to the environs of Eden. The contrast between "rain" (verse 5) and "streams" (verse 6) must not be overinterpreted as an indication that rain never fell upon Earth or the environs of Eden until the Flood. The Hebrew word used for rain is *matar,* and it refers to any kind of liquid precipitation.[1] The Hebrew word for "streams" is *'ed.* It can mean "mist," "vapor," or "flood," as well as "stream."[2] Mist, of course, would be encompassed by the word *matar,* and the two words, *matar* and *'ed,* could be synonymous here.

With certainty we can deduce from Genesis 2 that Earth at one time had no water cycle (before the second creation day) and that the region of Eden, just prior to God's preparation of the garden, was watered by streams and perhaps mist. If Eden were situated somewhere on the mid- to southern Mesopotamian plain, this description would fit the meteorological conditions we currently see.

The continuity of clouds and rain from Genesis 1 through Genesis 10 (and beyond) receives confirmation in Job 36:27-30, 37:13, 38:25-30, Psalm 104:3-6, Psalm 148:4-8, and Proverbs 8:28. These poetic reflections on the Genesis 1 creation events clarify that the "water above" (on the second creation day) was clouds and rain. Jumping ahead for a moment to the Flood account, we can draw some inferences about rainfall, based on the Psalms and on Genesis 2:5-6. The Bible makes no claim that the rainbow God showed Noah in Genesis 9 and the rain that caused it had never before been seen on Earth. The text does say that the rainbow was established by God as a sign, or symbol, of His promise that He would never again destroy by flood all humanity and all the soulish animals associated with humanity. (See chapters eighteen and nineteen for further discussion of the Flood account.)

God has made several covenants (binding commitments) with the human race, seven to be exact. As a seal or symbolic reminder of each of these seven covenants, God chose something familiar, something previously existing. Bread, wine, and water, for instance, serve as symbols of communion and baptism. Thus, the rainbow fits this pattern of something old and familiar adopted as a sign of something new.

Geologists have evidence that rain began falling on Earth long before the human era. Certain kinds of sedimentary deposits preserve the splash patterns of ancient raindrops, large and small, just as clearly as other sedimentary deposits show us the pattern of ancient waves lapping ocean beaches and lake shores. Thus, the Bible and the geological record agree that raindrops of all sizes have been falling from the sky throughout human history and for millions of years before.

Animals Came When?
Misinterpretation of Genesis 2:19 has raised many questions and doubts among skeptics and others, though the problem, once again, comes from failure to consider the context:

> Now the LORD God had formed out of the ground all the beasts of the field and all the birds of the air. He brought them to the man to see what he would name them; and whatever the man called each living creature, that was its name.

Some scholars, perhaps influenced directly or indirectly by the "higher critics" (see chapter ten), read into this passage that man's creation predated the creation of the animals, and the creation of the animals predated the creation of woman. Because Genesis 1 clearly claims that God created humans, male and female, *after* He created the mammals and birds, such a reading of Genesis 2 puts it in direct contradiction to Genesis 1, and a serious problem thus has been manufactured by faulty scholarship.

This supposed internal contradiction is routinely "exposed" in Western European schools and universities. Is it any wonder that the Bible holds so little attention and credibility among these Europeans?

The resolution of the supposed "problem" is simple. In chapter five I explained that verb tenses as English speakers know them do not exist in biblical Hebrew. Biblical Hebrew employs three verb forms. They express completed action, action not yet completed, and commands. The verb in Genesis 2:19 appears in the first form and simply indicates that the creation of the beasts and the birds occurred sometime in the past. The text says nothing about when such creatures were created relative to the creation of the first man. They could have been made either before or after the man, from a grammatical perspective.

Sequencing of physical events is not the purpose of Genesis 2. That purpose has already been achieved in Genesis 1, and the writer clearly has laid such issues to rest. The focus has shifted to other matters.

Naming of the Animals

To those who wonder how Adam could possibly name several million animal species and still have time left to get acquainted with Eve and raise children with her, some help comes from a review of Genesis 1:24-25 and the Hebrew word *nephesh*. Notice the similarity between the list of Day Six animals and the list of animals (with the addition, of course, of the birds from Day Five) in Genesis 2:20, the verse in question:

> So the man gave names to all the livestock, the birds of the air and all the beasts of the field.

The Hebrew words employed here for the creatures include *behema*, *'op*, and *hayya*, words for long-legged land mammals and birds.[3-4]

Animal population specialists have tallied 9,500 bird species and 4,500 mammal species to date.[5] They anticipate that several hundred more species will be discovered in future field studies, especially bird species. Fossils of recently extinct species reveal that birds and mammals have suffered very high extinction rates at the hand of humans. Ecologists estimate that double the current number of bird and mammal species existed at the advent of the human race.[6] Assuming that ground-hugging mammals and sea mammals account for about one-third of all mammal species, about 20,000 bird species and about 6,000 long-legged land mammal species inhabited Earth when Adam arrived. Bird and mammal species' ranges of travel, according to fossil finds, were much larger at the advent of humanity than now. So we can reasonably conclude that as many as 4,500 bird and mammal species inhabited the environs of Eden.

If Adam were to examine a member (or members) of each species (the Hebrew word for "kind" used in Genesis 1:11,12,21,

24,25 could have a broader definition than our English word "species") for thirty to sixty minutes to ascertain its characteristics before assigning an appropriate name, he would need about a year to complete his task (given a forty-hour work week). A year may seem long to us, but to Adam it represented a tiny fraction of his life expectancy. He had insufficient time to age before meeting Eve but sufficient time to gain appreciation for his need for a partner.

Some interpreters suggest that before he fell into sin Adam manifested extremely high mental capacities and thus could examine and name animals at hyperspeed.[7-10] However, we find no hint of this possibility in the text. Furthermore, enhanced mental capabilities would seem to offer little speed advantage in the examining and naming of animals.[11]

Eve from Adam's Rib?

A popular mistranslation of Genesis 2:20-21 has led to a centuries-old, still-popular myth—that God made Eve from one of Adam's ribs. A careful rendering of the Hebrew text reveals a different scenario: First, God put Adam into a deep sleep, such as the sleep induced by anesthesia. While Adam slept, God removed a portion, something like a biopsy, from Adam's side and used that tissue in constructing Eve.

The text does not say that God made Eve totally and only from the tissue God took from Adam. It does suggest that the portion taken from Adam served a significant and substantial role in God's creation of Eve.

Current understanding of genetics makes us aware of what a shortcut this biopsy from Adam would represent. That biopsy would include a complete blueprint of all of Adam's cells, biochemical machinery, and morphology. With just a few million modifications here and there, the blueprint for Eve would be complete. The New Testament sheds some light on why God may have chosen to construct Eve from Adam's tissue sample:

> In the Lord . . . woman is not independent of man, nor is man independent of woman. For as woman came from man, so also man is born of woman.[12]

God created men and women as interdependent beings. In His divine foreknowledge of how men and women would later struggle over the superiority issue, God chose a means for creating the human race, male and female, that would make clear to all cultures and all generations their equal but distinct interdependence.

Adam's "Helper"

Many women and men take offense at Eve's designation as a "helper" for Adam. Again, the English word choice, with its "underling" modern connotation, creates the problem. *'Ezer* is the Hebrew word for "helper" in Genesis 2:18, 20. The Hebrews used this word with reference to a military ally (see, for example, 2 Chronicles 28:16 and Psalm 121:1-2), an ally that is essential for victory.[13] As Genesis 1 reveals, God's job assignment for humanity exceeds the limits of an individual, and as Genesis 3 reveals, humanity must face a daunting foe, a literal "enemy force," both within and without. By himself Adam lacked the resources to deal with the challenges and the enemy. He needed an ally, the right kind of ally.

In war, allies are different from one another, offering different assets necessary for victory. But regardless of what they have to contribute, they are necessary and equally valuable partners.

Together, Adam and Eve, men and women, can conquer. Divided and embattled, they fail.

Adam's Introduction to the Creation

Genesis 1 introduces us to all three "layers" of God's amazing, brand-new creative work, each set apart by the use of the verb *bara*: the physical creation, the soulish creation, and the spiritual creation. In Genesis 2 we read an account of God's introducing Adam in this same order to these three creation layers.

Adam first met the plants and soil of the special garden God prepared for him and his future mate. In tending to them, Adam must have begun to learn what he would need to know to manage the physical resources of Earth. At the same time he experienced the enjoyment that comes from working a magnificent garden. As enjoyable as the gardening may have been for him, however, God had something more wonderful in store.

God next brought to Adam all the birds and mammals of Eden, and Adam discovered the splendors of God's soulish creation. In naming these creatures Adam experienced a quality of relationship he had not known with the plants. Unlike the plants, these creatures could communicate with him, and with each other, and their intriguing behavior reflected their capacities for reasoning, choosing, and feeling. These creatures as yet had no fear of humans (Genesis 9:2), so, as much as we enjoy animals today, whether viewing them in the wild or caring for them as pets, Adam would have enjoyed these creatures even more. At the same time, Adam began to learn about the needs of the various animals and to realize the awesome responsibility, as well as the privilege and joy, of providing and caring for them. But as wonderful as this new level of relationship must have been, God had something still more wonderful in store.

Finally, God introduced Adam to Eve, a fellow spirit creature. Adam's exclamation upon seeing Eve for the first time makes clear that he was delighted. At long last, a creature he could enjoy at all levels, a creature that would help him explore, as he helped her, and she helped him, the height and depth and breadth of human capacities—body, soul, and spirit!

This step-by-step introduction communicates as effectively to us as it did to Adam and Eve God's desire that humanity appreciate and enjoy everything He created, from the stars in the sky to the starfish in the sea, from the moon in the heavens to the dirt beneath our feet, from the most timid animal to the fellow-creature who looks and acts and thinks and feels as we do. I believe He wanted Adam and Eve to understand the full extent of their responsibility and authority and capacity for enjoyment. After all, they had the capability, under God's guidance, to extend the conditions of Eden over much of the land area of Earth.

EDEN: GLOBAL OR LOCAL?

Some Bible interpreters try to claim that Eden was a paradise that encompassed the entire surface of planet Earth.[14-17] There are several textual clues, however, that Eden is limited to just one geographical locale on Earth. First, Genesis 2 informs us that after God created Adam from the dust of the earth He placed him in Eden. Second, the same chapter tells us God planted the Garden of Eden "in the east." Third, in Genesis 4 we discover that God banished Cain to the land of Nod which was "east of Eden." Fourth, Genesis 2 names four rivers, two of which are identifiable today, as flowing through Eden.

Given that Eden is a local piece of geography, Adam's perspective on life and death was somewhat different from Eve's before their fall into sin. Eve only knew of Eden. Adam was placed into Eden. Adam, unlike Eve, experienced the difference between the wild creation and the tamed creation.

Eden's Location

The Genesis text tells us that God prepared and planted this garden "in the east."[18] Given that Moses, the likely writer of this account, considered Canaan (Israel today), or possibly Sinai, as the center of his compass, we can reasonably conclude that Eden must have been located somewhere east of Canaan or Sinai.

The text also tells us that Eden was watered by a river that flowed through it[19] and then divided. The river's four head streams are identified: the Pishon, the Gihon, the Tigris, and the Euphrates.[20] The Tigris and Euphrates have been identified throughout human history as the two primary rivers flowing through Mesopotamia. These rivers and others in the large, flat valley area frequently changed course and split into smaller streams. Satellite photographs identify many dry riverbeds throughout Mesopotamia where water at one time flowed. These or others long lost from view could be the beds of the Pishon and the Gihon.

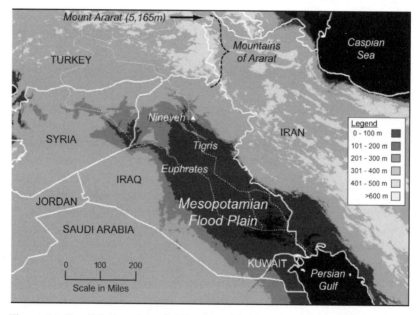

Figure 9.1: Possible Locations for Garden of Eden (within line of dashes)
There are two places today where the Tigris and Euphrates rivers come close together. Since these rivers and their tributaries change course frequently, other locations for Eden are possible.

At two locations (see map on previous page), one just north of the ruins of ancient Babylon and another in the Armenian highlands (the mountains of Ararat mentioned in chapter eighteen), the Tigris and Euphrates currently come close to each other. Modern geography, thus, suggests the possibility that the Garden of Eden was located in the south-central portion of the Mesopotamian plain or in the foothills just to the north of it.

Adam and Eve in Paradise

The garden's name, Eden, means "delight," and what a delightful place it must have been! What Adam and Eve experienced and possessed in the Garden of Eden—a garden designed and planted by God Himself—defines the word *paradise*, the word consistently chosen for Eden by the Jewish scholars who first translated the Old Testament into Greek. Its fruit trees both "pleased the eye" and yielded "good food." Its perfect watering system made it verdant and gorgeous. (How many gardeners among us struggle to get the watering just right?)

Eden offered more than a perfect haven for plants and animals. It contained other riches as well: "gold, aromatic resin, and onyx," treasures of great value to ancient civilizations. This list of items gives us only a sampling of the garden's riches, not a complete inventory. It serves primarily to suggest that everything prized by humankind could be found in abundance in Eden.

In Eden our first parents had access to "the tree of life." The fruit and leaves of this tree guaranteed them perfect health and well-being.[21] (Note: The text does not tell us explicitly to what degree Adam and Eve, before sinning, experienced the effects of aging, illness, or injury.)

Adam and Eve were free to enjoy all the riches of God's creation to the fullest in Eden. They enjoyed perfect peace and harmony with the animals, which approached them without fear or hesitation. Imagine being able to play with one of the great cats or ride on the back of a rhinoceros!

Better yet, the man and woman enjoyed perfect peace and harmony and fearlessness with each other, continuously, at all levels—physical, mental, emotional, volitional, and spiritual. Even better still, they enjoyed peace and harmony and fellowship with God. He was with them, available to them, loving them perfectly and completely, and they knew it. If they needed guidance or direction or answers to questions of any kind, they could ask and receive.

The second chapter of Genesis ends with the profound statement that Eden was free from shame. Because of shame, none of us today really knows what perfect peace and harmony feels like, looks like, or sounds like. When we submit our lives to Jesus Christ's authority and receive His pardon for all our sins, we begin to experience the kind of love, acceptance, and inward transformation that helps erase our shame. But we live in a sinful world. We have experienced the effects of evil—our own and others'—and we still struggle (and fail) to resist temptation. Our thoughts and motives are tainted. In Eden, before sin, Adam and Eve did not face this struggle, nor did they ever feel embarrassed or bad.

As idyllic as Eden must have been, God understood its limits and had something better in His plans. Eden's delights were limited to what is possible within the matter, energy, and space-time dimensions of the universe and within the laws of physics governing it. More important, Adam and Eve's respect for God's authority and wisdom remained untested. The potential for self-exaltation and for usurpation lurked beneath the surface. God prepared a test, the seemingly tragic results of which would eventually expel humanity from earthly paradise. God, however, by stepping back into human history, redeems and prepares people[22] who so choose to receive an indescribably superior paradise: the new creation.[23-24]

CHAPTER TEN

MODERN CRITICISM ARISES

The first scholars to seriously attack the Genesis creation accounts for "internal inconsistency" were Richard Simon, an Oratorian priest, writing in 1678,[1] and Campegius Vitringa, a Dutch Reformed theologian, writing in 1707.[2] Their arguments fell on deaf ears, for the most part. Contemporaries ignored them and later generations forgot them. But the questions they raised eventually occurred to others.

The Birth of Higher Criticism

Jean Astruc, a physician in the French royal court, had the means, influence, and motivation to spread his ideas about the Genesis creation accounts. Though these ideas did not originate with him, he garnered the title as founder of "critical" studies of the Old Testament.

In 1753 Astruc published his first treatise undermining the credibility of Genesis. Unfortunately, his education and position kept people from questioning his credibility and his intellectual honesty. Even a cursory glance at his personal history—his recanting of his family's Huguenot faith, a series of illicit relationships, and his swindling of several widows and their families—reveals possible motives for discrediting the Bible.[3] Enough of his peers had similar motives to make them eagerly receptive to his work.

Astruc asserted that Moses had borrowed and interwoven material from several independent sources in his writing of Genesis. To support this conclusion, he relied on the claim that Genesis contained two contradictory creation narratives, which "obviously" came from different sources.[4-6]

Soon after Astruc's ideas began circulating, Johann Eichhorn, perhaps the most famous theologian of the time, published these same conclusions, though he credited a later-born scribe, not Moses, with the compilation of conflicting narratives.[7] Eichhorn's publications make no reference to Astruc, but in a later book, *Introduction to the Old Testament*, he acknowledged his dependence on Astruc's material.[8] Eichhorn went on to popularize the notion that emerging geological research not only contradicted both Genesis chronologies but also the creation date for the heavens and the earth widely accepted by the church, the one proposed by Irish Anglican Archbishop James Ussher (4004 B.C.).

Soon Eichhorn and his German colleagues were bursting with ideas for publication. They theorized that much of the Old Testament represented a compilation of late, unreliable documents dating from 800 to 500 B.C. They argued that the biblical accounts of creation were edited versions of myths Hebrews borrowed from neighboring cultures.

We are left to wonder about the research methodology and presuppositions employed by Astruc, Eichhorn, and the emerging "higher critics." But their exegetical approach can only be described as simplistic. They presumed that the order in which various creation events appeared on the Bible page represented the chronology of the text. For the most part, they ignored verb choice, verb forms, contextual cues, indicators of parenthetical comment, and virtually all other syntactic features. The order of Genesis creation events they deduced[9-10] appears in Table 10.1.

Table 10.1: Genesis Creation Events According to the Higher Critics

Genesis 1 order of events	Genesis 2 order of events
1. heavens and earth created	1. heavens and earth created
2. light created	2. plant life created
3. light divided from darkness	3. man (male only) created
4. heaven ("firmament") created	4. animal life created
5. land separated from water	5. woman made from man's side
6. plant life created	
7. sun, moon, and stars created	
8. animal life created	
9. man (male and female) created	

Most notably, these critics placed the creation of virtually everything but the "heavens and earth" in contradictory positions on the two lists. And, of course, they showed contradictions with well-established scientific concepts.

Higher Criticism Matures

The views on Genesis published by the German higher critics prompted many theologians and other intellectuals around the world to conclude that the Bible is unreliable, both internally and externally. For them, the search for God either ended or took a significant turn toward subjectivity—blind "faith" divorced from reason and fact.

This brand of faith is exalted and promoted among many theologians and religious groups of all kinds even today. Many, if not most, churches fail to teach a biblical definition of faith. According to abundant scriptural discussion, faith is founded on well-tested fact and on what God has clearly done. It encompasses the mind as well as the will and emotions. It implies trusting on the basis of being "convinced," not on the basis of wishful thinking or separation of mind from heart, as if that were really possible. (See Isaiah 50:10; 1 Thessalonians 5:21; Hebrews 11:1; also examples in Exodus 4:5; 19:9; Isaiah 41:20; 43:9-10; John 11:15,42; 13:19; 14:29; 19:35; and 20:31.)

Early Response to the Higher Critics

Some Protestants took what seemed a less drastic, more reasonable position. They deemed the Bible an extremely complex set of books, each book composed of several documents varying in quality and from disparate sources. Thus, they viewed their critical task as sifting the truth of God from the human myth and error, the wheat from the chaff, the gold from the dross. Their most conservative constituents formalized this theological position: the Bible is true and reliable as a guide to doctrine and practice (the practice of worship and human relationships, responsibilities, and government), but not as a text of history and science. The miracles may be considered legends.

One can easily imagine the reaction of individuals and churches holding tenaciously to the view that the Bible is the divinely inspired Word of God from cover to cover. They condemned the notion that people can stand in judgment over the Bible, choosing which parts are true and worthy to be followed and which parts can justifiably be ignored. While seeing through the interpretive errors in the higher critics' conclusion that Genesis 2 contradicts Genesis 1, they made little comment about the supposed external contradictions. Perhaps because they felt uncertain about tackling science and scientists, they initially made little if any response to claims that Genesis and science irreconcilably contradict each other.

Most Christian fundamentalists of the nineteenth century clung to the Protestant creed *Sola Scriptura*, which they interpreted to mean that a believer need give heed only to the words of the Bible, for these alone are true and trustworthy. Typically, they regarded what science and scientists had to say as suspect, deserving little time and attention.

The Great Divide

The (seemingly) contrasting positions on faith reflected a growing schism in the Protestant community. One camp, often labeled conservative or fundamentalist, resolutely held the Bible as their sole authority, taking what they called a "high" view of Scripture. Some held the Bible so high as to make their interpretations of it objects of worship. Typically the "high view" Christians gave far more serious attention to their understanding of the words of the Bible than to the words of scientists about the facts of nature.

The other camp, often labeled liberal or modernist, viewed the Bible as an important literary work, "inspired," but not in the strictest sense. They certainly had no respect for its history, geography, anthropology, astronomy, or comments on other scientific matters. This disrespect, of course, often carried over into theology.

A Counterreaction

The higher critics and their disciples, astounded that so many Protestants would willingly ignore their claims of external inconsistency and contradiction, viewed the conservative response (of ignoring science) as a defensive maneuver. Assuming that these traditionalists had tacitly caved in to science's insurmountable challenges, they assessed their own position as strong and the others' as hopelessly weak.

For two centuries, higher criticism theologians and their followers in the church have tended to view Christian conservatives as naive, unsophisticated, and intellectually inferior. This opinion was fostered in part by the success of the Enlightenment.

Atheist and agnostic scholars at European universities heaped abundant praise on the higher critics for their ground-breaking scholarship. Perhaps unconscious of the sense of "triumph" over Christian theism, which these nontheistic scholars felt and expressed, many of the higher critics and their lay followers received the accolades as further proof of their own intellectual and educational prowess—and of the strength of their theological perspective.

Scientific Reaction

Curiously, more than a few Christian fundamentalists of the late nineteenth century adopted Darwin's theory of biological evolution.[11] Their voices, however, were quickly muffled or forgotten.

Physical scientists, especially those who participated in church, though typically not sympathetic to Darwin's claims, felt more than astounded that so many conservative Christians would choose to ignore modern advances in the geological and astronomical sciences. They were both appalled and incensed. Many could not fathom how their work, which they saw as contributing to the body of truth, could be so easily shunned. Most were shocked that science and scientists could be given so little credit. They were especially surprised that Bible verses promoting natural theology, the study of God through research on nature, would be so quickly glossed over. The latter move seemed no different from the higher critics' tactic of choosing which parts of the Bible to follow and which to ignore.

The result? The majority of Western scientists in the nineteenth century either joined the followers of the higher critics or left the church altogether, calling themselves scientific agnostics. This move further convinced the higher critics that they were on the right track. Unfortunately, the polarization and alienation between scientists and conservative Christians increasingly isolated that segment of the Protestant community. It kept them away from some of the most convincing evidences in support of their conviction about the reliability of the Bible.

Peace at Any Price

Abhorring the conflict between scientists and theologians and between the higher critics and conservatives, not to mention the turmoil among the laity over the Genesis creation accounts, a growing informal coalition of church leaders and scientists proposed that scholars and lay people alike back off from "overinterpreting" Genesis 1 and 2. All the conflict and turmoil could end, they suggested, if everyone would just agree to acknowledge that the Genesis creation accounts are no more than poetic ballads intended to communicate the beauty and harmony of nature. That is, they claimed Genesis 1 and 2 were metaphorical devices to express God's enjoyment of nature and His exhortation to humanity to join Him in appreciating the wonders of the natural realm.

Given the lack of any significant voice for the reconciliation of Genesis 1 and 2 with established scientific data, the appeal of these exegetical pacifists carried weight, at least for a while. Who, after all, could deny the artistry in the composition of Genesis 1 and 2? But who would challenge the obvious fallacy that beauty denotes fantasy? (One group certainly did, and their efforts are summarized in the next chapter. To them, the peacemakers had sounded a battle cry.) And who would mistake elegant prose for poetry?

Poetic accounts of creation do exist in the Bible. Their style and structure stand in marked contrast to Genesis 1 and 2. The most famous, Psalm 104, is a song about the majesty, power, and wisdom of God in creating and shaping the heavens and the earth for humanity. That song clearly implies that God performed mighty works in nature in an orderly, planned fashion. For the composer of Psalm 104, Genesis 1 and 2 were not devoid of scientific content. He made specific reference to those chapters in concrete, scientific terms. So did King Solomon. In Proverbs 8:22-31 Solomon created powerfully evocative metaphors to describe God's attributes using material from the Genesis creation account. Other poetic accounts of creation in the Bible—such as Job 36–41 and Psalms 8, 19, 33, and 148—reflect on Genesis 1 and 2 as a nonfiction prose, a literally true record of events.

Critique of the Critics

Many conservative Protestant theologians have devoted their careers to researching the theological and exegetical claims of higher criticism theologians. Today, several textbooks present a thorough history, new research findings, and careful analysis of the flaws in the higher critics' suppositions.[12-14] While I recommend these books, my approach in this book is to remove the basis for conflict, the "need" for a higher critical approach, by demonstrating that a literal reading of the Genesis creation chapters integrates perfectly with the established scientific record.

CHAPTER ELEVEN

GENESIS AND "CREATION SCIENCE"

The twentieth century saw the rise of a new champion for the reliability of the Genesis creation story: the "creation scientist." Accepting the assumption of higher critics and other scholars that no resolution is possible between the established scientific record and a literal reading of Genesis, these science-trained Christians sought to discredit accepted scientific notions and reestablish science in terms that would appear to be in concordance with their particular interpretation, which they deemed the only correct interpretation, of the opening chapters of Genesis.

Invention of Flood Geology

The founders of scientific creationism were initially drawn together in defense of the Genesis Flood account. The precipitating event was the 1923 publication of a book by George McCready Price entitled *The New Geology*.[1] Price, a Seventh-Day Adventist layman and amateur geologist, wanted to combat the incursion of "evolutionary" teachings (defined as the belief that Earth and life date back further than a few thousand years) into Christian churches.

Price insisted that Genesis 6–9 reports a relatively recent Flood inundating all the land masses of the planet. The Genesis Flood, he claimed, could account for all the geologic features on all the continents, all the fossils ever found, and all Earth's limestone, coal, oil, gas, and topsoil deposits. According to Price, the sediments, fossils, and fossil fuels were laid down quickly in the great Flood catastrophe, not through hundreds of events over hundreds of millions of years.

Price cared little that his views found no support among science professionals and scholars. Scientists, in his opinion, suffered from such a severe case of "university-itis"[2] that their findings and conclusions would always and only fit the reigning paradigms, Darwinism in particular. His anti-intellectual, anti-science bias still echoes in the churches today.

Price thought he had invented a weapon not just for the destruction of evolutionism (the belief that life-forms become progressively more advanced through natural processes) but for any and all theories accepting the geologic time scales that scientific research revealed. These included the gap theory (the interpretation of a gap of billions of years between Genesis 1:1 and six twenty-four-hour creation days) and the day-age theory (the interpretation of the six creation days of Genesis 1 as six long periods of time). The gap and day-age theories he called "creation on the installment plan."[3] He denounced the gap theory as "heretical"[4] and the day-age theory as a "libel on Moses."[5] The latter he viewed as an attack on the cherished Seventh-Day Adventist doctrine of the Sabbath.[5]

Price's book and ideas received an enormous boost from the Scopes trial (1925), the prosecution of a Tennessee educator for teaching biological evolution in a public school. Fundamentalist and conservative Christians, stinging from the humiliation of their champion, prosecuting attorney William Jennings Bryan, desperately sought some way to bring the evolutionists down a notch. Price's book, his fervor, and his considerable skills as a public speaker made him the new David, courageously taking on the Goliath of evolutionism.

Ramm's Appeal

By the 1950s some credentialed scientists in the Christian community were becoming alarmed at the growing popularity of Price's "Flood geology." Bernard Ramm, an accomplished scholar in the philosophy of science, wrote *The Christian View of Science and Scripture* (1955)[6] to alert Christian scientists to the growing popularity of Price's views and to warn them that such views had already become "the backbone of much Fundamentalist thought about geology, creation, and the flood."[7] He urged his readers to act quickly to repudiate Price's notion of a recent creation (all creation packed into 144 hours less than ten thousand years ago), which he called "narrow bibliolatry,"[8] and to adopt what he termed "progressive creationism."

Ramm's appeal backfired, perhaps because of his inflammatory reference to "narrow bibliolatry," which many conservative Christians took as an attack on the Bible. His broad definition of progressive creationism[9] too closely paralleled the higher critics' view. Ramm denied not only twenty-four-hour creation days but also six extended creation periods, or "day-ages."[10] He also denied the recent appearance of humanity[11] and the scientific accuracy of Genesis 1,[12] preferring to view this story as something other than a factual chronology.[13] For these reasons—and because the list of "great creative acts" Ramm and his followers accepted kept shrinking through the years—Ramm's work served to heighten rather than limit the popularity of Flood geology in conservative Christian churches.

A Response to Ramm

Ramm's movement toward the camps of higher critics and evolutionists (albeit "theistic" evolutionists) so thoroughly upset John C. Whitcomb, Jr., professor of theology at Grace Theological Seminary, and Henry M. Morris,[14] chairman of the department of civil engineering at Virginia Polytechnic Institute, that they published a rebuttal in 1961, *The Genesis Flood*.[15] This thick treatise sought to put some scientific meat on the bones of Price's Flood geology and to establish both Flood geology and recent "special" creation (the creation of the universe, Earth, and all life by divine miracles in the last ten thousand years or less) as the *only* orthodox interpretation of Genesis. Though many reviewers justifiably termed the book an update of Price's earlier work, the authors made scant reference to Price or his book. They seemed to recognize the importance of distancing themselves from Price's Seventh-Day Adventist connection and his lack of scientific credentials.

The Genesis Flood, like *The New Geology*, gained a tremendous boost from a new sense of desperation in the fundamentalist (ultraconservative) Christian camp. These Christians were finding fewer ears sympathetic to their ridiculing of science and scientists. Science was experiencing far too much success and offered far too much economic benefit during the 1950s for anyone to make headway with such disparagement. These Christians felt the need of a scientific response to what they perceived as an anti-Christian scientific establishment.

The Genesis Flood appeared to deliver the goods. Written by educators with earned doctorates (Ph.D. and Th.D.) from accredited institutions, the book was filled with explanatory footnotes and references to the scientific literature. Even its thickness and small print gave it the look of a weighty tome. To the layman, *The Genesis Flood* appeared a well-researched, well-documented science text-book. To most Christian fundamentalists, Whitcomb and Morris seemed to offer the scientific and intellectual respectability they desperately wanted.

Flood Geology Captures the Church

Stimulated by the publication of *The Genesis Flood,* genetics professor Walter Lammerts began communicating with Morris and eight other Christian fundamentalist scientists. In 1963 these ten formed the Creation Research Society (CRS). This team of scientifically trained Christians brought about a spectacular revival of Flood geology and recent creationism. Within ten years the CRS boasted 450 members with graduate science degrees, several self-sustained research projects, an education program that had successfully penetrated the majority of America's conservative (fundamentalist and evangelical) Christian churches and schools, and journals, books, and pamphlets distributed in the tens of thousands.

By the early 1970s the CRS began to splinter over differences in personalities, opinions, and objectives. This splintering, however, served only to multiply the CRS's success. One organization promoting belief in creation became several organizations, reaching many more people in many more places.

The rising star among these new creationist organizations, the Institute for Creation Research (ICR), was founded in 1972 by Henry Morris. Labeling its beliefs in Flood geology and recent, six-day creation of the universe and Earth as "creation science" or "scientific creationism," ICR scientists began to promote their message aggressively on university campuses. They sponsored public debates with nontheistic professors drawing crowds of several thousand. Their "Back to Genesis" seminars at churches drew (and still draw) thousands more. The ICR's team has prepared dozens of books (and other materials) on scientific creationism covering the spectrum from preschool to graduate level. In 1981 the ICR began offering graduate degrees in creation science.

By that time nearly every conservative church in America had been influenced by the teachings of the CRS and its daughter organizations. And the movement had begun to spread to other nations and other continents. Henry Morris's books have been translated into twenty or more languages, and societies along the lines of the CRS and the ICR have formed in more than a dozen nations, including Australia, Canada, Russia, South Africa, and the United Kingdom. Much of ICR's success has come from its tireless attempts to defend the scientific accuracy of the Bible.

By the 1990s the teachings of these organizations became so predominant that the news media, the American Association for the Advancement of Science, and the National Academy of Sciences now define "creation," "creationist," "creationism," and even "evangelical Christianity" according to the tenets of Flood geology. In the words of science historian Ronald Numbers, "their once marginal views, inspired by the visions of an Adventist prophetess [Ellen White], now define the very essence of creationism."[16]

Anti-Evolutionists Embrace Evolutionism

One irony for the creation scientists (also known as Flood geologists) cannot be overlooked: the approach they chose to crush the serpent of evolutionism forces them to embrace the principles of evolutionism more tightly than any atheist biologist would. Genesis 1 clearly states that beyond the sixth creation day God ceased to introduce new life-forms on Earth. Yet the creation scientists' views on the Fall (Genesis 3) and the Flood (Genesis 6–9) require the introduction of a huge number of new species of animal life in just a few hundred years.

Creation scientists teach that all animals ate only plants until Adam and Eve rebelled against God's authority.[17-19] Because carnivorous activity involves animal death, they presume it must be one of the evil results of human sin. Accordingly, they propose that meat-eating creatures alive now and evident in the fossil record must have evolved in just several hundred years or less, by natural processes alone, from the plant-eating creatures![19]

The size of Noah's ark and the limited number of humans on board (eight) present an equally serious problem for them. Even if all the animals aboard hibernated for the duration of the Flood, the maximum carrying capacity by their estimates for the ark would be about thirty thousand pairs of land animals.[20] But the fossil record indicates the existence of at least a half billion such species,[21] more than five million of which live on Earth today,[22] and at least two million more lived in the era immediately after the Flood, as they date it. The problem grows worse. Shortly after the Flood, they say, a large proportion of the thirty thousand species on board — dinosaurs, trilobites, and so on — went extinct; so the remaining few thousand species must have evolved by rapid and efficient natural processes alone into seven million or more species.

Ironically, creation scientists (quietly) propose an efficiency of natural biological evolution[23] greater than even the most optimistic Darwinist would dare to suggest. They face the embarrassment of a complete lack of evidence for their position. If naturalistic evolutionary processes actually did proceed at such a rapid rate, they would, of course, be observable in real time, in our time.

Fear of the Millions

Confidence in the superefficiency of evolution makes creation scientists' extreme dogmatism on the age issue understandable. If Darwinian processes work as smoothly and rapidly as creation scientists believe, a million- or billion-year-old Earth would seem to remove any need for God's involvement in the creation of life, the opposite conclusion to the one they desire to defend.

From the creation scientists' perspective, any concession that Earth or the universe may be significantly older than ten thousand years damages what they see as *the* biblical belief system, and thus overturns the foundation of their faith. No wonder otherwise compassionate, morally upright people, even fellow Christians, attack those who propose an ancient universe and Earth.[24-25] No wonder they cannot seriously investigate the scientific evidence for Earth's antiquity.[26]

While creation scientists call themselves anti-evolutionists, they do not reject natural biological evolution as impossible in principle. Indeed, they appeal to it to explain the present diversity of animal life from a small number of post-Flood animal species. They also appeal to evolutionary processes to produce, in the short time span between the creation and the Flood, a wide variety of carnivorous adaptations from fauna that were completely herbivorous. With such rapid evolution of animal forms, the question begs to be asked whether this view really needs supernatural creation at all. The rapid evolutionary processes which young-earth advocates invoke are inadequate to account for the great diversity of life-forms found on Earth today and in the fossil record *only* if the pre-human history of Earth is kept very short. In this sense, creation scientists are anti-evolutionists, though their position might better be labeled "short-timescale macroevolutionism."

CHAPTER TWELVE

HOW FAR THE FALL
GENESIS 3

Angels witnessed the creation days, Job tells us.[1] We can surmise that Lucifer turned to evil, and with him a third of the angels,[2] before the events of Eden. Perhaps his rebellion occurred even before a part or all of God's six-day creation work on Earth. God, the Creator of the angelic hosts, could have kept Satan and Satan's allies away from Eden and away from Earth. Under God's guidance, Adam and Eve and their descendants could have spread the wonders of Eden throughout the whole world. Humanity could have enjoyed earthly paradise for all time.

God had other plans, however. According to all that we learn in Scripture and stretch to understand, God wanted something far better than earthly Eden for his unique body-soul-spirit creatures, the human race. But the path to that something better, the new creation[3] with its unimaginable goodness[4] and its total absence from even the threat of evil,[5] would be hard—and costly—more so for God than for us. And along that path lay essential tests and training that encompassed the humans' whole being—body, soul, and spirit.[6]

Adam and Eve's Departure from Eden

God informed Adam and Eve that one tree only was forbidden to them. He let them know that if they ever violated His authority by eating of the fruit of that one tree, which He called "the tree of the knowledge of good and evil," they would in that moment experience death.[7] We who read this warning today think immediately of physical death, of course. Perhaps Adam and Eve did too, but they may have understood from one of their unrecorded conversations with God the deeper meaning of this "death." (Satan apparently knew.) We see that they expressed no surprise at finding themselves still living and breathing once they had eaten the forbidden fruit. Whether this response came from their believing the serpent's words or God's we do not know.

Reflecting the fearless harmony of all living creatures in the garden, Eve showed no fear when the serpent approached her and spoke. We can surmise from later contextual clues that the serpent served as a tool in Satan's hand. His communication reflected the mind of Satan and his voice surely came from a supernatural source. Later, in Moses' time, Balaam's donkey similarly was used by a supernatural being.[8]

The text matter-of-factly portrays, through narration mostly, the profound change that occurred in that simple act of reaching out for and biting into the fruit. Suddenly Adam and Eve became aware of their nakedness. A sense of vulnerability and shame sent them running for cover, to hide from each other and from God. Fear has interfered with all our relationships ever since. What a loss! We see the humans hiding from responsibility as well, and the first account of blaming holds a mirror before our faces.

Some critics seem thrown, even outraged, that so undramatic an action as biting into some fruit could possibly carry such horrendous consequences: the curses spelled out by God in the verses that follow and banishment from the garden. But these critics miss the point. They fail to recognize the terrible danger and consequences involved in the creature's expression of autonomy from the Creator.

Upon Adam and Eve's grave experience of loss, the loss of an open, free, and trusting relationship with God, God took action to ensure that they would not live forever in this "broken" condition, which we recognize as the spiritual death of which He warned. He cut off their access to the Tree of Life. God had prepared a way out, a way through, this tragic dilemma. Death of the earthly body would become a part of His strategy for deliverance.[9] By this strategy, God would be able to deliver humanity, anyone who chooses, from the far worse consequence of eternal spiritual death.

God sent Adam and Eve away from the garden. Now, because of sin (rebellion against God's authority), the Tree of Life became a danger to them, as did their once easy life in the garden. God knew that Adam and Eve needed the extra work and pain afforded by life outside Eden. They and their offspring needed training and preparation for their future life in the new creation. They would become part of God's plan for redeeming humanity from this dreadful condition of spiritual, hence moral, weakness.

Did the Fall Change Physics?

From our human perspective certain conditions we see in the post-Fall world seem so bad that we can hardly believe God created or planned them to be this way. Many Christians presume that the natural tendency toward decay (the second law of thermodynamics), for example, and carnivorous activity by various animal species must be attributable to human evil, not to God's goodness. In that case, these conditions did not exist before Adam and Eve's sin. Human rebellion, they say, ruined God's creation.

NonChristians also wrestle with this perspective. An all-loving, all-powerful God, they argue, would not have designed a system that includes waste and disorder (again, the second law of thermodynamics). Nor, they claim, would such a God create a natural order that involves animals killing other animals for food. The cruel, bloodthirsty, and wasteful characteristics of the natural realm, they conclude, suggest either a God who is not there or a God who does not care.

NonChristians, especially those with some science education, reject the proposition that neither carnivorous activity nor increasing entropy (decay and disorder that naturally increases with time) existed before the advent of humans. The livers and teeth of ancient sharks and the teeth and limbs of *Tyrannosaurus rex*, for example, are designed exclusively for the consumption and processing of animal, not vegetable, matter. And without entropy that increases, no living thing, plant or animal, would be able to process energy to perform work. All the catalytic and metabolic reactions that are essential for physical life to exist would fail. The existence of stars, including the sun, would be impossible. Deposits of coal, oil, gas, and topsoil would not exist without entropy that increases through time. Even such simple geologic formations as moraine, talus, and alluvial silt result from entropy's increase.

A careful reading of Genesis 3 offers invaluable insights. First, the account does *not* say that Eve's sin created the experience of pain. Rather, it says that Eve's pain in childbearing, physical or otherwise, would be greatly increased (verse 16). Second, the account does *not* say that Adam now had to work for the first time. Rather, it says that because of what Adam had done, his work would be much harder and less efficient than it was before. The problems and distractions brought on by sin would hinder his management efforts. Thorns and thistles would grow out of control and make food-gathering hard, sweaty work (compare Genesis 2:15 and 3:17-19).

What changed, the world or the people and their relationship to it? Genesis 3 indicates the latter. Because of broken relationships with God and each other, Adam and Eve would be less efficient and pro-ductive, not to mention less joyful, in all their efforts. Consequently, there would be more pain and work in both their lives.

Driven from the garden, Adam and Eve found themselves in the untamed world for the first time. Before the Fall, they lived in God's specially prepared garden. After the Fall, they had to face the world outside with *all* its natural characteristics. An untended wilderness would be much more difficult to manage than a divinely established garden.

Returning to the discussion of physical laws, we recognize that Adam would have had no managing or tending to do at all before the Fall if the thermodynamic laws were not already in effect. Physical work of any kind—even eating and digesting food—involves the second law of thermodynamics.[10] This law describes the process whereby food is converted to work energy, or to movement of any kind. Adam and Eve surely ate and moved, talked and walked, before the Fall (see Genesis 2:16; 3:2-6).

Before man or any of the plants and animals were created, God made the stars and the sun (see Genesis 1:1-16). These heav-enly bodies represent a near-perfect expression of the second law of thermodynamics, which can also be defined as the flow of heat from hot bodies to cold bodies. Stars radiate heat very efficiently. They rank among the most entropic (heat-radiating) entities in the universe. Thus, Genesis implicitly affirms the operation of the second law of thermodynamics before man's fall.

In a letter to the church at Rome, the apostle Paul describes how this physical law affects the entire creation:

> The creation was subjected to frustration, not by its own choice, but by the will of the one who subjected it, in hope that the creation itself will be liberated from its bondage to decay and brought into the glorious freedom of the children of God. We know that the whole creation has been groaning as in the pains of childbirth right up to the present time.[11]

This passage refers to "the whole creation," the entire universe, "right up to the present time." General relativity, now one of the best-established principles in all physics,[12-13] tells us that the entire creation includes all the matter and energy in the universe *and* all the space-time dimensions along which its matter and energy are distributed.[14-18] In fact, the matter and energy are inseparable from the space-time dimensions of the cosmos. Thus, Paul's words can reasonably be interpreted to mean that the second thermodynamic law has been in effect since the creation of the universe and throughout the whole of the universe.

Cosmological research goes so far as to demonstrate that unless the universe were both extremely entropic and extremely homogeneous (meaning that entropy must be roughly the same everywhere in the cosmos) throughout the whole of its existence, physical life would not be possible. The cosmic entropy level stands as but one of the thirty-four features of the universe discovered so far that must be exquisitely fine-tuned for life's chemical components even to exist.[19] If the second law of thermodynamics had not been in effect from the first moment of creation until now, the cosmos would be devoid of stars, planets, and moons.[20] A cosmos without stars, planets, and moons is a cosmos without physical life.

When we consider that the second thermodynamic law is essential for life's existence, essential for eating and mobility and countless other activities that most of us agree are enjoyable and good, we see no reason to suggest that the law should be judged as bad. Thermodynamic laws were included when God declared His creation "very good" (Genesis 1:31).

We must be careful, however, not to confuse God's very good creation with His best creation, or more accurately, His ultimate goal for His creation. In the new creation there will be no thermodynamic laws—no decay, no frustration, no groaning, no grieving (see Revelation 21:1-5). The thermodynamic laws are good, in spite of the "decay," "frustration," and "groaning," because they are part of God's strategy for preparing His creation to enjoy the blessings and rewards of the new creation.

Carnivorous Activity

The Bible makes no explicit statements about animal behavior and eating habits before the time of Adam and Eve. Genesis 1:24-25 identifies two different kinds of long-legged land mammals, those that are easily domesticated and those that are wild, or more difficult to tame. As we know them today, the first group is herbivorous and the second, carnivorous. While the domesticated herbivores serve our agricultural industry well, we tend to choose our pets from among the wild carnivores.

The digestive system of these creatures makes a crucial difference in our relationship possibilities (as does intelligence, of course). The carnivores, such as dogs and cats, spend only a brief portion of their day eating. They have such control over their elimination that they can be housebroken. Eating and digesting food does not interfere with their playful activity—they run and jump and play games with us, and may even do our bidding if we make the effort to train them. They even express delight in seeing us and sadness in our leaving them. Compared with the herbivores, which spend many hours a day in the eating-digesting process, carnivores are more active, social, and agile.

We humans can maintain a normal level of activity eating only fruit and vegetable products, but only for this simple reason: we possess the intellect and technology to process vegetable matter into high-calorie, highly nutritive, low-fiber form. The only option for large, active mammals in the wild is to eat herbivores, the one significant natural source of processed vegetable matter. They could not survive or thrive otherwise.

What about the "hunted" herbivores? They actually benefit too. Carnivorous activity maximizes the quality of life for the herbivores as a whole. As game wardens will verify, a lack of carnivorous activity leads to the spread of disease, to starvation, and to genetic decline. Without the help of predators, game wardens find themselves forced to thin out the herbivore population in order to maintain its health and vitality.

We should note, too, that God made herbivores difficult to hunt in one way or another, some by their size, some by their speed, and some by other means of defense. We humans are the ones able (and willing, I'm sad to say) to kill the best individuals within a species. The carnivorous animals go after the weakest, sickest, and most genetically damaged individuals. Thus, they protect and enhance the quality of the herbivore species.

Sometime in the future, when Jesus Christ reigns for a time on Earth and His followers serve alongside Him in managing the planet, carnivores will no longer eat herbivores, according to Isaiah 65:25.

This change most likely results from Christ's bringing peace and harmony among all humans and between human beings and the animals so that under God's authority we can provide the carnivores with all the processed, nutritionally adequate food they need. During this time, referred to as the Millennium by many Bible scholars, God will remove all human excuses for sin—including our carnivorous activity—to demonstrate, once and for all, that our weakness lies within us, not in our external environment (see Jeremiah 17:9-10).

When Death Entered

Whatever difficulty we may face in acknowledging that thermodynamic laws and carnivorous activity are good, we find a greater challenge still in understanding the "good" of physical death. Whether we speak about plant death, animal death, or human death, death seems a terrible thing. How can anyone say death is good? Let me offer five points for consideration.

First, we tend to forget that death, decay, pain, suffering, and carnivorous activity will all come to an end. None of these conditions will exist in the new creation.[21-22] However, each of them plays a vital part in the permanent conquest of evil. Also, they provide a basis for testing and training humans for their future participation in and enjoyment of the new creation.[23]

Second, evil existed *before* the fall of Adam and Eve. Satan had already manifested evil by his accusations and prideful rebellion against God (see Genesis 3:1-15). Before Adam and Eve were created, possibly even before God began to transform the formless and empty Earth (see Job 38:7), Satan shattered his rightful relationship with God. Thus, he experienced spiritual death, *eternal* spiritual death because his life is not bound by the limits of our universe's time line.

For humans, God uses physical death as one tool for restraining the spread of evil. Wicked people are limited by physical death in the amount of malice and evil they can spread. They also are limited by death in the number of righteous people they can torture or kill. Physical death for humans who choose God's gift of redemption provides a way for the eternal part, the core part of their beings, to enjoy eternal life with God, no longer bound within the limits of physical life. Physical death for us, though it represents a naturally frightening crossover from the tangibly familiar to the unfamiliar, can bring potential benefit to our spiritual nature.

Third, we must refrain from assuming that plants and animals approach death the same way humans do. God has endowed them with an instinct to live, an instinct that keeps them working hard enough to survive the rigors of their existence on this planet. However, because of our spiritual nature, physical death has a meaning for us humans—a drama, we might say—unparalleled in the animal kingdom. We are the only species, past or present, on Earth that faces upon physical death divine judgment.[24-25] Because birds and mammals are soulish beings, physical death for them holds more trauma than it does for the lower animals. Because the lower animals are much more sensitive to their environment than plants are, they recoil from death more than plants do.

Fourth, death sustains the life of every animal. Eating, which makes animal life possible, requires the death of some other living thing. For example, when herbivores eat, plants or plant parts die. And, by the way, botanists did not originate the claim that plants experience life and death. The Bible said so first.[26-27]

Fifth, to reject the reality of physical death among plants and animals before the creation of Adam and Eve defies both the scientific and the biblical data. Life can be reliably dated back to 3.86 billion years ago.[28-29] And, unless God is a capricious trickster, which the Bible certainly denies,[30] we can accept the testimony of billions of fossils throughout the last 3.5 billion years of geologic history. The existence of limestone, marble, coal, oil, gas, kerogen, peat, coral reefs, and guano deposits in great abundance on Earth tell of millions of generations of past life and death (see chapter eighteen). Even the young-earth interpretation of Genesis 1 places the plants before the animals, and the animals before the humans, by a matter of days and hours. If any animal moved or ate, something else had to die.

In Romans 5:12, which speaks of death as the result of sin, the text limits that death to human beings. It clearly specifies specifies the spiritual death of humans, "death through sin . . . came to all men because all sinned" (for which physical death follows as a God-bestowed blessing), not the physical death of plant and animal species. Likewise, 1 Corinthians 15:20-23 (the only other Bible passage directly addressing death as a result of sin) does not extend the death brought by Adam's sin beyond the human species. Plants and non-human animals cannot sin and cannot die through sin. Rather, the same kind of rebellion or sin nature was incurred, and passed to every human, as when Adam and Eve first chose to place their own inclination above God's wise command.

CHAPTER THIRTEEN

CAIN'S WIFE AND CITY
GENESIS 4

Genesis 4 at first glance seems to report that Adam and Eve had only three sons: Cain, Abel, and Seth. This reading of the text leads to some questions and doubts among Bible readers of all ages everywhere. Even the youngest readers realize that if the human race is to continue, Cain and his brother Seth must find wives. But the problem grows more complicated: After murdering Abel, Cain was banished to an eastward land called Nod.[1] (Seth was not born until after Cain's departure.[2]) There, Cain not only found a wife, apparently, but found enough people, by the time his son Enoch was born, to build and populate a city. The question ringing in readers' minds, the question asked of Christian apologists more often than almost any other, is this: where did Cain's wife and all these other people come from?

Was God Surprised?
Before answering the questions about Cain's wife and city, the issue of God's power and knowledge in the matter needs addressing. Many skeptics claim that Genesis 4 proves that the Christian God is not all-powerful and all-knowing. By the questions God poses to Cain (verses 6, 7, 9, 10) these skeptics conclude that either God was ignorant of Cain's intentions and eventual murder or that He had no power to stop Cain.

That the conclusions are incorrect is clear from the context. God did not ask His questions out of ignorance or weakness. In posing the questions God was appealing to Cain's conscience and responsibility. As every parent knows, the best way to correct and restore a child caught in bad behavior is to ask questions.

After Cain refused to tell God why he was angry, God told him (verse 7). After Cain refused to tell God of the whereabouts of his brother Abel, God told him (verse 10). God obviously knew.

In disciplining Cain, God first appealed to Cain's conscience by asking a question. Second, He explained to Cain the benefits of obedience. Third, He pointed out the consequences of rebellion. Fourth, He reminded Cain of the power of temptation and sin in his life as well as the resources he had to overcome them. Last of all, He left it up to Cain to decide, right or wrong. Yes, God could have prevented Cain's crimes, but God was much more motivated that Cain and all other human beings would grow in character. Human character growth cannot happen unless God permits the exercise of human free choice. Most parents understand this about their children, and God in Genesis 4 gives them a manual.

Finding the People

The second step in answering the questions about Cain's wife and city requires looking ahead a few verses. Adam and probably Eve, too, lived several hundred years. The text tells us that Adam lived 930 years, 800 of them after Seth's birth, and had "other sons and daughters"—too many to list by name, apparently. The genealogy of Genesis 5 indicates that every descendant of Adam down to Lamech had "other sons and daughters" whose names do not appear in this record. Some of the offspring chosen for the record were born when their fathers were sixty-five, some after their father turned five hundred. This gives us a rough idea of the extent of the ancients' childbearing years.

Considering the long life spans recorded in Genesis 5 (these are discussed in chapter fifteen) and assuming that couples remained reproductive for about two-thirds of their life spans, we see in the era before the Flood the possibility of a veritable population explosion. Without effective birth-control options and perhaps only the vaguest notion of how the reproduction process worked, the first pair alone would have had at least 150 children. And their children would have begun raising families at a similar rate while they, Adam and Eve, were still having more sons and daughters, and so would their grandchildren, great-grandchildren, great-great-grandchildren, and so forth.

The potential population growth during Adam's life span appears in Table 13.1. According to simple mathematics, if Cain waited to marry until he was about sixty or seventy years old, he probably had several women to choose from, providing some migrated eastward to Nod with other family members. If he waited another two hundred years to build a city, he could have had at least a few thousand people to help him, again assuming some migration occurred. Cain may have had sisters or nieces from whom to choose a wife even before his banishment and the birth of Seth. The text does not tell us.

Table 13.1: Expected Population Growth in Adam's Lifetime
According to Genesis 5, life spans from Adam to Noah averaged 912 years. Each of the patriarchs mentioned had "other sons and daughters" in addition to the sons recorded by name. The table calculations are based on:

- life span = nine hundred years
- first child comes at age forty
- childbearing years = six hundred
- one child every four years during childbearing years

Adam's Age	Reproducing Couples	Children Born	Total Population
0	1	0	2
40	1	10	12
80	6	30	42
120	21	100	142
160	71	352	494
200	247	1210	1704
240	852	4180	5884
280	2942	14,450	20,334
320	10,167	49,892	70,226
360	35,113	172,358	242,584
400	121,292	595,378	837,962
440	418,980	2,056,530	2,894,492
480	1,447,245	7,103,862	9,998,364
520	4,999,176	24,538,536	34,536,930
560	17,268,444	84,762,338	119,299,368
600	59,649,613	292,790,780	412,090,500
640	206,045,003	1,011,374,120	1,423,465,830
680	711,732,063	3,493,544,650	4,917,014,660
720	2,459,504,388	12,067,585,000	16,984,600,000
760	8,492,300,000	41,685,303,000	58,669,903,000

Archeological evidence from the pre-Flood era provides no indication that the pre-Flood population ever became as large as the mathematical chart above suggests is possible. Infant mortality may have been one factor suppressing growth, but this problem alone seems vastly inadequate to explain the lack of a population explosion.

Cain's Sin

Murder is the theme that glares from Genesis 4. Not only did Cain commit murder, but so did his descendants, and these murderers showed a frightening lack of conscience. Four times God spoke to Cain, initially to warn Cain against carrying out his evil plan and later to elicit a confession of responsibility (Genesis 4:6-15). Four times Cain rejected God's appeal. At the time of his banishment from home territory, he expressed the fear that he would be killed by anyone who found him (presumably his brothers, sisters, nieces, nephews). By the time Lamech came along a few generations later, murder had apparently become something to brag about (Genesis 4:23-24).

Genesis 4 hints that wanton murder prevented the pre-Flood human population from really taking off. The sin of Cain seems to have grown out of control. The estimated numbers, even if trimmed back to a conservative extreme (consider that couples with the likelihood of bearing over 150 children would see only a handful survive), indicate that murder must have become the leading cause of death for pre-Flood people. As many as nine out of ten, and perhaps more, must have been murder victims.

Even the earliest commentaries on Genesis 4–6 support this interpretation. The Jewish scholar Josephus writing in the first century A.D. states:

> Nay, even while Adam was alive, it came to pass that the posterity of Cain became exceedingly wicked, every one successively dying one after another more wicked than the former. They were intolerable in war, and vehement in robberies; and if anyone were slow to murder people, yet was he bold in his profligate behavior, in acting unjustly and doing injuries for gain.[3]

If this scenario has merit, it helps explain the extreme language used in Genesis 6 to describe the evil into which the pre-Flood people had fallen (see chapter seventeen). Because God-fearing people, such as Abel, were more likely to be murdered than those who were malicious, we can begin to imagine why Noah's contemporaries manifested such chilling irreverence and why so few righteous remained. It explains God's decision to use a flood and an ark for rescue. Humanity lay in danger of self-extermination. It explains further the strong language God used with Noah in Genesis 9:6, commanding

Noah's descendants to exercise whatever means were necessary, up to the death penalty, to restrain the sin of murder.

We can surmise from the story of Cain and his descendants in Genesis 4 that rampant murder took several generations to develop. Thus, the population numbers we used to suggest where Cain found marriage candidates and the citizens to fill a city would still hold, with some moderate revision perhaps.

The "Incest" Problem
As recorded in the book of Genesis, no law of conscience or society forbade marriage between brothers and sisters or other close relatives (except parents and children, Genesis 19:30-38) in the early centuries of human history. Even at the time of Abraham, the practice of marrying siblings continued.[4]

Sometime later, however, when God established a set of moral and civil laws for the emerging nation of Israel, He ruled out marriage between siblings (Leviticus 18:6-18). The timing of this command makes perfect sense from a biological perspective. Genetic defects as a result of intrafamily marriage develop slowly. They would present no risk until after the first several dozen generations.

Cain's Mark
Genesis 4 tells us that God placed a mark on Cain to warn others against avenging the blood of Abel. The necessity of this mark indicates that the population had grown, or would soon grow, large enough that Cain ran two risks: first, of being recognized and killed in revenge and, second, of not being recognized and being killed randomly.

The text says nothing about what kind of mark Cain received and makes no suggestion of its being passed on to his progeny. This chapter provides no basis whatsoever for identifying a race or ethnic group as bearers of Cain's mark.[5] (For a discussion of the origin of the races, see chapter twenty.)

Warning for Today
In many Scripture portions, we read that horrible wickedness, as bad as the wickedness of Noah's time, will again overtake humanity. The era when evil rises to such proportions the Bible writers refer to as the "last days." One indicator that these last days may be approaching comes from current statistics on murder and violent

crime worldwide. In fact, for the first time we know of since the Flood, murder has become the leading cause of death among humans.

This statistic may seem inflated compared with reports from newscasters in the popular news media. They typically give numbers for their communities or for the United States only, and they fail to include the killing of living humans before birth. Though the abortion rate decreased slightly in the United States in the mid-1990s, still one individual in four experiences death by murder—counting abortion as murder—in this civilized, "Christian" nation. The figures for the rest of the world's nations are in many cases worse. In the case of Eastern Europe, Russia, and the People's Republic of China, the figures are *much* worse.

God is yet holding back His judgment against the hard-hearted peoples of Earth, including some who call themselves His people. He patiently waits for those who will turn to Him in grief and repentance, recognizing the need for divine mercy.

CHAPTER FOURTEEN

DATING THE ORIGIN OF HUMANITY
GENESIS 5

Once the Bible became available in English, some British church leaders busied themselves with figuring out the precise date when God created Adam (and Eve, presumably). Genesis 5, together with Genesis 11, served as the basis for their calculations. The math seemed relatively simple and straightforward. Add the ages of the fathers to the ages of their sons and work backward from the fairly well-established date for Abraham. Cambridge University's Vice-Chancellor John Lightfoot and the Anglican Archbishop of Ireland, James Ussher, actually became caught up in a race to see who could publish an accurate date first. By the middle of the seventeenth century, they announced to the world that Adam was created in 4004 B.C.[1-2] Lightfoot really went overboard, citing the month, the day, and the time of day,[2] but few expressed suspicion about the validity of his and Ussher's claims. Before long their date spread throughout Christendom and beyond as if it were part of the Bible text itself. By the nineteenth century, it had reached the margin notes of most English Bibles.

Unfortunately, the more widely and deeply this date became entrenched in published Bibles and Christian thinking, the wider and deeper became the credibility gap between educated people and biblical faith. For the first time the Bible became an object of ridicule.

The genealogies in Genesis 5 and 11 can be misleading to Westerners who know little about Jewish culture and tradition. The formula in Genesis 5, "when X had lived Y years, he became the father of Z," combined with the statement in Genesis 7:6 that Noah was six hundred years old when the Flood struck, adds up (in the British way of thinking) to a total of 1,656 years between Adam's creation and the Flood. Similarly, Genesis 11 combined with the statement in Genesis 12:4 that Abraham was seventy-five years old when he left Haran, indicates that only 353 years passed between the Flood event and the birth of Abraham. These numbers tell us that God created Adam precisely 2,009 years before the birth of Abraham. Since we know with some certainty that Abraham was born in or about 2000 B.C., we see "proof" that Lightfoot and Ussher's date comes close to, if not right on, the mark.

The first Christian missionaries to China experienced shock and dismay when they encountered Chinese historical accounts placing Chinese national origins earlier than 4004 B.C.[3] No wonder these missionaries faced rejection, loss of their credibility, and resistance to their message. The same reaction comes today from American Indians, who date their origin to 9500 B.C.; Australian Aborigines, who date back to 25,000 B.C.; and Europeans, who date advanced cave art back to 30,000 B.C. All are firmly established dates.

Gaps in Biblical Genealogies
Lightfoot and Ussher in their calculations and Western thinking presumed that Genesis 5 and 11 present meticulously *complete* genealogical records. Most Jewish scholars never published a date for Adam because they knew their cultural heritage. The Old Testament (and New Testament) genealogies are considered *adequate* lists of descendants, not complete lists. Hebrew genealogies tend to focus on the heroes or notables (famous as well as infamous) within a family line. Therefore, gaps are expected.

An example appears in the genealogy of Matthew 1:8:

> Asa the father of Jehoshaphat, Jehoshaphat the father of Jehoram, Jehoram the father of Uzziah.

However, 1 Chronicles 3:10-12 reads differently:

> Asa his son, Jehoshaphat his son, Jehoram his son, Ahaziah his son, Joash his son, Amaziah his son, Azariah [also called Uzziah] his son.

Matthew leaves out at least three generations: Ahaziah, Joash, and Amaziah. Why?

Bible scholars cite some reasons for the seeming discrepancy. In many biblical lists of descendants, cadence and pattern hold great importance. In his genealogy Matthew presented three groups of fourteen generations each: fourteen generations from Abraham to David; another fourteen from David to the Babylonian exile; and a third set of fourteen from the Babylonian exile to Jesus, "who is called Christ." To maintain the pattern of three fourteens, Matthew dropped names from the list of descendants as he deemed appropriate.

Matthew's subtraction of names does not, however, invalidate Matthew's genealogy. In biblical Hebrew *'ab* ("father") can be used to mean grandfather, great-grandfather, great-great-grandfather, and so on, while *ben* ("son") can be used for grandson, great-grandson, great-great-grandson, and so on.[4] Thus, the "father" of Uzziah can be understood as Uzziah's great-great-grandfather. Matthew lists for us, from his perspective, the fourteen most significant names in the list of descendants for each of the three Old Testament eras of Jewish history.

A similar pattern appears in Genesis 5 and 11. From Adam to Noah, Genesis 5 lists ten names. From Shem (Noah's son) to Abraham, Genesis 11 lists ten names. Just as with the Matthew 1 list, we discover that these Genesis lists of descendants are incomplete. The parallel genealogy in Luke 3, for example, includes eleven names from Shem to Abraham, adding the name Cainan between Arphaxad and Shelah. As we see in the case of Matthew's three fourteens, maintaining the two tens of Genesis requires dropping names from the list of descendants.

The existence of gaps in the Genesis genealogies should not be construed as flaws. The gaps mean we must treat them as we would abbreviations. The words translated into English say this: "When X had lived Y years, he became the father of Z." Someone reading the same passage in Hebrew would see a second possibility: "When X had lived Y years, he became the father of a family line that included or culminated in Z."

Exactly how many gaps may exist in the Genesis genealogies has been the subject of much debate among Old Testament scholars. Some argue for a very loose limit on the number of gaps. They suggest that Adam may have been an Australopithecine created some four or five million years ago and from whom modern man evolved. Most Bible scholars, however, see reasons to put a much tighter limit on the gaps. Aside from their observation that the Bible portrays Adam as an individual strikingly similar to ourselves, they point out that parallel genealogies in Scripture usually overlap significantly, holding a majority of names in common. The lack of great discordance in these parallel genealogies argues for relatively few and small gaps. Scholars in this camp date Adam's creation somewhere in the tens of thousands of years ago (but less than a hundred thousand years ago).

Dating Spirit Expression

According to Genesis, the distinguishing feature of humanity is our spiritual nature. The spirit distinguishes the human race as the one and only earthly species aware of God and with the innate desire and capacity for relationship with Him. The one convincing evidence of this unique spiritual quality must have something to do with worship. All known human societies, wherever and whenever they have existed, however large or small, technologically sophisticated or not, have engaged in religious worship involving temples, altars, icons, and other unique relics.

Anthropologists usually identify other characteristics, such as burial practices, tool use, art, and music as expressions of the spirituality of humans. Certainly human beings can and do express worship through music, art, tools, and burial practices, but these forms of expression do not always represent worship. We can think of examples from each of these categories of expression that have nothing to do with worship but rather express our emotions or our minds, the characteristics we hold in common with the birds and mammalian species (see chapter six). Keen observers of nature know that bower birds, elephants, chimpanzees, gorilla, and zebra finches engage in music, tool use, art, and even burial practices.

Bipedal, tool-using, comparatively large-brained primates (called hominids by anthropologists) may have roamed Earth as long ago as 1.5 million years,[5-7] but religious relics and altars date back only as far as twenty-four thousand years, at most,[8-9] and art containing indisputable spiritual content just five thousand years.[10] Thus, the archeological date for the beginning of spirit expression agrees with the biblical date.

Biochemical Dates for Eve and Noah

Two portions of human genetic material do not recombine (mix up) in reproduction: (1) most of the mitochondrial DNA (that is, DNA that resides in specialized structures, called *mitochondria,* outside the cell's nucleus); and (2) a large segment of the Y-chromosome. Though both men and women carry mitochondrial DNA, all of us get nearly all of our mitochondrial DNA from our mothers only. Only men carry the Y-chromosome segment. That is, males receive a large portion of the Y-chromosome from their fathers only.

If all humans descended from one woman and one man without God's supernatural intervention, the only explanation for variation in these portions of human mitochondrial DNA and the Y-chromosome is natural mutation. (The only way my mitochondrial DNA can differ from my mother's and my Y-chromosome from my father's is if I experience a natural mutation.) Measuring the natural mutation rate in this genetic material should be possible, then, via observation of real-time changes. By comparing samples of currently living humans with some well-dated ancient human DNA,[11-12] and by noting the range of DNA differences among individuals from all of the people groups of the world, researchers could then estimate the total time required for these differences to have developed.

Natural mutation rates, however, have proved difficult to measure. One study of Jewish males worldwide provides some useful information, especially in tracing the genetic history of Jews since Moses.[13] But increased intermarriage between Jews and Gentiles at the exodus from Egypt and later during the Diaspora (worldwide dispersion after Rome's destruction of Jerusalem) weakens the conclusions. A more recent study on Japanese males yields a veritable treasure.[14] The advantages of the latter study include the centuries-long stability of this island population and the availability of ancient DNA samples from the Jomon and Yayoi tribes, who first colonized the Japanese isles.

With reasonably reliable figures for the natural DNA mutations, rates derived from this research, from another study on the Finnish population,[15] and from more studies currently underway, we can explore dates for the common ancestor of all humans.[16] In 1995 a Y-chromosome research project—one which examined a hundred times more nucleotide base pairs than any previous study—fixed the date for the most recent common ancestor of all human males at somewhere between 35,000 and 47,000 B.C.[17] This finding represents a significant breakthrough in physical anthropology. The recent date eliminates the possibility that modern humans evolved from another bipedal primate species (meaning that humans must be specially created). This date has been questioned, however, for its lack of consistency with the date derived from mitochondrial DNA analysis. Mitochondrial DNA results typically place the most recent common ancestor of all women somewhere between a few thousand and a few tens of thousands of years earlier.

While scientists ponder the reason for this discrepancy, Genesis provides an explanation. Genesis reveals that we can expect to find a much earlier date for the most recent common ancestor of all women than for the most recent common ancestor of all men because of what happened in the Flood. Of the eight people on board Noah's ark, the four men were blood-related but not the four women. Thus, the most recent common ancestor for the four men on Noah's ark (and for all men since) was Noah; the most recent common ancestor for the four women on the ark, Noah's wife and daughters-in-law, could go back all the way to Eve. The difference in the two biochemical dates roughly fits the time frame suggested by the Genesis 5 genealogy.

So far, of course, the fit is only approximate. The biochemical studies have relied on relatively small population samples, a few dozen individuals or fewer, and typically (with one notable exception) on a relatively small number of nucleotide base pairs (several hundred). Genesis 5 and 11, as indicated above, also deliver only approximate dates for Eve and for Noah. And one additional factor should be mentioned: Genesis 10 indicates that God may have intervened at some point shortly after the Flood, imposing some additional genetic diversity (see chapter twenty).

Neandertal's Morphology

Until the mid-1990s, anthropology courses routinely taught that no significant anatomical differences distinguish modern humans from Neandertals (the *h* after the *t* has now been dropped). Based on this assertion, most anthropology professors, including some well-known creation scientists,[18-19] have argued that Neandertals should be considered part of the human species, descendants of Adam (though no shred of evidence credibly links Neandertals with spiritual activity[20]). With complete fossil skeletons of some Neandertal individuals dating back at least a hundred thousand years, this view places the origin of the human race at some time previous to a hundred thousand years ago, a conclusion that has compelled some Christians to attack fossil-dating methods.

So-called insignificant anatomical distinctions between modern humans and Neandertals were noticed when the first Neandertal fossils were uncovered. For example, while modern humans possess a circular hole at the skull's base for passage of the spinal cord, the Neandertals' spinal hole was oval; humans have a triangular lower jawbone, Neandertals had a squarish one; and Neandertals had a unique bony protrusion near the rear of the lower jawbone, apparently to accommodate a large chewing muscle.[21] Researchers assumed these differences arose in the maturation process as a result of environmental differences and that young children of both modern humans and Neandertals were anatomically the same.

This assumption was shattered recently by the discovery of a Neandertal infant's skeletal remains.[21-22] This infant possessed the same three anatomical distinctives found in the adult Neandertal fossils.

An even more dramatic demonstration of anatomical difference between Neandertals and modern humans comes from a study done by distinguished American anthropologists Jeffrey Schwartz and Ian Tattersall. These men measured the nasal characteristics of thirteen different Neandertal skulls kept in museums around the world.

They were stunned to discover that Neandertals possessed enormous nasal bones and huge sinus cavities compared to modern humans, and had no tear ducts. The nasal bones and sinus cavities alone showed such major differences as to argue conclusively against any biological link between modern humans and Neandertals.[23-24] From the standpoint of morphology, modern humans cannot have descended from Neandertals.

The nasal bones and sinus cavities of Neandertals are so large and so distinct that Schwartz and Tattersall go on to conclude that Neandertals cannot be biologically related to any known primate species or any known mammalian species. Just as modern humans appear to have been specially created, so too do Neandertals. The naturalistic explanation for Neandertals currently rests on a set of "unknown" intermediate species.

Neandertal's Biochemistry

A spectacular advance in biochemical technology has brought further breakthroughs in Neandertal research. Analysis of recently recovered

Neandertal DNA confirms Schwartz and Tattersall's conclusion that the human race neither descended from nor bears any biological connection to the Neandertal species.[25]

As one of the great ironies of our time, the DNA sample used in this breakthrough study was taken from the very first Neandertal skeleton (dated as between 40,000 to 100,000 years old) ever found. That skeleton was dug from a limestone quarry in Neandertal, Germany in 1856, and its impact on Charles Darwin, his descent of man hypothesis, and the tide of history has been enormous.

The search for a Neandertal DNA sample lasted about thirty years.[26] Through painstaking effort the research team located about fifty copies of the Neandertal skeleton's mitochondrial DNA in strings of about 100 nucleotide pairs each. Matching pieces of the strands with other pieces, they ended up with a DNA fragment 379 nucleotide pairs long, all from a part of the mitochondrial DNA that does not recombine in the reproductive process.

When the Neandertal DNA fragment was compared with a DNA strand of 986 nucleotide pairs from living humans of diverse ethnic backgrounds, the difference was enormous—an average of twenty-six nucleotide links in the DNA chain differed completely.[27-28] Modern humans differed from one another in an average of just eight links of the chain, and all of the observed differences among humans were independent of the twenty-six observed for the recovered Neandertal DNA. The researchers considered these findings conclusive: Neandertals could not have made any contribution to the human gene pool.

As elegant and painstaking as the research on the German Neandertal specimen was, and as high acclaim and little criticism the work received, the scientific community yearned for confirmation. Such confirmation came when members of the same research team and others in 1999 published their analysis on a different fragment from the same skeleton.[29] They got essentially the same results as the first research effort and concluded that their analysis gave "no support to the notion that Neandertals should have contributed mtDNA to the modern human gene pool."[30]

Two research teams, one from the University of Glasgow and the other from the University of Stockholm, produced truly independent confirmation when they independently isolated and sequenced mitochondrial DNA from a different Neandertal skeleton.[31-32] This skeleton, about 29,000 years old, was an infant found in the Caucasus Mountains which is the easternmost part of the

Neandertal range. Both the Glasgow and Stockholm teams reported identical results, results which were consistent with the earlier studies done on the German Neandertal specimen, namely, there was no possibility of a genetic link between the Neandertals and humans.

As this book edition went to press, mitochondrial DNA was recovered from a third Neandertal skeleton, a Croatian specimen dated as older than 42,000 years.[33] Similarly to those analyzing the other two Neandertal skeletons, the team studying the Croatian skeleton concluded that "Neandertals did not end up contributing mtDNA to the contemporary human gene pool."[34]

Since the three Neandertal skeletons from which mitochondrial DNA has been recovered are so diverse in their geographical sites, their ages, and their levels of maturation when they died, a determination of the genetic diversity for the entire Neandertal species can be done. Such a determination established that Neandertals, like humans, manifest a very low species-wide diversity in their mitochondrial DNA.[35] In fact, the diversity is so low that it forces the conclusion that Neandertals, like humans, expanded rapidly from just a few individuals over the course of just a few tens of thousands of years. Such a conclusion defies a natural evolutionary explanation but is perfectly consistent with separate special creations for each of the Neandertal and human species.

The Data Converge

A quick review of the data shows that the fossil and archeological dates for the origin of humanity are consistent with the dates for the most ancient religious artifacts. The biochemical history of humans proves consistent with these dates and with new evidence that the Neandertals were morphologically and biochemically distinct. All the dates and data fit the roughly estimated biblical dates for the creation of Adam and Eve. Chapters fifteen and twenty discuss the consistency of these dates with new scientific estimates for the date of the Flood, the origin of different races of humanity, and human migration into the Americas.

CHAPTER FIFTEEN

THE POSSIBILITY OF LONG LIFE SPANS
GENESIS 5–6

Some readers who make their way through the first few chapters of Genesis and encounter the long life spans in the list of Adam's descendants become convinced that the book is fictional, or legendary at best, whether in part or in whole. Other readers, convinced that the book must be the true Word of God, conclude that the ancient Hebrew "year" must have been very much shorter than a year as we know it today.

The average life span of the patriarchs listed in Genesis 5 (with the exception of Enoch, who went to heaven without passing through death) was 912 years. According to Genesis 5:27, Methuselah lived 969 years, about eight times longer than the oldest human on record in the twentieth century, with all our learned and technologically advanced means to extend life. How can these numbers be credible?

Defining "Year"
Whatever the answer to this question, it lies beyond Hebrew definitions and time measures. Stories from the ancient Akkadian and Sumerian cultures also tell of extraordinarily long life spans. Only rough dates or ages appear in these accounts, but they claim that their most ancient kings lived thousands of years.

Fourth-century Babylonian historian Berosus drew from archives in Marduk's temple to name ten kings who lived before a great deluge, ten kings who reigned thousands of years each. The Weld-Blundell prism, which dates back to the third millennium B.C., and the Nippur tablets also list ten pre-Flood kings who lived thousands of years.

Not a trace of evidence can be found in either biblical or

extrabiblical texts to indicate that the ancients or pre-Flood peoples counted their years significantly differently from the way we count them today. The Genesis 5 genealogy records that both Mahalalel and Enoch became fathers in their sixty-fifth year. If pre-Flood "years" roughly equaled ten years today, the ages given for Mahalel and Enoch make no sense, nor does the Genesis 6:3 reference to the shortening of human life spans to about 120 years or less (currently, less than one person in a billion lives past 116 years).

Astronomers have investigated the possibility that Earth's rotation period has changed significantly, that it was several times more rapid (hence, the days shorter) several thousand years ago. Research shows no evidence of significant change and ample evidence of extreme stability within the last few million years.

Agricultural references further indicate that the ancients counted years as moderns do. Their survival depended on their success in growing food, and their success in growing food depended on knowing the seasons and the right times to plant and harvest. Biblical and extrabiblical references to the seasons show no possibility for confusion on this issue.

Both Mesopotamian records (circa 1500 B.C.) and the Old Testament clearly state that a calendar year consisted of twelve thirty-day months. The Mesopotamians and other ancients also showed awareness that their twelve thirty-day months fell short of an actual year by a little more than five days. Ancient civilizations employed astronomers and equipped them with transit instruments for measuring time. These early astronomers were able to measure a year's duration to a precision as close as a few minutes. Though some variations can be found from one society to another, the ancients typically celebrated a set of festival days every few years or so to make up the extra days and reset their calendars.

Implicit Evidence for Long Life Spans

Virtually all world civilization textbooks attest to the rapid rise of the most ancient civilizations in the Fertile Crescent of Mesopotamia. The Bible explicitly describes rapid advances in pre-Flood technology.[1] Long life spans would effectively promote a high rate of advance. A 900-year life gives an individual opportunity to discover and apply knowledge, to pass along that knowledge, and to work with others to refine it and find new applications for it. Knowledge and experience could, thus, multiply. And that seems to describe the history of ancient peoples. Post-Flood peoples, by contrast, show evidence of starts and stops and restarts in their progress, technological and otherwise. The use of various metals, for example, frequently appears, then disappears, then reappears later in the archeological record. This change in the rate and smoothness of advance makes sense if human life spans dropped dramatically around the time of the Flood.

We see in the Genesis text a change of dietary law after the Flood. This change, too, correlates with a change in life expectancy. God informed Noah after the Flood that the people need no longer restrict their diet to green plants. They could now eat animals, though fear of humans would drive many creatures away (Genesis 9:2-3). As chapter nine mentions, a diet that includes meat adds higher concentrations of heavy elements to the body (anywhere from ten to ten thousand times more than a vegetarian diet). These higher levels would prove detrimental to health, even life-threatening, after a few hundred years. But for people living only 120 years or less, the new limit God set at the time of the Flood (Genesis 6:3), the health risk becomes negligible (except where industrial pollution is extremely high).

Recent research demonstrates two more benefits of a vegetarian diet for people living before the Flood. Caloric restriction (reducing the number of calories consumed on a day-to-day basis) has been shown to extend the mean and maximum life spans of many species, including mammals, by 20 to 40 percent.[2-3] Similarly, minimizing the intake of oxidants and maximizing the intake of anti-oxidants can increase the mean life spans of some species by as much as 40 percent.[4] Typically, meats are rich in oxidants whereas certain vegetables are rich in anti-oxidants. Caloric binging usually is more difficult on a vegetarian diet than it is with a meat diet. A well-designed vegetarian diet, therefore, could significantly enhance longevity by preventing caloric overload and reducing oxidative stress on human tissues and cells.

How to Live 900 Years

Until recently no one could begin to explain scientifically how the pre-Flood peoples were able to live 900 years or more. Several canopy theories, derived from mention of the "mist" or "streams" watering the Garden of Eden (Genesis 2:6), rose in popularity. However, such hypotheses fail the test of plausibility. Any canopy substantial enough to protect humanity from various forms of life-shortening radiation would either collapse (as in fall to the ground) or dissipate into outer space. Worse yet, any such covering would establish atmospheric conditions unsuitable for life, particularly for advanced life. Neither historical nor scientific evidences for the existence of such a canopy has been found (see page 157).

Genesis 6 states simply that God shortened the life span of humanity to 120 years. Genesis nowhere states *how* God effected this change. The answers we seek will have to come through scientific investigation. A reasonable place to start this inquiry would be to identify what factors limit the human life span. Sixteen have been discovered thus far, and Table 15.1 lists them. Among the sixteen, we find three that could realistically account for the great difference in survivability: (1) radiation from radioisotopes (for example, uranium, radium, and thorium) in igneous rocks; (2) cosmic radiation; and (3) telomerase activity (forestalling natural chromosome shortening by adding nucleotide base pairs to the ends of DNA).

Table 15.1: Major Factors Limiting Human Life Spans

1. war and murder
2. accidents
3. disease
4. famine or inadequate nutrition
5. high metabolic rates
6. internal oxidative stress
7. environmental stress
8. inadequate exercise
9. chemical carcinogens
10. heavy element accumulation in tissues
11. high caloric intake
12. ultraviolet radiation
13. solar x-ray radiation
14. radioisotope decay radiation
15. cosmic radiation
16. telomerase activity (forestalling natural chromosome shortening by adding nucleotide base pairs to the ends of DNA)

If the pre-Flood peoples lived in geographic locations or dwellings well isolated from igneous rocks, their exposure to radiation from radioisotope decay could have been lessened. Genesis 6–11 (see chapter eighteen) indicates that indeed their habitation was limited to regions for which that possibility existed.

Cosmic radiation would have affected humans wherever they lived on the planet. Harmful cosmic rays come from quasars, black holes, neutron stars, supernovae (giant star explosions) and their remnants, and novae (star explosions). Quasars are so extremely distant that their cosmic ray flux is small compared to cosmic ray sources in our galaxy. The black holes and neutron stars in our galaxy actually result from supernovae. Novae occur hundreds of times more frequently than supernovae, but novae pack tens of thousands of times less wallop. The percentage of high-energy particles they emit is tiny in comparison to supernovae emissions. Consequently, the radiation from novae does less damage and subsides more quickly than does radiation from supernovae. The bottom line is that supernovae are by far the prime contributor to cosmic rays incident upon the earth.

Except in our galaxy's halo, where supernova events are rare, supernovae (and their remnants, of course) are distributed fairly evenly throughout our galaxy. Until recently most astronomers assumed, on the basis of this even distribution, that the level of cosmic radiation was roughly constant in recent time and everywhere the same throughout the galaxy. This assumption was challenged in 1996 by two astronomers who analyzed all of the available data from air-shower experiments (forty years of measurements of cosmic ray impacts on Earth's atmosphere). Their findings indicate that much of the heavy nuclei cosmic rays striking Earth must be coming from a recent, nearby supernova—a supernova closer than three thousand light-years and younger than one hundred thousand years.[5-6] Only one known supernova fits this profile.

Evaluating Vela's Impact
The only known supernova eruption that could possibly be implicated in the shortening of human life spans and maintenance of short life spans is that of the Vela supernova. This one event occurred so near Earth that at maximum light it would have outshone the full moon. Only about thirteen hundred light-years away, the Vela is more than three times closer to Earth than the next nearest human-era supernova event, an eruption that occurred in A.D. 1016. Vela is more than five times closer than the Crab eruption, the third closest, which occurred in A.D. 1054.

Because of its magnitude and proximity to Earth, the Vela bathed and still bathes Earth with thirty times more cosmic radiation than either the A.D. 1016 or the Crab eruption events.

In 1981 geophysicist G. Robert Brakenridge published a paper entitled "Terrestrial Paleoenvironmental Effects of a Late Quaternary-Age Supernova."[7] In this study Brakenridge explains two of the effects Vela would likely have produced: (1) its impact on the upper atmosphere would have brought about several months of global cooling; (2) its damage to the ozone layer would have increased ultraviolet radiation for that same period by two to ten times. He then documents geological evidence that both effects were felt roughly around 9000 B.C. and notes that some diatom and plankton species disappeared at about the same time.

Brakenridge sought to determine a date for the eruption of the Vela supernova. He measured the positions and velocities of material ejected from the supernova relative to the position of the neutron core remaining after the eruption. The date he calculated lies between 8,500 and 14,500 years ago. However, Brakenridge assumed that the neutron star core remaining after the eruption had not moved across our line of sight, and his calculation failed to take into account the possibility that the quantity of gas and dust in the Vela's vicinity could have disturbed significantly the motions of the ejecta. Brakenridge's figures, then, must be corrected for such effects, and the corrections render his dates as an extreme lower limit on the time since the eruption.

Further adjustments continue as researchers learn more. Calculations done in 1995 by three German X-ray astronomers place the date of the Vela eruption at 18,000 ± 9,000 years ago or 31,000 ± 6,000 years ago.[8] (The difference between the two dates arises from two different methods for determining the movement of the neutron star relative to the supernova's ejecta.) A more recent study by four British radio astronomers measures the rate at which Vela supernova's neutron star core (a pulsar) is spinning down.[9] The date the British team reports is 22,000 to 29,000 years ago.

The techniques used by both the British and German teams have the potential of delivering much more accurate results. For now, we must be content with a date for the Vela supernova eruption somewhere between about 20,000 and 30,000 years ago. Given that the Vela supernova plays a major role in shortening human life spans, this measurement, even without the refinements to come, may rank as our most accurate means for determining when (approximately) the Flood occurred. As chapter eighteen will amplify, this rough date for the Vela seems consistent with the timing of humanity's post-Flood spread from the region of Mesopotamia into all parts of the world.

Testing the Vela Hypothesis

Theoretically, researchers could test the conclusion that radiation from the Vela supernova significantly shortened (and keeps short) human life spans. The test would require raising a human (from the time of conception) in a radiation-free environment, with a nutritious vegetarian diet, a healthy lifestyle, protection from war, crime, disease, carcinogens, and accidents. If this human lived 900 years or more, future generations of us would know we were right about Vela's impact.

From a practical perspective, this experiment appears impossible. We cannot find a feasible way to shield a person from radiation. If we shield a person from cosmic rays by permanently keeping that individual several hundred feet underground, we then expose that person to radiation from the decay of radioisotopes in the earth's crust. Typically, the damage from this radioisotope radiation exceeds that from the cosmic rays avoided. The one exception would be the possibility of living inside a very thick, deep underground salt deposit. But who would volunteer to live in such confined quarters for hundreds of years and continuously avoid all the other factors listed in Table 15.1?

Researchers could, on the other hand, try the opposite approach, exposing advanced life to radiation roughly equivalent to that of a much closer (than Vela) supernova event and observe the consequences over several years, even several generations. Ethical concerns, of course, rule out this option.

Experiments similar to the latter have been performed, inadvertently, however, in war and nuclear accidents. Hiroshima, Nagasaki, Three Mile Island, and Chernobyl come to mind, but other radiation disasters have occurred as well. In each case the damage has been devastating, and it strongly supports the hypothesis that the Vela supernova did play a significant role in shortening human life.

Role of Telomerase

Recent study of human cells may render this discussion of the Vela supernova partly academic. Cells of complex organisms are limited to the number of replications they can undergo. For those cells that make up the differentiated tissues and the different organs and appendages (the somatic cells), the telomere region of each chromosome within a given cell is not fully replicated during cell division. Therefore, each chromosome becomes shorter and shorter as the number of cell divisions increase. Eventually, the chromosomes become so short that important genes fail to get replicated, which actually prevents cell division from occurring for the next generation. Once such cells are unable to reproduce, damaged cells cannot be replaced. The organism then dies from the failure of organs, tissues, and appendages to perform their life-essential functions. What this means for human beings today is that no matter how healthy and safe a lifestyle a person leads, he or she will not live beyond about 120 years.

There is one way, though, past this biochemical life span limit. There is an enzyme called telomerase that adds nucleotide base pairs to the ends of DNA so that the chromosomes are not shortened. Allowing this enzyme to work in all somatic cells, however, does carry a significant risk. Because telomerase sustains cell reproduction, if normal cells turn cancerous, then the resulting tumors could grow unchecked. In other words, the lack of telomerase in most somatic cells is one of the best defenses available to complex organisms to hold in check the development and spread of tumors and cancers.

What this means is that too much telomerase activity typically will bring about an earlier demise for a complex organism through the spread of cancers and tumors.[10-11] But, too little telomerase activity typically results in an earlier demise from organ and tissue failures.[12] Given the cancer-inducing factors present within an organism's environment, there is an ideal telomerase activity level for maximizing the organism's life span.

Currently, we live in a radiation environment that rather strongly induces the growth of tumors and cancers. Therefore, it is important for us that telomerase activity be kept relatively low. Before the Vela supernova eruption, the level of cancer-inducing radiation was much less. We can speculate, then, that before the Vela eruption, God fixed telomerase activity at a level that permitted life spans of 900+ years, a safe level given lesser cosmic radiation at that time. After the Vela eruption, God (it seems) lowered human telomerase activity to protect us from the effects of increased radiation exposure.

God possibly may have altered some other biochemical pathways as well. Certain genes activate the production of specialized proteins that operate so as to magnify the longevity-enhancing benefits of caloric restriction and high anti-oxidant consumption.[13-14] That is, by manipulating human genes God could have increased the life extension possible through a controlled vegetarian diet in a low-radiation environment. The current benefits of a lack of the above-mentioned specialized proteins in a high radiation environment where meat is being consumed are as yet uncertain.

Genesis 11 indicates that the change in life span did not happen instantaneously. The life spans recorded there testify to an exponential decline over the generations from Noah (950 years) down to Nahor (148 years).[15] This exponential drop in human life spans may reflect God's response to the exponentially increasing effects of Vela radiation (currently we lack the data to give us an accurate profile of these effects), or it may reflect God's allowance for humanity's difficulties in adjusting to change. Or it may reflect both.

God's Good Intentions

None of these possible life-shortening scenarios implies that God simply reacted to (or sat back and watched) natural disasters. Rather, Genesis 6 states that God acted purposefully to shorten human life spans. Shorter life spans served to limit the spread of human wickedness. An exceptionally evil person can hurt or destroy a great many righteous people in 900 years. In fact, the long human life spans of the pre-Flood peoples may help explain why only one family among the entire human race was deemed salvageable by the time of Noah's six-hundredth birthday. The Vela supernova may represent one of God's chosen methods for achieving an important goal.

Whether the Vela supernova and reset telomerase activity offers a full, partial, or minor contribution to the explanation of humanity's life span change remains to be seen. Nonetheless, they help demonstrate that what has sometimes been considered a scientific and historical absurdity—the 900+ years of Methuselah and his peers— really can prove scientifically and historically plausible.

CHAPTER SIXTEEN

SONS OF GOD AND THE NEPHILIM
GENESIS 6

Genesis 6 opens with some brief contextual details setting the scene for the expansive Flood narrative. But these details seem so strange, so mysterious, that they present an apologetics challenge almost as great as the Flood story itself. In this case, unlike that of the Genesis 5 life spans, the solution to the mystery must come largely from the pages of Scripture, though science does play a significant role.

The time frame is characterized by a growing population. Apparently, at least some of the exponential increase expected from the multiplication of Adam's descendants (see Table 13.1 on page 103) had begun to shoot up, despite metastasizing violence. The main characters include the "sons of God" and the "daughters of men," initially. Apparently the "sons" were so captivated by the "daughters'" beauty that they "married any of them they chose" (verses 1-2). So far, the story seems straightforward and comprehensible, though we may wonder who these "sons" could be.

In the next moment we are thrown by the sudden interjection of God's rebuke, His declaration that human life will be shortened from hundreds of years down to 120, at most, because He does not wish to "contend with man forever." The reference to contention suggests a struggle, perhaps God leading one way, humanity pulling another, like a mule resisting its master. Here is our first clue that relations between the sons of God and daughters of men may be displeasing to God.

Then comes mention of the Nephilim:

The Nephilim were on the earth in those days—and also afterward—when the sons of God went to the daughters of men and had children by them. They were the heroes of old, men of renown.[1]

In the next stroke of the pen, the narrator moves on to explain, from God's perspective, the necessity of the universally destructive Flood. The writer of this account apparently assumed his readers' familiarity with these characters, all of them, and did not waste ink elaborating on them. The Nephilim, after all, appear many times in the biblical narratives up until the days of King David.[2] Modern readers, however, must do the necessary homework, looking to other passages in the Bible for help in understanding this text. If we find insufficient information for drawing firm conclusions, we can accept the obvious: the interpretation of this passage has no crucial bearing on our relationship with God or confidence in the reliability of His Word.

A reasonable interpretation will offer consistency—biblical, historical, and scientific. The demonstration of such consistency, by itself, adequately answers the attacks of skeptics and scoffers. The degree of confidence we place in any proposed interpretation will be determined by the degree of consistency it manifests on all three fronts.

I am aware of three interpretations (one is a blend of the other two) that demonstrate sufficient consistency to answer the charges of those who doubt biblical accuracy on this issue. All three date back to the Ante-Nicene church fathers (church leaders writing before A.D. 325). I have added some new scientific and exegetical observations. More data, if and when available, will be helpful in refining or revising all perspectives.

Identifying the Nephilim

The interpretation preferred by most Bible scholars[3-6] today identifies none of the characters mentioned, including the Nephilim, as possessing any supernatural qualities. These scholars view the sons of God and their offspring (by the daughters of men), the Nephilim, as purely human. The account reduces to God's imposition of a sexual restriction between the sons of God, whom they presume to be males in the godly line of Seth, and the daughters of men, presumably female descendants in the ungodly line of Cain. While no mention of any such prohibition appears anywhere in the Genesis text, the principle certainly can be deduced from passages found in Ezra and 2 Corinthians.[7]

The textual support for the intended separation of the Cainites from the Sethites rests upon Genesis 4:1-24 exclusively dealing with Cain and his descendants while Genesis 4:25–5:32 deals exclusively with Seth and his descendants. Genesis 4:1–24 says nothing good about the line of Cain whereas Genesis 4:25-5:32 says nothing bad about the line of Seth. Minor but significant points are that Enosh's associates (Enosh is Seth's son) "call on the name of the Lord" (Genesis 4:26) and that the name of Lamech's daughter, Naamah, (Genesis 4:22) means "beautiful."

As for the Nephilim who appear both before and after the Flood, they are taken to be wicked men of great renown and strength in battle. No scholar disputes the wicked nature of the Nephilim. The Hebrew root of nephilim, means "to fall." This name, then, indicates the Nephilim were fallen ones morally. In the post-Flood era the Bible identifies them as existing with the wicked Canaanite and Philistine populations.

A check of cross-references to the Nephilim in other parts of Scripture, however, raises doubts about the consistency of interpreting them as strictly human. They go by alternate names, including the Rephaim (or sons of Rapha), Anakites, and Anakim, and they are referred to as "the giants." All are male.

The chilling descriptions of the Nephilim focus on their superhuman size and strength. Goliath, identified in 1 Samuel 21 and 1 Chronicles 20 as a descendant of Rapha, stood six and a half cubits (at least nine feet, nine inches) tall and demonstrated great mobility and strength in battle while carrying at least 250 pounds of armor and weapons.[8] Og, the king of Bashan, had to sleep in an iron bed measuring nine by four cubits (at least thirteen and a half feet by six feet).[9] The Hebrews' use of three different cubits makes for difficulty in rendering precise values, but we can establish approximate lower limits at least. The three types of cubits included the common, the royal, and the long, measuring (respectively) about eighteen, twenty, and twenty-two inches.[10-11]

"Giants" also are described in extrabiblical literature. The Greeks, Romans, Phoenicians, Mesopotamians, and Egyptians, for example, all wrote stories of famous heroes, men of supernatural size and strength. Greek literature is especially rich in this respect, and the Philistines who settled in the coastal plain of Canaan came from Greece or Crete. In all their accounts, the superheros came from the sexual union between immortal "gods" and mortal humans. These giants resemble the biblical Nephilim in their penchant for fighting[12] and in their tendency to manifest birth defects.[13] The extrabiblical stories differ from the biblical ones, however, in attributing virtue and immortality to at least a few of the giants. The biblical Nephilim are evil and mortal, without exception.

In addition to the enormous weight of weapons and armor the Nephilim were able to carry, their great stature, if our values for biblical cubits are accurate, supersedes human capabilities and the limits of biological engineering. The bone mass necessary to support the muscles and resist the effects of gravity rises geometrically with height (just as the weight of a building's supporting beams goes up geometrically with the length of the span they support). This ratio implies an increasingly severe loss of mobility and stamina once human height exceeds about eight feet.

We see verification of this loss in the case of the tallest documented modern human, a victim of a growth-hormone malfunction who reached eight feet, eleven inches.[14] This man moved so slowly and with such difficulty that he could not participate in sports. He died at age forty from physical exhaustion.

The sport of basketball provides further verification. The ease with which a player can score a basket goes up with the square of his height (because the range of shooting angles that will score increases with the square of the height from which the ball leaves the player's hands). Thus, even a one inch height advantage is huge. This explains why seven-foot tall players tend to be much higher scorers than six-foot tall players. However, basketball players who are seven and a half feet tall tend to move, jump, and dodge with less strength, quickness, and fluidity than those only seven feet tall. Evidently, the shooting advantage gained from the extra half foot of height is not enough to overcome the loss of mobility, agility, and stamina as a result of the increased height.

Given human physiological limits, the Nephilim must have been in some way superhuman. Strictly human bodies cannot manifest this combination of size, power, agility, and endurance. One way to maintain a strictly human interpretation for the Nephilim would be to call into question the weights and measures of David's and Moses' time. This approach presents difficulties, however, in view of the archeological evidence and it raises the additional problem of why Saul, a soldier who was "an impressive young man without equal" and "a head taller" than any other Israelite,[15] was so terrified of Goliath.

Sons of God in the Old Testament

The Hebrew words for "sons of God" can refer either to humans or to angels.[16] The "sons of men" and the "daughters of men" can refer only to humans.

Outside the Genesis 6 passage, all Old Testament references to "sons of God" appear in the book of Job. In Job 1:6 and 2:1, the sons of God, or "the angels," present themselves before the Lord, and Satan comes along with them. The location, "before the Lord," appears to be heaven, not Earth. When God asks Satan where he has come from, he replies, "From roaming through the earth and going back and forth in it." In Job 38:7 the sons of God are addressed as witnesses to the laying of Earth's foundations. No human was present when that event took place. Many modern translations of Scripture simply render the "sons of God" phrase in each of these Job passages as "angels."

One Old Testament verse, Hosea 1:10, refers to "sons of the living God." This phrase refers to human beings, Jews in particular, but in the context of future events. It refers to those Israelites who will partake in salvation through the redemptive sacrifice of the coming Messiah.

Single Old Testament references to "children of the LORD your God"[17] and "His children"[18] occur in Deuteronomy and clearly refer to human beings. The Hebrew word for "children" is the same as the word for "sons." However, neither of the two Deuteronomy phrases is identical to the "sons of God" phrase used in Job and Genesis. The two Deuteronomy expressions appear to fit well as variants of the 357 references in the Torah (Genesis–Deuteronomy) to "children of Israel." Thus, the Old Testament provides no conclusive evidence that the phrase "sons of God" refers to Old Testament era human beings (see Appendix C).

Those holding a human interpretation for the Genesis 6 sons of God make the point that three occurrences in just one book (besides the Genesis 6 references) hardly seem a strong enough foundation on which to rest a doctrinal point. Moreover, it seems strange that "sons of God" would be used anywhere in the Bible for evil angels. Job 38:7 has the sons of God shouting for joy over God's creative work, strange behavior indeed for fallen angels. The counter from the other side is that the Bible does not specify exactly when before Eden the angelic rebellion occurred and that sons of God is a generic term for all angels. This latter point seems supported by a similar term for the angels, literally in the Hebrew, "the mighty ones" used in Psalm 29:1 and 89:7. The implication is that sons of God may be a generic term for all the supernatural beings God created.

Both sides of the debate argue that "sons of God" is an inappropriate term for the other's interpretation. Outside of Genesis 6 Moses (in the first five books of the Bible) refers to angels fifteen times, and he consistently identifies them with the Hebrew word for "angels," *mal'ak*. They always are called angels, not once sons of God. Therefore, if Genesis 6:2,4 really does refer to angels, why would he not use that word? Likewise, those disputing a human interpretation state that if Genesis 6:2,4 really does refer to the descendants of Seth, why was not the phrase "sons of Seth" used?

Sons of God in the New Testament

The New Testament usage presents a contrast that seems to make sense because of the change Christ has brought about through His death and resurrection. All eight uses of the Greek phrase "sons of God" apply to humans. The equivalent expression, "children of God," also applies exclusively to humans, and it appears six times. Four more passages refer to "sons" without including, but certainly implying, "of God": Luke 6:35, Galatians 4:4-7, Hebrews 2:10, and Hebrews 12:7. In all eighteen cases (see Appendix C), the designation "sons of God" (or the equivalent "children of God") applies to a particular group of people, who have received Jesus Christ as their Lord and Savior and, thus, have received the permanent indwelling presence of the Holy Spirit. (The Luke 6:35 and John 1:12 references point to the future fulfillment of a promise that those who welcome and receive Christ will gain the right to become sons of God.) Evidently, these humans alone can rightfully be called, in the New Testament context, "sons of God" ("children of God"). This title went into effect for humans only after Pentecost (see Acts 2,8,10), when the Holy Spirit "sealed" the new covenant God established with all who put their trust in Him.

If only post-Pentecost believers can be called sons of God, it seems inconsistent that the sons of God in Genesis 6 would refer to humans. Those arguing for a human interpretation in Genesis 6 counter that a scriptural pattern in the usage of the term does not necessarily prove a scriptural doctrine. Nowhere does the Bible explicitly state that human sons of God must have partaken of the Pentecost experience. In the twenty-three biblical occurrences of "sons [or daughters] of men" and the nineteen to the equivalent "children of men" (see Appendix C) the phrase refers exclusively to humans.

Jesus, the Son of God and of Man

By referring to Himself as "the Son of Man" and "the Son of God," Jesus seems to be making an important point about the use of these titles. Jesus knew God as His Father, claimed for Himself roles, capacities, and authority that only God can claim, and demonstrated divine power, and yet He bore the title "Son of Man" until after His resurrection. From the resurrection onward, He never again called Himself (or was called by anyone else) the Son of Man. He took instead the title "Son of God."

The frequency and consistency of Jesus' use of these titles argues for their distinction. Until He completed the sacrifice that would transform willing humans into sons (or children) of God, the title Son of God apparently was inappropriate. Once His work was done, however, and the Spirit was sent in His place to live among us and *in* us who believe, human beings, for the first time since Eden, could be called sons and daughters of God.

Even great men of God such as Ezekiel and Daniel take only the "son of man" title. Only once in Scripture, previous to the Resurrection and to Pentecost, is a human being called a son of God. In the Luke 3 genealogy, Adam bears that title. (Adam for a time was unfallen.) However, once again, the argument that only post-Pentecost humans can be called sons of God comes by way of scriptural pattern, not by way of explicit doctrinal statement.

Angels and Sex

The primary objection to the notion that the sons of God were angels comes from our perception of angels as asexual beings. Genesis 6 indicates that the "sons of God" did engage in sexual intercourse with women and impregnated them. The objection to the angelic interpretation is based on three points: (1) nowhere in the Bible is sexual capacity explicitly attributed to angels; (2) not one case of a demon impregnating a woman or transmitting semen to a woman has been documented; and (3) Jesus explicitly declares in Matthew's gospel:

> "At the resurrection people will neither marry nor be given in marriage; they will be like the angels in heaven."[19]

Rejoinders to all three points have been published. Many scholars have pointed out that Jesus' explicit statement can be interpreted two ways: (1) it may indicate that angels have no capacity for sexual relations; or (2) it may indicate that angels in heaven simply do not engage in marital relations.

After all, God replaces earthly marriage relationships with far superior, extra-dimensional, "heavenly" relationships in His coming kingdom. When we humans enter heaven in our immortal bodies, the longing for oneness we express in sex will be completely satisfied. (Furthermore, reproduction to sustain Earth's population will no longer be necessary.) It seems reasonable that angels living in God's presence and experiencing His love have neither need nor desire for our earthly kind of marriage and the physical union that belongs to it.[20]

Angels who have broken their relationship with God through rebellion and who follow Satan instead of God have lost that unity, that oneness, and all the pleasures and joys of heaven. Their loss of place, purpose, and, more importantly, of relationship with God possibly might tempt these angels-turned-demons to seek the kind of union they observe among humans.

Paul made a subtle reference suggesting this possibility in 1 Corinthians 11:10. In his guidelines for propriety in worship, he instructed women believers to wear "a sign of authority" when the congregation meets, not only because it would demonstrate appropriate respect toward God and men, but also "because of the angels." The text does not elaborate on this point, and it has been interpreted in various ways, but it possibly could fit with the notion that angelic beings can, in some way, be influenced or tempted by women's behavior. We must remember, too, that sexual acts of various kinds were part of Greek and Roman worship in the temples of the gods.

While it is true that the transmission of semen from a demon to a human has never been documented, the sexual interest of demons seems consistent with a great body of documentation on occult practices. Evil spirits, and humans operating under their influence, manifest an obsession with sex to a level much higher than the average population.[21] The incidence of rape and sexual assault on women and men proves extremely high among those involved in occult encounters and practices.

Some have argued that angels are "bodiless, purely spiritual-beings and sexless."[22] The fact that angelic beings have the capacity to take on human form and perform concrete biological functions such as walking, talking, eating, and drinking finds ample support from biblical accounts, from Genesis to Revelation, from Abraham to John the apostle.[23] Several times angels in their encounters with humans were mistaken for men (never for women).[24] The men of Sodom even saw them as candidates for homosexual rape.[25]

However, one watershed question remains, even if reasons exist for believing that the sons of God who fathered strange offspring by the daughters of men could have been fallen angels: why is there no evidence, at least in modern times, for the fertilization of an ovum in demonic encounters?

The plausibility of the supernatural-sons-of-God interpretation rests heavily on this question, and the Bible offers no explicit answer. However, Jude 1:6-7 may offer a viable explanation:

> And the angels who did not keep their positions of authority but abandoned their own home—these he has kept in darkness, bound with everlasting chains for judgment on the great Day. In a similar way, Sodom and Gomorrah and the surrounding towns gave themselves up to sexual immorality and perversion.

Jude here associates the angels' offense with sexual debauchery of the worst magnitude known to humans.

Given the punishment Jude describes for these angels' (demons') behavior, we can better understand the reaction of demons Jesus cast out of people during His earthly ministry.[26] In many instances the demon or demons shrieked with terror at the prospect of being sent to the place of darkness and chains of which Jude spoke, "the Abyss," or "Tartarus" in the Greek New Testament. The demons begged Jesus not to send them there, pleading that they had done nothing to deserve that degree of punishment. In each case, though the demons were rebuked and sent away, Jesus accepted their appeal. Their judgment will come later.

If demons do possess the capacity to bear offspring by women, their inclination to do so might be restrained today by the threat of the terrible penalty—consignment to the Abyss—for doing so. Such an interpretation would contribute to our understanding of the Flood's necessity and of the mention of Nephilim in this Genesis 6 context. The Flood would have rid Earth of the evil and powerful Nephilim and of those women inclined to engage in sexual relations with demons.

Even the Flood, however, did not fully eradicate the problem of the Nephilim. It seems the sin that produced them recurred for a time after the Flood. The Nephilim receive mention again in Numbers, Deuteronomy, Joshua, Judges, and 1 and 2 Samuel. After the Flood, though, their number seems reduced and their distribution restricted to one locale, the land of Canaan. God destroyed these later "giants" by sending Abraham's descendants into Canaan and raising up Moses, Joshua, and, finally, David, with his thirty mighty warriors. Since the time of David's conquest, we see no evidence or suggestion of their return. One possible explanation, then, based on what we read in the New Testament, is that the threat of consignment to the Abyss for angels who cross a sexual boundary was instituted at or after David's time, or became heightened adequately since that time, to prevent a recurrence.

A third interpretation of Genesis 6 represents a blending of the prominent opposing views. This approach attempts to solve the sexual issues by hypothesizing a special kind of demon possession. The sons of God in Genesis 6 are presumed to be fallen angels who invade and possess human males in such a powerful way that the genes in the human semen were altered to produce the supernatural Nephilim. Further development and discussion of this view will be helpful, but as yet little appears in print.

Humans Judged for Angels' Sin?

A major objection to interpreting the sons of God in Genesis 6 as fallen angels arises from the seeming unfairness of God's judgment of humans for the sin of angels. This line of argument assumes, however, that the sole purpose of the Genesis Flood was to destroy the sons of God and the Nephilim.

I am persuaded by what follows in Genesis 6, specifically verses 5-13, that the sins of the sons of God and the Nephilim represent just part of all the evil pervading Noah's generation. We cannot blame all the evil of the pre-Flood peoples on the sons of God and the Nephilim. The rest of Earth's population had grown wicked through their own thoughts and actions. As the text records, "All the people on earth had corrupted their ways," and "every inclination of the thoughts" of every human heart "was only evil all the time."[27]

Recognizing that Genesis 6:2-4 represents but a parenthetical comment on the evil of the days just before the Genesis Flood should go a long way toward resolving the controversies surrounding the sons of God and the Nephilim. The three scenarios addressed here leave many questions unanswered, but they do fit with available information and contradict no information already available. Thus, the burden of proof returns to the side of the skeptic. The existence of an element of uncertainty no more detracts from the reliability of the whole text than does an unanswered question of science undermine our confidence in the whole body of established scientific knowledge.

CHAPTER SEVENTEEN

THE BOUNDARIES OF GOD'S WRATH
GENESIS 6

As much skepticism and ridicule as secularists may express about the scientific plausibility of the Genesis creation accounts, they tend to heap more derision on the Genesis Flood story. What they have heard or read strikes them as utterly preposterous. The story seems to contradict well-established science at every turn, and it appears even to go against the popular notion of the benevolent Christian God.

The problem is that Genesis 6–9, the account of the great Flood that destroyed everything and everyone in its path, has been approached time and again from the wrong angle. While I would agree that it bears significantly on geology, geophysics, meteorology, paleontology, biology, anthropology, and so forth, first and foremost it teaches about God's character, His judgment and mercy. It gives invaluable insights into the who, the how, the when, and the why of God's judgment.

Without such insights the scientific material of Genesis 6–9 cannot be interpreted correctly. The themes of divine judgment and mercy guide our understanding of the text's geological, geophysical, geographical, paleontological, biological, meteorological, anthropological, and other scientific content.

Sin's Damage

Jesus underlined a message about sin that the Jews missed. People today miss it still. He said that if we have broken one commandment, we have broken all the commandments.[1] He wants us to understand that "all have sinned and come short of the glory of God."[2] We all would repeat the sin of Adam and Eve if we were the ones in the garden, and we prove it every day. Sin is sin, and were it not for Christ's sacrificial atonement, no one would escape its penalty.

Sin describes the heart condition with which we are born,[3] that is, the tendency to rebel against God's authority. Sins are the acts that reflect our heart condition. Each act of sin, according to Scripture, does some damage to the one who commits it.[4] Sin "defiles," the Bible says, and we can easily recognize that some sins do more damage, are more "defiling," than others.[5] Some sins are so serious that they damage not only the person committing them but also the people, animals, and even things around that person. Sins against the body (murder, assault, fornication, adultery, and so on) do deeper harm than do sins outside the body (stealing, lying, cheating, and so on).[6] But all sin damages, and all sin grieves and offends the heart of God.

The extent of a sin's damage depends on the depth of degradation the sin expresses. Multiple and repeated sins compound the damage. Defilement begins and spreads in this order:

1. to the sinner (Romans 7:8-11)
2. then to his progeny (Exodus 20:5)
3. then to his soulish animals (Joshua 6:21)
4. then to his material goods (Numbers 16:23-33)
5. then to his inhabited land (Leviticus 18:24-28)

Defilement reaching as far as possessions and lands has not been seen on Earth since the time before Jesus' earthly ministry and the spread of the Holy Spirit's restraining, "convicting" influence. Even during Old Testament times, evil rarely descended to such depths. In the centuries since the church was born, horrible atrocities have occurred, not just among "primitive savages" but among savages in modern garb with technological tools of torture. But the world has not seen a repeat of Sodom, for example,[7] where a city's entire male population, young and old, violently pursued honored guests to commit homosexual rape against them.

People sometimes struggle to believe that the God of the Old Testament could be one and the same as the God of the New. They read accounts of wholesale destruction ordered by God and cannot imagine His actions as expressions of mercy or love. They cannot fathom that God's judgment in such instances compares with the work of a skilled surgeon removing a dangerous malignancy. God has not changed, but He has moved on to another stage in His plan to preserve and protect humanity from its hopeless sin condition.

In the Old Testament era God operated as needed to prepare and protect the way of His coming deliverance, more specifically of His coming Deliverer, from sin's penalty. Today, in the New Testament era, we look back on the deliverance Christ brought and we can receive the "deposit"[8] guaranteeing our ultimate deliverance, the indwelling Holy Spirit, who frees us from sin's power. The Spirit works in and through us to protect and prepare the way for that ultimate deliverance from sin's penalty, power, and presence.

All human behavior has changed, at least to some extent, because of God's presence among us in a new way, by His Spirit indwelling those who recognize and receive His Deliverer as their only hope. As Jesus explained, His followers are the salt of the earth,[9] a preservative protecting all society from the kind of reprobate (extremely wicked) behavior that occasionally plagued people during Old Testament times.

The Dangers of Reprobation

Reprobation, such as the whole of pre-Flood society (except Noah) manifested, developed over time and spread. Romans 1:18-32 outlines, step by step, how reprobation develops anywhere, anytime—and gains momentum. Verse 32 describes the final step of those who will not, and no longer can, turn back from evil:

> Although they know God's righteous decree that those
> who do such things [vile deeds] deserve death, they not
> only continue to do these very things but also approve of
> those who practice them.

Reprobates not only do evil, they also cheer on others who do evil. They enjoy recruiting others to live as they do, according to Peter:

> They seduce the unstable. . . . By appealing to the lustful
> desires of the sinful human nature, they entice people who
> are just escaping from those who live in error. They
> promise them freedom, while they themselves are slaves of
> depravity.[10]

Anyone exposed to depravity at close range for a long enough time will be affected—and infected—by it. Reprobates are, as Paul said, captives of Satan,[11] and they share Satan's desire to drag others into captivity.[12]

God's "wrath," or judgment, protects and preserves those who are not yet Satan's captives from those who are moving rapidly in that direction or are already there. God's skill as a surgeon is unmatched by that of the best human physician. He knows when and how to wield His scalpel. He knows how much or how little to remove to protect the viable tissue. He is an enemy to disease and a friend to health. He operates from the motive of mercy and love.

Antediluvian Depravity

Though we have no experience that enables us to picture the situation, Noah's contemporaries reached a degree of depravity that threatened to contaminate the planet irreversibly. The Hebrew language has two words to describe ultimate evil, *shachat*, meaning "morally putrid, totally decayed, spiritually gangrenous, destroyed and wasted";[13-14] and *chamas*, which means "seeking to gain through assault, physical attack, cheating, and/or oppression."[15-16] No other people or society warranted the use of such strong language. Their evil was, and remains, unprecedented (though the New Testament warns that society will return to a similar condition at "the time of the end").[17]

Some explanation for this wholesale reprobation appears in chapter thirteen. Contributing factors included violence and murder, initiated by Cain and copied by others. The long life spans, of course, favored the spread of violence and murder, for the percentage of perpetrators rose as more and more victims died, many righteous among them, and as the cycle of revenge escalated. We cannot know why God allowed conditions to reach such a deplorable state, but one of His reasons may have had something to do with demonstrating to all future generations that we humans lack the inner resources to save ourselves, to overcome evil with good. Another reason may have been to persuade us that short life spans benefit us under current conditions, as we await His ultimate deliverance.

The Flood account tells of God's grief and agonizing over humanity's corruption. With a heavy heart He cleansed the world to keep it from utter ruin. He found one man, just one, who with his family could keep the human race from self-extermination and further suffering in the process. The story has more to do with rescue than with wrath. God saved 100 percent of the noncancerous tissue in the body of humanity.

The Boundaries of God's Wrath

The limits of defilement identified above also define the limits of God's wrath. His judgment never goes beyond the boundaries of sin's damage. This principle becomes clear not only in this Flood account but also in God's instructions for the Israelite invasion of Canaan under Joshua's leadership. In the conquest of some Canaanite cities, God instructed the Israelites to kill only the Canaanite adults. In the conquest of other cities, God decreed death for the entire population but not for the soulish animals, the *nephesh* creatures tamed by the inhabitants. (The negative impact of evil humans on the birds and mammals living with them most of us have seen, and the Bible directly identifies,[18] but no amount of sin affects the behavior of insects and bacteria, for example.)

In the conquest of a few cities, God told the Israelites to destroy everything: people, their soulish animals, and in still rarer, more extreme cases, the people's possessions too. The extent of destruction was determined by the extent of defilement.

Such destruction always resulted, of course, in the death of some insects, plants, lizards, viruses, bacteria, and so on, in the immediate environment. Though they were untainted by reprobation, to save them was neither practical nor necessary. Unlike birds and mammals, these species multiply and reestablish themselves rapidly enough that any limited region of destruction would quickly recover.

In the rarest of cases, such as Sodom and Gomorrah, even the land was laid waste. To this day, despite the land's former fertility and abundant water supply, no crops or herds are raised in that region.

Before the book of Genesis was written, the Lord had a dialogue with Abraham that helped Abraham, and helps us, identify the limits of God's wrath.[19] The Lord promised Abraham that if only ten righteous people could be found in Sodom and Gomorrah, He would save the entire populace for the sake of those ten. The Lord also gave His word that in the destruction of those cities, He would first rescue the (fewer than ten) righteous people and any relatives who chose to go with them. God's wrath never falls upon the righteous (Jesus excepted).[20]

In a previous conversation the Lord had told Abraham that the time had not yet come to destroy the Amorite people.[21] Their wickedness had not yet developed to a degree that warranted destruction. His judgment would be held back until the wickedness of the Amorites reached universally reprobate proportions. This process, Abraham was told, would take another four hundred years.

Application to the Flood

This principle of conservation in God's acts of judgment would apply also to the Genesis Flood. It means that if human beings had spread as far as Antarctica, the Flood would cover Antarctica, destroying the Emperor penguins along with the people, except those Emperor penguins and people aboard the ark. If no people lived in Antarctica, God would have no reason to destroy the place or its penguins. Nor would Noah be required to take a pair of Emperor penguins aboard the ark.

The extent of the Genesis Flood, according to the principle laid out in Scripture, would be determined by the spread of human habitation. If, for example, humanity had spread throughout Africa, Asia, and Europe, only Africa, Asia, and Europe would be destroyed by the Flood. If only Mesopotamia had been settled, only Mesopotamia would be flooded. Such a geographically limited Flood would still be "universal" or "worldwide," given that people, not the globe, defined "world" among the ancients. Any flood that exterminates all human beings, all the soulish animals with whom they have contact, and all their material possessions—except those on board Noah's ark—would be universal and would achieve God's purpose in pouring out judgment.

CHAPTER EIGHTEEN

THE FLOOD: GLOBAL OR LOCAL?
GENESIS 7–8

One of the most hotly debated biblical issues of the past century has been the extent of the Genesis Flood. It stirs as much emotion and rancor as the discussion of biological evolution or the creation date for the universe. Chapter eleven provides at least some background for understanding the intensity of the conflict. To some Christians, a person's belief that the Flood covered the entire planet and all its high mountains (as they interpret the Genesis text) provides a reliable litmus test of his or her salvation, of membership in the body of Christ. They have drawn a line in the sand where it does not belong. The Bible tells us that a person's response to the truth, to the Holy Spirit's testimony about who Christ is and about who we humans are in relationship to Him, represents that line. As chapter seventeen demonstrates, the Flood account teaches us about God's character in the story of the catastrophe human wickedness brought upon the world.

Determining the extent of the great Flood that eradicated all humanity except Noah and his family will depend on discovering the extent to which the population (thus, the wickedness) had spread by Noah's time. My first approach to this determination is simple: Through science we can deduce that pre-Flood humans never settled Antarctica. They lacked the population pressure. They lacked the wealth. They lacked the technology. Even today, no nation has succeeded in establishing a self-sustaining colony on Antarctica. In a region where conditions favor the preservation of the past, we find no evidence—and no basis for assuming—that any people as early as the time of the Flood colonized or even visited Antarctica.

On this basis, and according to the principles of judgment God sets forth in the whole testimony of Scripture, we can reasonably and respectfully conclude that the Genesis Flood did not extend to Antarctica. However, if it did not reach Antarctica, it was nonetheless universal—it touched all the creatures God reached out to judge, no fewer and no more.

The hypothesis proposed by some Christians that Antarctica moved from the tropics to the South Pole during the Flood clashes with sound evidence. Antarctica's ice pack is too thick to have been laid down in only a few tens of thousands of years. Further, crowding that much tectonic activity into a single year would have destroyed the ark and killed all its living cargo.

Antarctica is an example, a test case. There were other major regions of the world not settled by humans at the time of the Flood—the whole Western Hemisphere, for one. In fact, as I will demonstrate shortly, the human race had remained localized to just the environs of Mesopotamia. That was the only place God needed to inundate—the region that constituted the whole world to the antediluvians.

A Modern Perspective

In the past century nearly everyone on Earth has begun to think globally. For about a month's salary most Americans and Europeans can visit any location on the planet. Decisions vital to our personal plans must take into account conditions in other nations.

Our global perspective naturally colors our interpretation of Scripture. When we encounter such phrases in Genesis 7 as "under the entire heavens" and "every living thing on the face of the earth," we see that face under the heavens as a sphere, a planet. However, in every one of the world's languages such expressions must always be understood in their reasonable context. What constitutes "the entire heavens" and "the face of the earth" in the perspective of ancient peoples? We must interpret in light of their frame of reference, not ours.

Another Bible story offers a helpful example: Genesis 41:56 tells of the famine that struck while Joseph served as prime minister over Egypt. The *King James Version* reads, "The famine was over all the face of the earth." We understand these words to signify that the famine devastated all the lands of the ancient Near East in and around Egypt. We do not interpret them globally, as implying that Australian Aborigines and American Indians came to Egypt to buy grain from Joseph. Likewise, when 1 Kings 10:24 states that "the whole world sought audience with Solomon to hear the wisdom God had put in his heart" we do not conclude that the New Zealand Maoris or the Patagonian natives sent yearly delegations to Jerusalem.

In the Flood account itself we find a similar example. In Genesis 8:5 the Flood waters are said to have receded enough so that the "tops of the mountains became visible." After forty more days of the Flood waters receding still farther, Noah releases a dove. Genesis 8:9 records that the "dove could find no place to set its feet because there was water over all the surface of the earth." Clearly, this implies that all of the earth or the whole world was inundated from the perspective of the dove but not from the perspective of Noah.

A New Testament example of "world" used to mean something less than the globe comes from Paul's letter to the Christians in Rome. He began by complimenting the Romans for their faith. Their faith was so exemplary that it was "being reported all over the world."[1] Did Paul mean in every region of the planet, or did he mean in the world defined by the boundaries of the Roman Empire? The latter represented "the whole world" for citizens of that empire, including Paul himself, though they were not ignorant of land and perhaps peoples beyond.

The apostle Peter made a specific comment on the extent of the Genesis Flood:

> By . . . waters also the world of that time was deluged and destroyed.[2]

The Greek word translated "world," *kosmos*, has these definitions: the whole universe, the whole planet Earth, the whole of humanity, or a portion of Earth.[3] An indication that the last definition applies in this verse comes from the qualifying phrase "of that time."

Scripture contains many more references to the whole world that we recognize to mean "the known world" rather than the entire planet. No one can reasonably say that to interpret "world" in the writer's context makes a lie of the text.

Failure to Fill the Earth
In Genesis 1 God instructed Adam and Eve to "multiply and fill the earth" and to manage wisely all of Earth's resources for the benefit of all life. That command required global occupation.

The failure of Adam and Eve's descendants to carry out this instruction seems indicated by God's words and actions recorded in

Genesis 9–11. In Genesis 9:7 God repeats the command to multiply and fill the earth first made in Genesis 1:28, and in doing so (9:4-6), He speaks directly and sharply to Noah about the need to put the brakes on murder. The firmness in His tone cannot be missed.

In Genesis 11 we see that God's command was ignored for many generations after Noah.[4] So recalcitrant in this matter were our progenitors that God intervened directly to propel them toward obedience for their own survival's sake. Since that time God has kept the nations geographically and politically separated to prevent a recurrence of the problem—and it is a problem for nations dominated by worldly rather than godly values to live together in some kind of harmony (see chapter twenty). The lesson of Babel must not be mistaken.

The conclusion we obviously can draw from these two episodes is that humanity had settled in only one geographical region. Not until a number of generations after Noah did humans begin to occupy the rest of the globe.

Limited Geography

Biblical clues to the geographical limits on human habitation can be found in the place-names Genesis mentions or does not mention. In Genesis 1–9 the text mentions place-names only in the environs of Mesopotamia. From Genesis 10 onward, we encounter references (by name or direction) to places beyond Mesopotamia, in fact, to places covering much of the Eastern hemisphere (see pages 169 to 171).

This sudden shift from narrow to wider geographical range after Genesis 10 strongly suggests that until the time of the Flood, human beings and their animals remained in and around Mesopotamia. Therefore, to fulfill His purpose in sending the deluge, God would need to flood only the Mesopotamian plain and perhaps some adjacent territories.

The Highest Mountains

The reference in Genesis 7:19-20 to the inundation of all mountains "under the whole heaven" proves a sticking point in the debate over the Flood's extent. The translators' wording of this passage explains why so many English-speaking Christians firmly conclude that the Flood must have been global. In the *King James Version*, the passage reads as follows:

> The waters prevailed exceedingly upon the earth; and all

the high hills, that were under the whole heaven, were covered. Fifteen cubits upward did the waters prevail; and the mountains were covered. And all flesh died that moved upon the earth.

In the *New International Version*, the passage reads this way:

They [the floodwaters] rose greatly on the earth, and all the high mountains under the entire heavens were covered. The waters rose and covered the mountains to a depth of more than twenty feet. Every living thing that moved on the earth perished.

The text certainly appears to claim that all land life on planet Earth was destroyed and that even Mount Everest was covered by more than twenty feet of water. A look at the Hebrew suggests that the translators may have struggled with the text, and some may have been influenced, unawares, by preconceptions about the story.

The Hebrew verb translated "covered" is *kasah*. This "covering" can be defined in any of three ways: "residing upon," "running over," or "falling upon."[5-6] The distinctions among these definitions are important. *Kasah* can be interpreted to mean that more than twenty feet of water stood, that is, remained, over the high hills or mountains; or it could mean that this quantity of water either ran over them as in a flash flood or fell upon them as rainfall. The context gives no clear indication which of the three meanings to choose. Not that the choice is significant for understanding the effects of such "covering." Any of the three scenarios would guarantee total destruction, no survivors.

The Hebrew words for "all the high mountains" are *kol heharim hugebohim*. Here again, because of Hebrew's small vocabulary (see pages 18 and 65), the words cover a wide range of meaning. *Har* is used for "hill," "hill country," or "mountain."[7] It could refer to a towering peak, which requires days for skilled mountaineers to ascend, or it could mean a small hill that children climb in their playtime. Anything in between is also possible.

The Hebrew adjective *gaboah* means "high," "exalted," "elevated," or "lifted above."[8-9] It applies to any elevation above the plain, from a landmark hill to a Mount Ararat. Genesis 7:19 describes Noah's inability to see anything but water, horizon to horizon, from his viewpoint on the ark's upper deck. If the ark were floating anywhere near the middle of the vast Mesopotamian plain on water as deep as two or three hundred feet, no hills or mountains would be visible from it.

Noah would see nothing but water. The high mountain ranges surrounding the Mesopotamian valley would lie beyond Noah's line of sight. His view was limited, of course, as everyone's is, by Earth's curvature, atmospheric conditions, aging eyes, and other factors. Those who drive through wide valleys such as California's San Joaquin (much narrower than the Mesopotamian valley) typically cannot see from the valley's middle the towering peaks beyond.

This interpretation that the Flood covered the essential region of the planet rather than the whole globe receives added support in Genesis 8:5:

> The waters continued to recede until the tenth month, and
> on the first day of the tenth month, the tops of the mountains
> [or hills] became visible.

The text speaks only of the region visible to Noah, not of the peaks beyond his horizon. At first, neither the raven nor the dove Noah released could fly far enough to find a landing place. A week later, when Noah sent the dove out again, it recovered a leaf from an olive tree. Olive trees do not grow at Earth's highest elevations, and yet this tree lived. We can reasonably assume that the *har* Noah finally saw were low-lying hills or foothills.

Supporting the conclusion that Genesis 7:19 speaks only of the region visible to Noah, we have the contrast in Genesis 8 between Noah and the dove's perspective on the receding waters of the Flood. In Genesis 8:5 the Flood waters have receded sufficiently for Noah from his perspective on top of the ark to see the hills and/or mountains on his horizon. A little later, in Genesis 8:9 Noah releases a dove. The text records in Genesis 8:9 that from the perspective of the dove "the waters were on the face of the whole earth." Therefore, right in the context of the Genesis chapters describing the Flood we have a clear example of "the face of the whole earth" meaning much less than the entire surface of planet Earth.

Genesis 8:1 describes how God removed the floodwaters from the land: He sent a wind. This removal technique perfectly suits the requirements of water removal from a gigantic flat plain such as Mesopotamia. Water even tens of feet deep would flow very inefficiently toward the ocean, but a wind would significantly speed up its movement. Wind also speeds natural evaporation.

Thus, wind would prove an effective means for removing water from an expansive, low-lying plain. It would prove of little if any use, however, in removing the waters of a global Flood. Such a quantity of water could not possibly recede to any location on or around the planet by the means described in just eleven months. A Flood universal to all of humanity inhabiting one geographical region certainly could, especially with a supernatural assist.

The Ark's Landing Place

For reasons I do not understand, nearly everyone with whom I have spoken or whose material I have read on the subject of the Genesis Flood—from Bible teachers to Bible mockers—asserts that the ark came to rest on Mount Ararat. Given Ararat's elevation, 16,946 feet (5,165 meters) above sea level, no wonder people are convinced that the Bible teaches a global Flood!

This pervasive misconception about the ark's resting place may arise (though I find this notion hard to believe) merely from a careless reading of the text. Genesis 8:4 reports that the ark came to rest on the "mountains" (plural) of Ararat, not on Mount Ararat. The distinction makes a huge interpretive difference. The entire Ararat range, actually a complex of ranges, extends from the vicinity north and east of Mount Ararat all the way down to the foothills skirting the Mesopotamian plain (see map in chapter nineteen on page 170). It covers more than 100,000 square miles (250,000 square kilometers).

Noah's ark could have come to rest anywhere within this enormous region. Genesis 8:4 does not require a global Flood interpretation.

Finding the Water

Few readers seem to catch the significance of statements about the source of the floodwater. In one respect the text itself rules out the global Flood interpretation by telling us where the water came from (Genesis 7) and where it returned (Genesis 8), namely, earthly sources. The quantity of water on, in, and around our planet comes nowhere near the amount required for global inundation.

According to Genesis 7:11-12, the floodwaters came from "the springs of the great deep" and "the floodgates of the heavens." The respective Hebrew phrases are *ma'yenoth tehom rabah* and *'aruboth hashamayim*. These terms refer to subterranean reservoirs, today called aquifers, and to heavy rain clouds.

Like most desert plains, Mesopotamia has the characteristics that would favor formation of an enormous aquifer. Certain well-timed geologic events could bring all that water to the surface. And while rain as we know it virtually never falls in Mesopotamia, an "act of God" could certainly bring it to the region and sustain the 40-day torrent which Genesis records.

To describe the receding of the floodwaters, the writer employs four different Hebrew words: *shakak, shub, kaser,* and *qalal,* which mean, respectively, "subsided or abated"; "returned to its original place or condition"; "diminished or lessened"; and "lowered or flowed away."[10-12] These verbs indicate that the floodwaters returned to the places from which they came, the aquifers and the clouds. Apparently, the floodwaters remain on Earth to this day. God moved the water from one location on Earth to another and later returned it. To cover Mount Everest (elevation 29,029 feet, or 8,848 meters) with water would require four and a half times the total water resources of the entire planet. Furthermore, such flooding would be pointless if no one inhabited that region.

Forcing a Fit

Some global Flood proponents who acknowledge the problem of a grossly inadequate water supply propose that Earth's surface was "smoothed," or flattened, by the Flood, thus reducing the water requirement. More specifically, they claim that during the forty days and nights when the floodwaters rose, Earth's mountains radically eroded from their lofty heights of ten, fifteen, and even twenty thousand feet to just one or two thousand feet, perhaps less. Meanwhile, the ocean basins filled with the silt of such erosion, forcing them up from their depths of ten, twenty, and thirty thousand feet to just a few thousand feet, perhaps less.

Other global Flood advocates simply presume that previous to the Flood all the continental land masses lay no more than a few hundred feet above sea level. While this explanation removes the appeal to extreme erosion, it requires that during the forty days and nights the ocean basins were quickly and sufficiently uplifted so as to inundate all the continents and islands.

All global Flood proponents posit that planet Earth during the eleven months following the forty days and nights of flooding was radically transformed. It changed, they state, from possessing very little vertical relief either in the oceans or on the continents to its present condition of mountains reaching to 29,000 feet above sea level and ocean basins dipping down to 38,000 feet below sea level. The mechanisms driving this drastic activity, they say, included plate tectonics and volcanic eruptions. In other words, Earth's crust buckled over the course of eleven months by tens of thousands of vertical feet as a result of gigantic earthquakes and volcanoes.

As drastic as all this vertical displacement is, it pales in comparison to the horizontal crustal plate movements global Flood proponents insist must have occurred during the several months following the Flood. Recognizing the overwhelming geophysical evidence that exists for massive movements of the continents including a supercontinent splitting into the seven continents that now grace our planet's surface, they claim that much, if not all, of this continental movement took place not over hundreds of millions of years but during the eleven-month time span following the Flood. That is, depending where one resides on the earth they propose something between 3,000 and 6,000 miles of plate tectonic movement took place in under a year.

While colorful, this proposition fails the test of plausibility on several counts. First, neither Genesis nor geophysics offers a hint that such drastic upheavals took place. The primary energy source for driving tectonics and vulcanism is heat from the decay of long-lived radiometric elements, and the primary energy source for erosion is Earth's rotation rate. Neither could have been dramatically increased without scientists today being aware of such past increases. For that matter, neither scientists nor anyone else would be alive today if such events took place at the time of the Flood. Second, the ark, though seaworthy for a massive Mesopotamian flood, would have broken under the stresses of such cataclysmic events as vertical displacements of Earth's crust by more than 200 feet per day and horizontal displacements by more than 60,000 feet per day. Anything more than just one foot of erosion or one foot of tectonic uplift per day is sufficient to destroy most cities. Though the ark was floating, such movement would produce sufficient G-forces to shatter the ark and its occupants. At a minimum the atmospheric dust and debris, not to mention heat, ashes, and gases released from such catastrophic events, would shut down photosynthetic processes for many years. Further, the text explicitly states that God "sent a wind over the earth" as His primary means to disperse the floodwaters. This reference to the wind suggests that God used evaporation, rather than geologic upheaval, to return the floodwaters to their original places.

Noah and his family's post-Flood activities also argue against this geologic cataclysm hypothesis. Genesis records that Noah and his family began profitable agriculture immediately after leaving the ark—impossible if such extreme erosion and tectonics rearranged the landscape. We recall, too, that an olive leaf was available to be plucked by the dove while the floodwaters were still receding. No olive tree, let alone its leaves, would have survived tens of thousands of feet of erosion, tectonics, and vulcanism packed into a few months or even a few years.

The effects of such monstrous erosion, tectonics, and vulcanism would be easily measurable by geophysicists today if it has occurred.[13-14] The fault lines scarring the earth would be many times more numerous, larger, and active than what we see. Also, the earthquake aftershocks from thousands of miles of tectonic displacement would have made cities, agriculture, and even the mere existence of human beings impossible during the decades following the Flood. Neither the Bible nor any of the other 200+ Flood accounts found in the ancient cultures of the world gives the slightest hint of such post-Flood catastrophes.

Slow Animal Evolution

A global Flood would mean, of course, that all land animals (and sea animals and plants, too, given the cataclysm scenario) alive today or living at any time since the Flood descended from the pairs aboard Noah's vessel. The account gives us the ark's dimensions (Genesis 6:15-16), so we have a basis for testing this notion. Even using the most generous cubit imaginable, we discover that the ark was too small to accommodate a pair of every land animal species currently existing (not to mention those that have become extinct). Nor could eight people possibly care for that number of animal pairs, feeding them and cleaning up after them for the required length of time, even if some or all of the animals went into some kind of hibernation.

Global Flood proponents who recognize this problem conclude that Noah took only pairs of each family, order, or genus rather than a pair of every species. Millions of animal species arose after the Flood, they say, through biological evolution. A few thousand pairs rapidly became millions, by natural processes. In their book, *The Genesis Flood*, Morris and Whitcomb suggest, for example, that zebras, horses, and several other horselike species evolved from a single pair of horselike creatures on the ark.[15] In their magazine, *Creation Ex Nihilo*, the organization, Answers In Genesis, suggests that the entire cat family—tigers, lions, leopards, cheetahs, panthers, bobcats, and even the ancestors of housecats—evolved from a single cat pair on Noah's ark.[16]

This conclusion merely trades one impossibility for another. Animals, especially animals as advanced as horses, zebras, and cats, simply do not and cannot evolve at this rapid rate. Such rates of change would mean that biologists today could witness thousands of animal species in the field developing from others. Many would love to see even one such occurrence, but as yet it is debatable whether they have.[17] (See "Speciation, Extinction, and Genesis 1 Accuracy" below.)

SPECIATION, EXTINCTION, AND GENESIS 1 ACCURACY

According to the fossil record, as many as a half-billion to a billion new species of life arose between the Cambrian explosion (circa 543 million years ago) and the arrival of human beings (circa 30,000 to 50,000 years ago)—an average of one or two new species per year. Since the coming of humans, however, the rate of speciation has dropped to a virtual zero (see page 64). The rate of extinctions due to natural causes (such as the second law of thermodynamics), discounting human impact on the environment, has remained about the same: about one species per year under normal conditions and many more per year during environmental catastrophes.

While scientists still seek an explanation for this change in speciation rate (and constancy of extinction rate), the Bible offers one: for six days God created and on the seventh day He ceased. Throughout six creation epochs or creation days (see pages 27 to 58), God created new species and replaced species that went extinct through the normal operation of physical laws (thermodynamics, gravity, electromagnetism, and so forth) and through environmental changes preparatory to humans' arrival and survival. During the seventh epoch, that is, the seventh day of God's creation week, which began immediately after the creation of Adam and Eve and continues until God completes the conquest of evil, God ceased from His work of creating new species of life. Therefore, the speciation rate we see today reflects the operation of natural processes; the eons prior to humans, the six creation periods, reflect the supernatural hand of God along with the natural processes.

Although in most scientific disciplines the present is the key to the past, in biology that key sticks in one lock. It works well in the door to extinctions but not in the door to speciation. Studying speciation today shows us natural processes and a roughly zero rate. Studying speciation in the fossils shows us these same processes and something more. Genesis identifies the "something more."

The "Day" Connection

Impetus for interpreting the Genesis deluge as a global event comes from the desire to explain how the entire fossil record and all Earth's geologic features could be compacted into a 144-hour creation week a few thousand years ago. This degree of compacting, however, defies many of the established laws and principles of physics, geology, paleontology, geophysics, and other scientific disciplines.

The global Flood view requires that all of Earth's species lived on the planet at once and that virtually all fossils were laid down at the time (and by the cataclysm) of the Genesis Flood. This view contradicts research showing that Earth cannot support all its species at one time. A planet with a diameter of eight thousand miles (thirteen thousand kilometers) can support only a certain number of inhabitants and their habitats. The maximum carrying capacity of Earth under the most ideal conditions the laws of physics permit is about fifty million species. The fossil record bears witness to at least a half-billion species—some paleontologists say many more than a billion.

Origin of Biodeposits

Science says that Earth's fossil-fuel deposits built up gradually during a period of several hundred million years in Earth's history. Global Flood proponents say that all fossil-fuel deposits were laid down during the year of the Flood. How do the existing, measurable quantities of such fuel—coal, oil, and gas—compare with the maximum quantity that could be laid down in a year, or even two years or five or ten? The figures do not come close. When we calculate the energy potential of all the plant matter (mostly forests) on Earth today—not even waiting for that organic material to convert to fossil fuel (a process that would enormously reduce the total potential)—it adds up to less than one-tenth the energy potential contained in Earth's coal reserves alone (what is left after centuries of industrialization).[18]

Global Flood proponents respond to this inequity by noting that Earth receives enough energy from the sun in just twenty-two days to match the amount available in our fossil-fuel reserves. The problem with this reply is that it fails to consider how much solar energy is lost in the process of converting solar energy into fossil fuel. That process involves two steps: first the conversion of solar energy into plant food (photosynthesis), then the conversion of plant matter into fossil fuel. The first conversion retains less than a tenth of a percent of the solar energy. The second step retains less than one percent of that tenth of a percent. Again, the numbers argue against any short-term deposition.

Feeling the pinch of these physical limitations, some global Flood advocates suggest the possibility that at the time of the Flood, Earth carried a much greater biomass (abundance of life). The problem here lies in the contradictory evidence from both paleontology and physics, among other disciplines. We see no indications of a radically larger biomass in the Flood's time frame, and we can calculate from the laws of physics that Earth, right now, carries a biomass close to its theoretical upper limit.

The total mass of all life on Earth is limited, of course, by the flow of solar energy to Earth. The total quantity of solar energy reaching us, a quantity that remains relatively constant, limits the amount of vegetation and therefore all life that Earth can sustain. (See "Did a Life-Enhancing Canopy Surround the Earth?" below.)

DID A LIFE-ENHANCING CANOPY SURROUND THE EARTH?

Most global Flood proponents attempt to explain long life spans (prior to the Flood) and huge deposits of hydrocarbons by proposing that a thick water canopy surrounded Earth. They claim such a canopy would shield life from radiation, greatly extending human longevity; would create a warm, humid environment to augment Earth's biomass; and, once collapsed, would suddenly inundate the entire surface of the planet, destroying all life (except on the ark) and even Earth's topography.

This hypothesis fails every test of plausibility. First, a canopy with enough water to cover the planet would either dissipate to interplanetary space (if it were vaporous) or come crashing to Earth under the influence of gravity. A vapor canopy, even existing for a short time, would set up such a powerful greenhouse (heating) effect that no ice or liquid water would remain on Earth to sustain life, and the Flood would become unnecessary. If the canopy were liquid or ice, converting the ice to liquid or liquid to vapor would consume so much heat as to freeze all life on the planet. Again, the Flood would become unnecessary.

Increasing Earth's surface heat and humidity by a little would increase the total living biomass of Earth by only a small amount. Earth's surface area and the solar energy flow limit Earth's living biomass to a quantity far below what is needed to explain all of the planet's hydrocarbon reserves. And, although a vapor canopy would provide some protection against ultraviolet radiation, it would not impede the hard cosmic rays that fundamentally prevent human life spans beyond 120 years.

Neither science nor Scripture provides any compelling evidence that such a canopy existed.

A further blow to the notion that all biodeposits could have come from the Flood event comes from recent research into the quantity of kerogen on Earth. It turns out that fossil-fuel reserves (coal, oil, and gas) account for just a tiny fraction of the total organic deposits. Kerogen, a tarry residue left over from biological processes,[19-21] appears to be about a thousand times more abundant than all fossil-fuel reserves combined.[22] Almost all the limestone and marble also originate from biological activity, as does all of the planet's topsoil. The quantity of these resources, too, by far exceeds fossil-fuel quantities.

One detail from the biblical story itself suggests that at least some petroleum products were available a few decades before the Flood during the long ark-building process. In Genesis 6:14 we learn that Noah received instruction to coat the ark inside and out with *koper*, which Hebrew lexicons define as "asphalt, bitumen, pitch, or tar."[23] The ark needed an effective sealant to protect it against leaks, and, apparently, lots of this tarry substance was available for the job. Thus, at least some petroleum products formed before the Flood. While researchers agree with the global Flood theorists' notion that much fossil-fuel (and other organic) deposition occurs amid geological catastrophes, an abundance of data convinces them that these catastrophes number in the thousands, if not the millions, separated in time. A single, brief cataclysm could not account for what we see.

Worldwide Marine Deposits

Sedimentary layers and marine fossils are found on all seven continents, including the peaks of many mountain ranges. Even the summit of Mount Everest is littered with marine fossils. Some people see these as evidence of the global Flood. Geophysicists see them as evidence of plate tectonics. For example, the geology of the Indian subcontinent bears little resemblance to that of central Asia, right next to it. India belongs to a different piece of Earth's crust, and that piece is pushing northward into Asia at the rate of a few centimeters per year. The Himalayas, which emerge from this collision, rank as the fastest-growing mountains in the world. Currently they are rising at an average rate of fifteen millimeters per year above sea level. India, then, represents a relatively recent addition to Asia.

From its past location adjacent to Antarctica in the south Indian Ocean, the Indian subcontinent slowly began drifting north. As it approached Asia, the ocean floor between the two plates buckled up to form the Himalayas. This rising of that particular piece of ocean floor explains why marine fossils are so common on Mount Everest, much more common than on the lands to the north and south of the Himalayas. The beginning of this marine layer uplift predates the Genesis Flood by many millions of years. Because the uplift shows no major discontinuities, geophysicists reasonably conclude that it has been proceeding fairly continuously for approximately the past fifteen million years.[24]

Likewise, North America's vast alluvial plain has everything to do with events in the distant past and nothing to do with the Genesis Flood. The North American prairies lay for tens of millions of years under a huge shallow sea. This ancient sea explains the region's huge limestone and fossil-fuel deposits. A number of independent dating techniques show that the prairies emerged from under water more than 200 million years ago, long before the Genesis Flood.

The Availability of Flood Evidence

The Genesis Flood must have been enormous by anyone's interpretation of the biblical account. To float a ship 450 feet by 75 feet by 45 feet or larger takes a lot of water. The Genesis text says that the passengers aboard the ark could see no land from horizon to horizon.[25] At least six billion acre-feet of water would be required, according to best estimates.

Most skeptics (and even nonskeptics) assume that a Flood of such immense proportions would leave behind substantial evidence, a deposit that geologists today should be able to find. Several large alluvial flood deposits have been found in the Mesopotamian plain.[26] One or more could fit in the time range for the Genesis Flood. The lack of a precise enough date for the Flood, however, hinders any positive identification.

The assumption that clear evidence "should" remain must be challenged. The Flood, though massive, lasted but one year and ten days. A flood of such brief duration typically does not leave a deposit substantial enough to be positively identified thousands of years later.

As an example, consider the flooding that occurred in California's San Joaquin Valley in the 1970s. Parts of the valley lay under three to four feet of water for a few months. Ten years later, all geological evidence of the disaster had been erased. Similarly, a one-year Flood in the region of Mesopotamia, even to a depth of two or three hundred feet, may leave behind insufficient evidence for a positive geological identification ten to forty thousand years later.

Conclusion

Behind this lengthy, though still incomplete, discussion of geological and other issues relating to the Flood lies a dual purpose: first, to offer a biblically consistent and scientifically plausible interpretation of the Flood account for any Bible reader; and, second, to remove one major barrier, the "geophysically impossible" global Flood, on which many skeptics rest their rejection of the Bible's message.

Because this chapter covers so much material, a summary of the main points may prove helpful. These points all support the thesis that the Flood event described in Genesis 6–9 did, indeed, accomplish the ends God clearly intended—and explicitly stated—without covering the entire planet. It may be described, accurately, as universal (with respect to humans and the animals associated with them) but not as global:

1. Biblical phrases such as "under the entire heavens" and "the face of the earth" must be interpreted in the writer's (and most readers') context, as true where these terms are used elsewhere in Scripture. In Genesis 8 for Noah the "tops of the mountains became visible" (verse 5), but for the dove that he released at that time there was "water over all the surface of the earth" (verse 9).

2. The extent and spread of human population and, thus, of sin's impact was limited, not global. In fact, God rebuked the human race for its failure to spread out over the globe.

3. Genesis mentions no geographical place-names beyond Greater Mesopotamia until chapter ten.

4. Earth's water quantity supports a regional rather than global Flood. The floodwaters came from Earth's underground and atmospheric resources, which are plentiful but inadequate to cover the globe.

5. Mountain ranges and ocean basins cannot erode in forty days nor build up in eleven months, as would be required by one explanation of a global Flood, without leaving evidence easily visible today.

6. Not even an ark of steel armor plate could survive the rigors of a Flood gone global in forty days nor of the devastating effects of tens of thousands of feet of vertical tectonic activity and tens of millions of feet of horizontal tectonic activity within a year's time.

7. The creatures earmarked for rescue included only Noah, Noah's family, and birds and mammals that had significant contact with humanity (see chapter nineteen).

8. Genesis 7 does not necessarily claim that water stood above the highest mountains; rather, it says that an enormous deluge fell upon or ran over or covered the highest hills visible to Noah.

9. Genesis 8:4 records that the ark landed in the mountains (or hills) of Ararat, not specifically on top of Mount Ararat itself. The designated area encompasses more than one hundred thousand square miles.

10. Olive leaves do not grow at high altitudes, nor could they survive a global Flood.

11. The water of a global Flood could not recede in less than a year.

12. A strong wind (Genesis 8:1) would be useful for dissipating a regional but not a global Flood.

13. Earth cannot possibly support at one time the half-billion or more species of life the fossil record documents, which would be required according to the global Flood theory.

14. A recent global Flood cannot account for Earth's enormous deposits of kerogen, topsoil, limestone, marble, and fossil fuels.

15. Petroleum products were available before the Flood for Noah's use in sealing the ark (Genesis 6:14).

16. The million-plus land animal species on Earth today could not have evolved in just a few thousand years from the thirty thousand species—maximum—the ark could have carried.

17. No viable scientific evidence has ever been found for a recent, global Flood.

18. Psalm 104:9 states that when God made dry land appear on creation day 3 (Genesis 1:9) that "never again will they [the waters] cover the earth."

CHAPTER NINETEEN

THE ARK AND ITS PASSENGERS
GENESIS 6–9

Unrealistic depictions of Noah ushering giraffes, lions, alligators, pythons, polar bears, kangaroos, geese, orangutans, and elephants up the ramp of a big, round-bottomed wooden boat—so familiar in children's literature—stick firmly in our minds. These images raise questions and doubts among believers and fuel ridicule among skeptics. Even if we get past questions about the extent of the Flood and its damage, we face another host of issues needing plausible explanation:

♦ Where did Noah get the technology and resources to build such a huge vessel?

♦ How could eight people possibly care for all the ark's animals?[1] Even equipped with large shovels (if they had them), how could they possibly ever clean up after the ark's animals?[2]

♦ How could a wooden ship of the dimensions stipulated in Genesis possibly be seaworthy?[3-4]

♦ If the Flood was not global, why bother with the monstrous task of building an ark? Why would God not simply instruct Noah to move his family and flocks to high ground?

Learning about these issues—the ark's design and construction, its passengers and its cargo—can help assuage doubts about the credibility of the Flood story *without* resorting to the conclusion that it must be allegorical—or borrowed legend.

Why an Ark?

Consideration of the Flood's geographically limited (though universal with respect to people and their animals) destruction may cause us to wonder why God did not deal with Noah's situation as He did with Lot's later—rescue by evacuation.[5] God could have instructed Noah to pack up and depart to a region far away where Noah and those with him would be out of harm's way.

Two reasons stand out, but we can be sure God had many more that we do not know or cannot comprehend with our limited perspective. First, when God pours out judgment, He gives ample warning ahead of time. He sends a spokesperson, a prophet, and gives that prophet some kind of platform, pulpit, or focal point from which to be heard. For the antediluvians, Noah was that prophet and the scaffolding around the ark was his platform.

The efforts of a middle-aged (or slightly older) man, a distinguished patriarch, to build an enormous vessel in the middle of a desert plain that receives scant rainfall certainly would have commanded attention. Noah's persistent devotion to this immensely challenging project for one hundred years would have heightened the drama. As crowds gathered to jeer, not cheer, Noah patiently preached. He warned his listeners of impending doom if they failed to repent. He freely offered passage to anyone who would heed his warning and call upon God for mercy. Perhaps one reason for the enormous size of the ship was to demonstrate the sincerity of this offer.

The New Testament confirms that Noah gave time to being "a preacher of righteousness."[6] Noah "condemned the world,"[7] not so much with words as by the example of his faith as he, like God, "waited patiently."[8] He could have built the ark much faster if he had spent less time preaching, but the magnitude of the impending disaster compelled him to give more than ample warning to his contemporaries.

Lot's circumstances contrast with Noah's in several ways. Lot was not a native to Sodom. He moved there as an adult and served for some time as a leader, or "judge," in the city state. Thus, Lot had a ready platform from which to preach.[9] Sodom was small by comparison with Mesopotamia, and its population tiny by comparison with the whole of humanity. One short trip would remove Lot and his family from danger and from an area nonessential to humanity's survival. God had big plans, however, for Mesopotamia.

As it was for Noah and Lot, so it was for Moses, Isaiah, Jeremiah, Jonah and every other righteous man facing a wicked populace. God always sends a warning of impending doom. He always sends a prophet and a pulpit ahead of His judgment. He always offers rescue to those who will repent.

Building the Ark

Some skepticism about Noah's ability to construct the ark comes from the observation that until the late nineteenth century A.D., no nation had ever built such a huge vessel. No nation to this day has succeeded in constructing one from wood. The largest wooden vessels ever assembled were the clipper ships of the last century, a little more than three hundred feet long. When New England shipyards attempted to build longer vessels, they discovered they could not make them seaworthy. Their oak beams lacked the necessary tensile strength. How could Noah's engineering capability and resources outstrip those of modern shipbuilding professionals?

Again we must look more closely at contextual details. First, Noah's ark was not intended for sailing on the high seas. Rather, it had to be able to float on a flooded plain. The engineering requirements for a barge-type vessel differ significantly from those of a three-masted schooner. Second, Noah faced none of the economic constraints pressuring nineteenth-century shipbuilders, whose goal was to transport (across treacherous oceans) as much cargo weight for as few dollars as possible. They did not push their oak shipbuilding designs very far, for they soon discovered that for very large vessels, steel offered greater economy than oak. Unlike the New England shipbuilders, Noah could consider options other than oak and weight of materials.

According to the Genesis text, Noah used "gopher" wood to build the ark. This type of wood we cannot identify with any certainty. We do not even know all the different kinds of trees that might have grown along the banks of Mesopotamian rivers and in the adjacent territories and mountains. We do know that hardwoods such as walnut are much stronger than oak. Some tropical timbers are denser than water with tensile strengths matching that of some metals. Woods like these would have been more plentiful, we can surmise, in the era before construction of huge buildings and palaces. Therefore, access to timbers of the necessary strength probably presented no major problem for Noah.

Both Old and New Testament passages indicate that Noah held considerable stature in his community. From these hints we can surmise that his personnel resources were abundant, certainly adequate (of course, with God's help) to complete the construction project. And possibly, Noah may have employed many more people than just his family members to assist in the building. We can easily imagine the opportunity this large workforce would provide for attracting larger crowds to hear Noah's message.

Whether he used a large building crew or not, workers were available for Noah's use, as were all the necessary materials from hardwoods to a natural sealant to keep out the water. No insurmountable obstacles stood in Noah's way for successful construction of an ark of the dimensions the text delineates. While no one today would or *could* invest the time and resources Noah did, Noah acted in response to an urgent mission given him by God. Hence, for Noah, no personal sacrifice was too great.

Animals Rescued

Aid for the tough task of identifying which creatures the ark shielded comes from two sources: one, biblical teaching about God's judgment; and, two, studies of the Hebrew nouns used for animals in the account. Chapter seventeen discusses the limits of God's judgment as they accord with the limits of sin's defiling effect. God always preserves and protects whomever and whatever can be redeemed for the fulfillment of His plan and purpose. This conclusion seems consistent with the Hebrew words used in Genesis 6–9 to describe the animals destroyed — and yet spared for the future — amid the Flood's devastation. The text includes these seven words, defined in the *Theological Wordbook of the Old Testament*, for the animals aboard the ark:

- ♦ **basar:** flesh; animal musculature; mankind; creatures used in Jewish sacrifices[10]
- ♦ **behema:** beast; cattle; long-legged, four-footed mammal[11]
- ♦ **hayya:** living animal; wild, not domestic, animal[12]
- ♦ **nephesh:** soulish creature; person; mind; land creature with the breath of life; creature capable of expressing yearnings, emotions, passions, and will; self-aware creature[13]

♦ **op:** bird; fowl; insect; winged creature[14]
♦ **remes:** creeping living creature; short-legged land mammal such as a rodent; small reptile[15]
♦ **sippor:** bird; little bird[16]

All these words refer to birds and mammals, though some can be used a little more broadly. We see a high correlation between this list and the list of soulish animals God created on the fifth and sixth creation days, animals that held significance in the preparation of Earth for humankind. Clearly, the survival of these creatures would be important to the restoration and survival of human society after the Flood. Nothing in the Genesis text compels us to conclude that Noah's passengers included anything other than birds and mammals.

Animals Not Protected

Two additional Hebrew nouns apply to the creatures destroyed in the Flood but not among those preserved on the ark. They and their expanded lexical definitions are as follows:

♦ **sheres:** teeming, swarming prolific small animals; all the smaller sea creatures and land animals (as contrasted with birds and beasts); rodents, amphibians, smaller reptiles, flying insects, wriggling water animals[17]
♦ **yequm:** animals with standing; animals which subsist[18]

While *sheres* can refer to small mammals, most often it is used for small nonsoulish animals. Likewise, *yequm* can refer to all animals or just those that merely subsist.

In the Israelites' destruction of Jericho, or in any other judgment conflagration, other life-forms, in addition to those targeted, died in the catastrophe. So, too, we can assume the death of bacteria, insects, reptiles, and other creatures in the floodwaters (see pages 143 to 144). Their death does not mean, however, that their kinds would be eradicated from the face of the Earth. Though many decades would pass before the Mesopotamian plain, stripped of all of its soulish life, would be repopulated by spared pairs and their progeny and by the migration of other birds and mammals from adjacent regions, the bacteria and insects would return in a matter of weeks or months, at most.

Noah's Future

In addition to building the ark and preaching repentance, Noah's job included caring for a pair (male and female) of every bird and mammal species living in the region where human beings lived. He did not have to go out to find them and bring them in, however; God apparently intervened in some way to send the birds and animals to him. The reason for sheltering these animals probably had more to do with economics than with ecology. Few of the creatures on board would have had a habitat range as limited as the humans. Therefore, few of them faced imminent extinction from the Flood. We see that God commanded Noah to take on board seven pairs of those bird and mammal species domesticated for agricultural and economic purposes, creatures also used as sacrificial worship.

God could have made life simpler for Noah in the short run by making him wait for birds and mammals to return to Mesopotamia. Instead, he helped Noah take a stock of birds and mammals, more of some than of others, that would allow him and his family to restore rapidly their economy, culture, and worship.

The Ark's Cargo

Recognizing that many more bird and mammal species existed in Noah's day than exist today and that the ranges of these species were broad, we must conclude that the ark housed at least many hundreds of species, conceivably as many as several thousand. Noah was commanded by God to make provision not only for housing this zoo but also for feeding them—not just during the Flood but until post-Flood lands began producing sufficient food for them. The same went for his own family, as well.[19] In other words, he needed to pack an eighteen- to twenty-month food supply. Thus, the weight of food and fodder must have exceeded by several times the weight of the animals and people.

In addition, Noah's family would need to store all the supplies and tools to rebuild their homes and farms. The availability of wood might not be problematic, given the lumber in the ark itself and the olive leaf retrieved by the dove (signifying the proximity of trees). Nevertheless, the rebuilders would need tools and simple machines, ropes, precut stones, timbers, and pegs, plus materials for clothing, cooking, and sleeping.

Caring for the Ark's Passengers

If the ark's dimensions are converted from short cubits to feet (see page 129 for details on the three cubit standards in the Bible), the ark measured 450 feet long by 75 feet wide by 45 feet high (140 by 23 by 13.5 meters). A vessel of these dimensions could easily accommodate the three decks God told Noah to build.[20] Constructed in this way, it would offer generous cargo space, roomy pens or stalls for the animals, and adequate quarters for the human passengers. Food could be sorted and stored close to animals, fertilizer could be stored for future agricultural use, and still the ark would allow room for exercising the animals and for human recreation. At the same time, the ark would be small enough that eight people could tend to their chores without walking their legs off. (The image of Noah drowning in the excrement of the ark's animals is based on a faulty understanding of how many animals were on board.)

Given their hundred-year building, planning, and preparation time, Noah and his family could have adapted and installed many labor-saving devices. Dumb waiters, carts, chutes, rails, and simple plumbing could have greatly streamlined their efforts. In the course of using and modifying such things, Noah's family may have been planning and preparing for their days back on land, building better homes, farms, and industries.

The Search for Noah's Ark

In 1995 the Columbia Broadcasting System aired a two-hour, prime-time documentary on the Genesis Flood and the search for Noah's ark. In addition to confirming the widespread impression that Christianity requires belief in a global Flood (the producers rejected Christians' requests that they present alternate views), the program claimed to prove the discovery of Noah's ark near the summit of Mount Ararat. Atheists and skeptics had a field day exposing the bogus "evidences" presented in the documentary.[21-25] Their exposés *all* stated or implied that evangelical Christians rely on deception, fraud, and sloppy scholarship to promote their views.

Rather than explaining why the wood fragments displayed in that program could not be legitimate ark remnants, I prefer to focus on explaining why we should not *expect* archeology to recover any such artifacts. First, as chapter eighteen mentions, the text gives no specific location for the ark's landing site. Mount Ararat seems an unlikely place to search, given the mountain's height and the probable depth and breadth of the Flood. The Genesis text identifies the "hills" of Ararat—a huge region bordering the Mesopotamian plain—as the area where the ark came to rest.

A better place to look, if we were to waste money on such an endeavor, would be the Ararat hills just a few hundred feet above sea level some 20 to 50 miles (35 to 80 kilometers) north of Nineveh's ruins (see map below). But I do not recommend any search, both for current and for ancient economic reasons. The ark's gopher wood timbers were enormous and enormously valuable. No enterprising post-Flood society would have left such wood unexploited. Given the proximity of the ark's probable resting place to later cities, including Nineveh, built by Nimrod's generation shortly after the Flood, such high-quality precut lumber would surely have been used for construction. In fact, all the ark's timbers may have been raided even earlier.

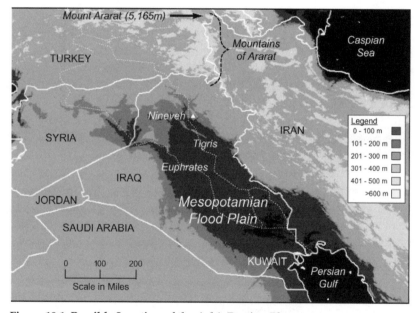

Figure 19.1: Possible Location of the Ark's Resting Place
The dotted line represents the contour of 600 feet above sea level for Mesopotamia as it currently exists.

To search the ruins of Nineveh and other ancient sites for ark remains would represent a further waste of time and money. All of the ancient Mesopotamian cities were burned to the ground more than once. Even if archeologists found traces of burned wood and sealant, they would have no way to make a positive identification of their find as the ark. I see the plausibility of the story itself and the supernatural accuracy of the entire biblical record as evidence enough to believe that the Genesis Flood really did occur as described.

Other Flood Stories

More than 200 distinct Flood stories abound in the lore of ancient civilizations, just as creation stories do. More than 85 percent of these mention a large vessel that saved the human race from extinction. The abundance of these Flood stories points to something more than just an interest in beginnings. It suggests that the memory of some unprecedented Flood catastrophe was firmly etched in the minds of ancient peoples.

One explanation that makes sense associates these Flood accounts with a common source. As with creation accounts, we see traces of a pattern: the greater the story's distance (in time and geography) from Mesopotamia, the greater the distortion relative to both the biblical record (Genesis 6–9) and the established scientific record. As with creation accounts, the least scientifically distorted of the nonbiblical accounts is the Babylonian one.

The *Gilgamesh Epic*

The same library of Ashurbanipal that contained the Babylonian creation story also contained the Babylonian Flood story, the *Gilgamesh Epic*,[26-27] a lengthy poem like the *Enuma Elish*. Like the *Enuma Elish*, the *Gilgamesh Epic* seems to be a reworking of the apparently older *Atra-hasis Epic* of Old Babylon.[28]

The Flood poem more closely resembles its Genesis counterpart than does the creation poem. It describes the building of a large multi-story ship sealed with pitch or tar. Like Noah of Genesis, Utnapishtim of the *Gilgamesh Epic* boards the ship with his whole family. The Gilgamesh Flood, like the Genesis Flood, destroys all humanity except those on board the ship, and its waters come mostly from a furious rainstorm.

Here the similarities end, however. The ark of Genesis had a stable shape for flotation. Utnapishtim's cubical ship (200 feet by 200 feet by 200 feet) would be neither seaworthy nor water stable. The rain of the Gilgamesh account lasts only six days, and instead of rescuing eight people and pairs of all the bird and mammal species associated with humanity aboard his boat, Utnapishtim is said to have ferried all his kinsmen, all his society's craftsmen, all the cattle and beasts of the field, and the seed of all living things.

The poem differs most profoundly from the Genesis account in its portrayal of the power(s) behind the Flood. The gods of Gilgamesh send the Flood not to protect mankind from its own evil but to destroy mankind for no apparent reason. Their action is arbitrary. Once the Flood is under way, the gods flee in terror to the upper reaches of heaven, where they crouch in fear like dogs. And then the Flood suddenly ends, in a matter of hours.

The Gilgamesh gods, like those of the *Enuma Elish*, seem obvious human constructs. They manifest ignorance, weakness, fear, and other human foibles. This difference and the obvious departure from scientific plausibility separate the *Gilgamesh Epic* from the Genesis Flood account, which stands all the more distinctly alone. The epic's very existence, however, lends additional credence to the Genesis story.

CHAPTER TWENTY

THE ORIGIN OF NATIONS AND RACES
GENESIS 9–11

Genesis 9–11 presents a brief history of the generations of humanity that arose and repopulated Earth soon after the Flood. Until recently science offered little evidence to support this history, but research in the late 1990s has brought such evidence to light and provides fascinating amplification.

These three Genesis chapters document the persistence of rebellion and autonomy despite their dire consequences. First, Adam and Eve and their progeny failed to "fill the earth" as God had commanded (Genesis 1:28). Then Noah and his descendants failed to obey that command. As chapter eighteen points out, the descendants of Adam and Eve neither multiplied to the degree God intended nor moved out of the environs of Mesopotamia. So when Noah left the ark to start over, God spoke to him in firm, direct terms about the importance of multiplying and spreading to all parts of Earth (Genesis 9:5-7). God instructed Noah to curtail murder for many reasons, including the unhindered multiplication and migration of his descendants.

Noah's immediate descendants did only slightly better in fulfilling this command than did Adam's. While they achieved some success in restraining murder, they resolutely refused to settle the regions beyond Mesopotamia. Unity and togetherness seemed more important to them than did following God's plan.

Dangers of Peace and Unity

All generations of humanity, including our own, have looked to political peace and unity among all peoples as the solution to humanity's ills. "Visualize world peace" appears on many bumper stickers. No one would argue that the world would benefit from peace and safety and harmony, but Christians recognize that these ideals cannot be achieved and maintained through human efforts alone, such as better leaders, better economies, better governments, better laws, and so on. God must bring the necessary change of heart and actions.

World peace and unity seem especially attractive to those personally familiar with the horrors of military conflict and terrorist actions. Some fifty-six million adults and children died in World Wars I and II,[1] and the number of war casualities since then is even greater. Few people realize that the Soviet Union, which suffered more losses in World War II than any other nation (sixteen million civilians and soldiers), killed several times more civilian and military personnel, approximately fifty-five million of the Soviet Union's own people, in the "peace" time afterward.[2-3] So-called peace and unity can lead to greater evil and suffering than conflict and disunity can. (This does not mean we should not advocate for peace, but rather we should promote peace and diversity or peace and unity under Christ.)

One reason for such carnage in times of peace and unity is that evil people, driven by greed and power, always try to exploit social peace and unity to rob and oppress others. The disaster that befell humanity and led to the Genesis Flood should serve as a stark warning to all generations of what happens when people unite to serve their own interests rather than to serve God's interests. Because we see some good in people, even in those who are not yet serving God, we assume that human good will prevail. But tests of history show otherwise.

An Analogy

A marketing analogy might help explain the risks of worldwide peace and unity (under human leadership). If one corporation acquires full control over a product everyone needs, we can anticipate what will happen: the price will go up and quality will go down. Free-market economies enact antitrust laws to keep monopolies from practicing this kind of exploitation. Competition among corporations forces them, to some degree, to keep product prices low and product quality high.

Typically, nations compete with one another for citizens and economic strength. "Brain drain" describes the loss of talented, well-educated citizens by one nation to another that offers such "brains" more opportunity for success and reward. Similarly, many nations constantly lure corporations to locate in their lands through tax incentives and educational programs designed to provide large pools of available, well-trained, efficient, and cost-effective personnel.

Eliminating national boundaries and uniting nations under a global banner may seem the right way to establish world peace and unity. Such peace and unity, however, eliminates competition for citizens and corporations. If only one nation exists, that nation can—and will under any leadership other than Christ's—oppress its citizens and corporations, and those citizens and corporations will have no recourse. If only one government exists for humanity, that government could control its citizens' lives to align with that government's goals. The government, really an elite group of people, becomes the final judge of what is "good" for itself and for everyone. Pride will command the world.

These principles help us understand the tragedy of the Soviet Union. Soviet leaders were able to lock out competition for people and enterprises. They even locked out foreign ideas and information. Thus, for a time, they got away with oppressing their citizens.

Biblical Warnings

The prophet Isaiah warned that true peace is impossible for people committed to their own ways rather than to God's:

> The wicked are like the tossing sea, which cannot rest, whose waves cast up mire and mud. "There is no peace," says my God, "for the wicked."[4]

> Their deeds are evil deeds, and acts of violence are in their hands. Their feet rush into sin; they are swift to shed innocent blood. Their thoughts are evil thoughts; ruin and destruction mark their ways. The way of peace they do not know; there is no justice in their paths. They have turned them into crooked roads; no one who walks in them will know peace.[5]

God also reveals His supernatural intervention to prevent world unification in Genesis and Daniel. He told Daniel that He halted Babylonia's attempt to dominate the world and that He would block the present empire (Media-Persia) and three future empires (Greece,

Rome, and an end-times empire yet to come) in their attempts.[6] The history of civilization documents the failure of one empire after another in its quest to control the world.

The danger of superficial peace and unity among peoples helps us understand Jesus' statement to His disciples:

> "Do you think I came to bring peace on earth? No, I tell you, but division."[7]

These words seem to contradict what the angels sang on the night of His birth,[8] but the contradiction is reconciled by what He said to His disciples just before His crucifixion:

> "Peace I leave with you; my peace I give you. I do not give to you as the world gives."[9]

Jesus came to offer humanity a peace very different from what the peoples of the world consider peace. He knew that real peace among human beings is possible only if people first make their peace with God.

The Origin of Nations

The opening verses of Genesis 10 report that after the Flood human population multiplied rapidly and civilization advanced just as rapidly. Not many generations after Noah's sons' time, a powerful prince by the name of Nimrod built eight cities throughout southern, central, and northern Mesopotamia.[10]

Genesis 11 also reports that the post-Flood population moved toward the verge of pre-Flood: intolerable depravity. They maintained a single language and a single nation.[11] They embarked on an ambitious building project, the construction of a huge city and a high tower in pursuit of two stated goals: (1) to express pride in their own achievements; and (2) to prevent human emigration beyond the boundaries of Mesopotamia:

> Come, let us build ourselves a city, with a tower that reaches to the heavens, so that we make a name for ourselves and not be scattered over the face of the whole earth.[12]

If God were to tolerate this blatant and persistent rebellion against Him,[13] and if the human race were to succeed in its two stated goals, only another mass destruction (such as the Flood) would curb humanity's evil and oppression.[14]

At this point God acted quickly. The text tells us He "confused their language."[15] No longer did everyone understand the same words. No longer could all the people come together and share ideas and plans. Given the confusion, people were inclined to find and stay close to anyone with whom they could meaningfully communicate. Nations likely formed along language lines.

Separation was achieved, but the scattering of the different language groups from Mesopotamia to all the habitable lands throughout the entire globe still lay ahead. Still ahead, too, was a guarantee they would stay scattered.

According to the text, God assigned each language group, or nation, its own territory as noted in the table of nations, Genesis 10:1-32, and proceeded to send them there. If the Vela supernova gives us a hint as to when the Flood occurred (between twenty thousand and thirty thousand years ago),[16-17] we can estimate that the movement of peoples from Mesopotamia to the far reaches of Asia, Africa, and Europe occurred during the era from about twenty thousand or thirty thousand to about fourteen thousand years ago. During that time, however, certain natural barriers, such as the Bering Strait, blocked global habitation.

Ancient Land Bridges Formed and Destroyed

Knowing how persistently human beings resisted spreading out, God also knew how to keep the newly formed nations apart. He had created the world and formed it in such a way as to produce land masses and oceans in just the right balance for life. He also fashioned its geography and geophysical forces so that, at just the right time and in just the right places, conditions would foster the separation of the peoples and ensure their staying separated.

With awe and amazement geographers note that virtually all Earth's continental land masses lie in climatic zones suitable for human habitation. Moreover, with the exception of frozen Antarctica, the continents and major islands are nearly contiguous. However, though the continents and islands are roughly contiguous, the barriers dividing some of them present a formidable challenge to people lacking modern transport vehicles. North and South America, for example, are cut off from Eurasia by the Bering Strait; Indonesia is separated from mainland Asia by the Strait of Malacca; Australia is divided from Indonesia by the Torres Strait; and the English Channel flows between Britain and the rest of Europe.

The Bering Strait constitutes fifty miles (eighty kilometers) of cold, treacherous sea between Alaska and Siberia. Even with modern ships, crossing that body of water is a risky venture. Previous to the twentieth century, except for one remarkable moment in history researchers have recently discovered, the Bering Strait effectively discouraged peoples living in the Americas from emigrating to Asia and vice versa.

A 1996 geological and paleontological study established that a land bridge briefly joined North America to Asia between forty thousand and eleven thousand years ago. A team of Arctic researchers found the remains of land vegetation across the full length of what is now the Bering Strait.[18] During most of these twenty-nine thousand years, temperatures remained too frigid to permit human migration across the bridge. For most of this epoch, Siberia and Alaska were as heavily blanketed with ice as Greenland is today. (The existence of such huge ice sheets explains why sea levels were so low.)

For a brief time, however, just before the Bering land bridge became inundated by rising seas from the melting of the continental ice sheets, a warm, moist climate came to the Bering bridge and to significant portions of Alaska and Siberia. Insect assemblages and plant fossils indicate that the period between fourteen thousand and eleven thousand years ago was especially favorable for human migration. The mean summer temperature at that period, as indicated by the insects and plants, ranged somewhere between 53°F and 56°F (11.5°C and 13°C),[19] not exactly balmy, but survivable. More importantly, these temperatures were warm enough to support food-bearing plants, and the team found the remains of such plants.

A study by another research team working in British Columbia indicates that other land bridges opened and closed at about the same time as did the Bering Strait bridge. The Hecate Strait, for instance, separating the Queen Charlotte Islands from the mainland of British Columbia, is a sixty-mile (one-hundred-kilometer) stretch of rough, cold sea. Challenge enough for large modern vessels, it would have proved more than a little daunting to natives in dugout canoes or other small vessels. Yet evidence of human habitation in the Queen Charlottes dates back to 10,200 years ago.[20]

A team of Canadian and American geologists and

paleoenvironmentalists combined an abundance of data from many sources to reconstruct the sea level and environmental history of the Hecate Strait region. They found that the floor of the Hecate Strait, relative to sea level, had once risen by as much as 502 feet (153 meters),[21] about half due to falling sea levels (lots of ocean water went into the continental ice sheets) and half from a huge bulging up of the underfloor, a reaction to the weight of the Cordilleran ice sheet pressing down on the British Columbia coastal mountain range.[22] With this much continental land mass pressed down by as much as 820 feet (250 meters), naturally something else had to go up, namely, the adjoining crustal material.

The research team's results demonstrated that a land bridge between the Canadian mainland and the Queen Charlottes formed as early as 14,600 years ago,[23] although the necessary plants and climate for long-term human habitation did not come until 13,000 years ago.[24] Between 10,000 and 9,500 years ago, the bulge in the Hecate Strait subsided and sea levels rose again, destroying the bridge.[25]

The speed with which the bridge formed and disappeared surprised the research team more than any other finding. The sea level rose and fell as rapidly as thirty-three feet (ten meters) per century,[26] giving some credence to Haida Indian legends of fast-rising seas in their early history.[27] The rapidity of the rise apparently prevented the organization of a concerted effort to evacuate the Queen Charlottes and return to the mainland. The Haidas remained cut off until Caucasian colonists made contact with them less than two hundred years ago.

In the Time of Peleg

The Haidas were not the only people cut off. Everywhere in the world sea levels were rapidly rising, widening all the straits separating the continents and great islands. The world became geographically divided and the human race geographically separated. However, Canadian and American geologists and paleoenvironmentalists were not the first to say so. More than 3,400 years ago, Moses wrote these words:

> Two sons were born to Eber: One was named Peleg,
> because in his time the earth was divided.[28]

This statement appears in the Semites' genealogy. It shows up halfway down the list from Shem to Abraham. Thus, the estimated biblical time of Peleg approximately fits the scientific dates for the collapse of the world's land bridges.

While the biblical statement of the earth's division in the time of Peleg is certainly consistent with the new discoveries of geographical separation, subsequent unity, and subsequent separation and with the larger context in Genesis 9–11 of God scattering humanity over the whole face of the planet, it is too dogmatic to state that Genesis claimed that the world became geographically separated in Peleg's time. This is the only verse in the Bible that refers to this event. The verse simply says that the earth was divided. It does not state in what way it was divided.

The Great Dividing

Here is the scenario that emerges from an integration of the scientific data with the biblical data: When Noah's descendants refused to "fill the Earth," God intervened to scatter them far beyond Mesopotamia. Thousands of years later, that scattering reached the geographical limits of the eastern hemisphere. Approximately fourteen thousand years ago, passable land bridges formed from the eastern to the western continents. For a few thousand years the scattering of humanity into all the habitable land masses of the planet continued. When that scattering was complete, about ten or eleven thousand years ago, the land bridges broke apart, preventing humanity from reuniting and repeating the sins of the pre-Flood and early post-Flood peoples.

As for Australia, Indonesia, New Guinea, and the British Isles, archeological evidence shows that humans settled them thousands of years earlier than they settled the Americas. The straits separating them from the larger land masses are warmer and calmer than Bering and Hecate. They may have been passable in boats. Some evidence suggests that earlier land or semi-land bridges may have existed in these locations. However, when the Bering and Hecate land bridges were disappearing, absolute sea levels were rising by about seventeen feet (five meters) per century.[29] This rise would have sufficiently broadened the straits separating Australia, Indonesia, New Guinea, and Britain from the Asian and European mainlands to hinder the return of their inhabitants.

This scenario demonstrates complete harmony between the biblical and scientific data.

The Origin of Races

The origin of humanity's different racial groups remains a mystery. Neither the Bible nor extrabiblical literature nor modern scientific research offers a direct explanation. One fact we can derive from Scripture: racial diversity existed by the time of the Jewish exodus from Egypt. Moses' relatives rebuked him for marrying a dark-skinned woman.[30] In some passages written later, the Bible contrasts the dark skin color of the Nubians and Ethiopians with the lighter complexions of the Egyptians, Jews, and Mesopotamians.[31]

This question cries for an answer: How did the human species develop such distinct skin colors and other more subtle differences in the relatively brief time from the days of Noah to the days of Moses? The usual answer that it happened in response to natural selection seems inadequate.

Genetic and anthropological research shows that natural selection cannot work as rapidly as necessary to offer a plausible explanation. Where skin-color options are available, marriage choice depends only weakly on skin color. Typically, small color differences present no barriers to marriage and large color differences generate only moderate effects, except where and when apartheid-type laws interfere.

Sun sensitivity works poorly as a selection effect. While dark-colored skin offers more protection against solar ultraviolet radiation damage, the advantage is too small to discourage people of light-colored skin from settling in the tropics. Nor is the biological cost of producing dark-colored skin high enough to give light-colored people a survival advantage over dark-colored people in the polar regions. Evidence for how weakly natural selection favors one skin color over another comes from the observation that dark-skinned Eskimos live in the arctic and fair-skinned Greeks live on Mediterranean isles.

These findings imply that natural selection cannot explain the development of racial diversity over just a few tens of thousands of years or less. At the risk of adopting what may seem a "God-of-the-gaps" approach, I can suggest an alternate explanation.

Given that Genesis 11 so explicitly describes God's personal intervention in breaking up destructive unity and in motivating people to spread throughout Earth's habitable land masses, God may have done more than diversify language at that time. He possibly may have introduced also some external changes—those we recognize as racial distinctives—to facilitate the peoples' separation.

The two types of change would seem to complement each other. Just as geographical barriers (mountains, rivers, straits, swamps, and so on) and distinct languages helped move and keep the nations apart, they might be even more effective with the addition of superficial but noticeable differences of skin, hair, eyes, and so forth. Time has proven that geographical barriers by themselves do not guarantee separation, nor do distinct languages by themselves, nor do racial distinctives by themselves, but the three together erect a barely adequate fence—at least they have until the late twentieth century. That this was God's intent seems indicated in Genesis 10:5,20,31 where the world's peoples are differentiated according to "their clans within their nations, each with its own language."

Questions about how God introduced these changes, as well as questions about how he "confused" the languages, we cannot answer from the biblical data. Clearly, the *how* holds less importance for us than the *why*. In time, scientific research may provide at least partial answers. Already it suggests some speculations.

Genetic research shows the possibilities of hybridization and breed development through selective pairing. Highly selective pairing among humans might have given some impetus to the development of racial diversity. On the other hand, God might have intervened, as He seems to have done in changing telomerase activity, by miraculously introducing something new, in this case new genetic material that would generate racial distinctives. God may have used a combination of these two methods or another entirely different means, but the changes happened in a way and in a time frame that science measures as impossible by natural means alone.

It's worth underlining that God's desire to separate the peoples of the world was due to His desires to: (1) restrain the evil that can come from a political monopoly; and (2) encourage people to "fill the earth" and "subdue it." This should not be taken as an indication that there is anything wrong in different peoples cooperating and mixing, as in trade and marriage.

Ham's Penalty

For many centuries certain sects of Christianity and Judaism have held the racist view that Noah's "curse" on his youngest son, Ham, marked the beginning of dark-skinned peoples. The incident for which Ham was penalized occurred shortly after the Flood at a time when Noah was harvesting the fruit from a vineyard he had planted (Genesis 9:18-27).

Noah became drunk from the wine of the harvest and slept off his drunkenness "uncovered" in the privacy of his tent. Ham walked in on his father and gazed on his father's nakedness. Then he walked outside and told his two brothers all about it. The two older brothers respectfully picked up a garment, walked into Noah's tent backward, and covered their father without looking at him. When Noah recovered and found out what Ham and his brothers had done, he pronounced this curse and this blessing:

> Cursed be Canaan [Ham's son]! The lowest of slaves will he be to his brothers. . . . Blessed be the LORD, the God of Shem! May Canaan be the slave of Shem. May God extend the territory of Japheth; may Japheth live in the tents of Shem, and may Canaan be his slave.[32]

These words imposed servitude on Ham's descendants through Canaan, no doubt shattering a father's dreams for his son and future generations of his lineage. However, the Genesis 9 text gives no hint, not even the faintest innuendo, that a change of skin color marked the change in Canaan's future. Nor does any Bible passage contain such a suggestion.

We can reasonably surmise that some details have been omitted from the story that comes to us. For some unspecified reason, the penalty fell only on Canaan, just one of Ham's sons. Ham's other named sons, Cush, Mizraim, and Put, were excluded. The historical record shows us that few if any of Canaan's descendants lived long on Earth. The Old Testament and extrabiblical records document that the nations moving in to occupy the ancient land of Canaan, the land held by Canaan's clans,[33] wiped out the inhabitants, Canaan's descendants.

There is no archaeological evidence whatsoever that the Canaanites had dark skin. They were later known as Phoenicians by the Greeks because from Tyre and Sidon they traded in purple dye (the Greek word for purple is *phoinix*) and purple-dyed cloth garments. The last of the Canaanites came to an end in the Roman-Punic wars when Carthage was destroyed.

Those who associate Canaan's curse with race invariably harbor a political agenda. Typically, they and their followers seek a basis for imposing a second-class or servant-class status on one or another of the peoples around them. Some, identifying Caucasians as descendants of Shem and Japheth, say Canaan's curse applies to certain African blacks. (Some blacks turn the tables and claim the sign of Canaan's curse is white skin.) Thus they trump up a biblical excuse for acquiring the territories of these people and for pressing them into servitude. Political ideology—and spiritual evil—rather than exegetical principles, drive their misinterpretation.

The Origin of Fermentation

Because some Christians look upon the consumption of wine or any other alcoholic beverage in any amount as sin, they have proposed an unlikely and unscientific interpretation of this Genesis 9 story about Noah. They suggest that Noah was surprised by his experience of drunkenness. Given Noah's righteous standing before God, he could not have known, they say, that the beverage he consumed would make him drunk. They imply, by this view, that fermentation never occurred on Earth till after the Flood. As entropy (the law of decay) and physical death are looked upon by some believers as evils introduced by humans' sin, so also fermentation seems to them the result of reprobate conditions at the time of the Flood. Specifically, some writers speculate that different atmospheric conditions before the Flood somehow would have inhibited the fermentation process.[34]

Here again the interpretation comes from some source other than sound exegesis of the text. The Bible in no instance labels fermentation or wine as evil. Jesus provided wine at the wedding feast in Cana, His first public miracle.[35] Paul instructed his disciple Timothy to take a little wine for his stomach's sake and not confine his fluid intake to water only.[36] The Bible does clearly forbid any drinking beyond "moderation," that is, drinking to the point of impairment, or drunkenness. The text gives no indication that Noah was taken by surprise, except by his son's behavior.

Also, the actions of Shem and Japheth seem to demonstrate a prior familiarity with the effects of fermentation. They responded to Noah's condition appropriately, and not with expressions of bewilderment or concern that their father might be seriously ill. They showed confidence that, if their father took the opportunity to sleep, he would get better soon.

The view that fermentation began after the Flood contradicts abundant evidence for continuity in the operation of physical laws (see pages 95 to 100). The laws of physics are not changed at any point in the Genesis chronology. God's Word in Genesis and God's Word in nature (see Psalm 19:1-4) agree in testifying to the stability of such laws. Bacteria, molds, fungi, and yeasts, all operating according to the laws of physics, play a vital role in the survival of higher plants and animals. God created them in time to support the existence of these other plants and animals. According to what we learn in Genesis 1, neither they nor the physical processes involved in fermentation could have been new at the time of the Flood. Perhaps few people realize that for many domesticated animals, including some mentioned in Genesis previous to the Flood, fermentation constitutes an essential part of the digestive process.

Wheat Reveals Agriculture's Spread
DNA "fingerprinting" helps with investigations beyond the criminal courtroom. In one recent case, this research technique was applied to the study of agriculture's origin, and the results provide a significant corroboration of biblical historicity.

That study compared the genes of wild wheat to those of cultivated wheat.[37-38] It indicates that the launch of organized, large-scale agriculture began at about 9000 B.C. The location for this launch was near the Karacadaq Mountains in Southern Turkey where the Tigris and Euphrates Rivers run close together. This site is consistent with the cradle of human civilization, namely the center of Mesopotamia's fertile crescent, and with both the probable landing spot for Noah's ark and the traditional location for the Garden of Eden. The date is consistent with the Bible's claims for the dawning and spread of advanced civilization after the Flood.

The same DNA analysis also outlines the spread of organized agriculture throughout Mesopotamia's fertile crescent (9000 to 8000 B.C.), to Persia, the Nile Delta, India, and Greece (8000 to 6000 B.C.), and beyond to south central Europe, the remainder of Egypt, southern Russia, and Arabia (6000 to 5000 B.C.). As the map in Figure 20.1 demonstrates, this spread is consistent with the biblical chronology outlined in Genesis 10–11 for the spread of advanced human civilization.

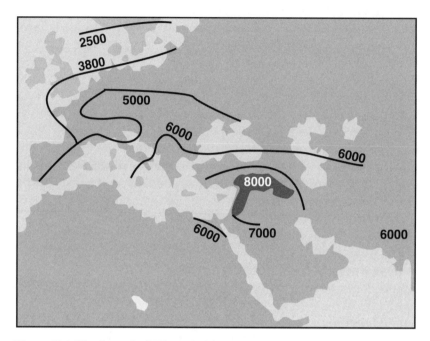

Figure 20:1: The Spread of Wheat Cultivation
Wheat cultivation expands from its launch point in northern Mesopotamia some 11,000 years ago to the whole of the fertile crescent by 10,000 years ago, to Persia, Egypt, India, and Greece by 8,000 years ago, and beyond in the succeeding millennia. Dates on the map are in years before Christ.

Spread of Goat Domestication

Two American anthropologists, Melinda Zeder and Brian Hesse, have pinpointed the initial domestication of goats as taking place 10,000 years ago in the Zagros Mountains located in western Iran and northeastern Iraq.[39] The new research finding was accomplished through studies and careful dating of goat skeletons. Clear evidence of organized goat domestication, Zeder and Hesse point out, would be the slaughtering of most of the subadult males for meat and the preserving of most of the females for milk and breeding. By contrast, human hunters of wild goats would select large males and females for prey. Therefore, a comparison of the sizes of goat skeletons for both sexes and the carbon-14 dating of the bones yields both the date and the location for the origin of large-scale goat domestication.

The date and the location for the origin of goat domestication matches well the date and location for the domestication of wheat. The Karacadaq highlands are just slightly west of the Zagros highlands. The two dates are identical given the uncertainties in the measurements. Both the wheat and goat domestication evidence fits consistently with the biblical record for the spread of human civilization after the Genesis Flood.

The End of Primeval History

The genealogy in Genesis 11:10-32 is a sort of bridge from the primeval past to a past that feels—and indeed is—much nearer to us. As I have evinced, Noah and his sons likely lived twenty to thirty thousand years ago. The scattering of peoples following the Tower of Babel debacle probably took place between thirty thousand and eleven thousand years ago. Abraham, on the other hand, was born only about four thousand years ago. Until now, belief in biblical events that occurred from patriarchal times onward was much more widespread than belief in more ancient biblical events. That was because historical and scientific evidence was abundant for the former and virtually nonexistent for the latter. However, thanks to several new discoveries, there is now a strong basis for belief in both.

We in the age of modern science are fortunate to have a burgeoning body of scientific evidence that confirms the accuracy and reliability of the first eleven chapters of the Bible. We should not be afraid of what future scientific endeavor will tell us, and neither should we accept an uninformed dismissal of biblical claims. Science can help us understand that God made all that is, destroyed nearly all human life by water when the human race had become too wicked, and is still working out His plan for our good.

CHAPTER TWENTY-ONE

DISPELLING MYTH ABOUT GENESIS

Observers of human culture acknowledge that every society known to humanity tells its own "story about the beginning." These stories, according to any dictionary, help define the word *myth*: "a traditional story of unknown origin, ostensibly with a historical basis, but serving usually to explain some phenomenon of nature, the origin of man, or the customs, institutions, religious rites, etc. of a people: myths usually involve the exploits of gods and heroes."[1] Widely held opinion among educated people worldwide, including many theologians, categorizes the Genesis "beginning story" with all the rest of beginning stories (though of course it has enjoyed much broader dissemination and impact than the others). They say it belongs to the same genre. It reflects a universal psychological need. Old Testament theologian Ellen van Wolde of the Netherlands beautifully expresses the view in her recent book, *Stories of the Beginning: Genesis 1–11 and Other Creation Stories*:

> Without a story about the beginning, human beings face chaos, and their origin seems to be an abyss. In order to provide a foundation for existence, the beginning was filled with meaning. Moreover, every culture attaches a meaning to the beginning, often in the form of stories. These are not stories in the sense of tales, but realities in which people live. These are stories which give people roots. In Western culture Genesis is *the* story of the beginning. Other cultures tell different stories of how it all began, and we read them with great amazement. We follow their traces with fascination into the past. Where no person ever was, what no ear

ever heard, we create by constantly reading afresh the story of our own beginning.[2]

Who can help but agree with her observation that the beginning is "filled with meaning," that it provides a foundation for existence? That point is, in fact, a central theme of this book. My own movement toward personal faith in Christ, the Savior and Creator, began with a reading of the biblical account of the beginning of the universe, Earth, life, and human history. Its message gave new meaning to my existence. But why? Van Wolde further observes that creation "tales" become "the realities in which people live," realities "we create," in her words. At this point an alarm goes off in my thinking.

How do tales become reality? How do people create reality? Is humanly created reality, reality? These questions may be among the most important any of us ever contemplates. The answer spells the difference between subjective truth and objective truth. It also spells the difference between Christianity and all other worldviews, both religious and nonreligious, theistic and atheistic. The answer: tales become reality through "blind faith," not "biblical faith."

Reading the Bible as a young scientist, I remember feeling thrilled, humbled, surprised, and enormously relieved to discover that God commands us to believe based on objective evidence. Biblical faith, like the faith exercised by scientists, must be "informed" faith, belief rooted in testable facts and logic, though not based on *absolute* proof. Too many people accept the erroneous notion that absolute proof is what scientists seek and find. Some demand absolute proof of God's existence and of the reliability of Scripture as a condition of faith in Christ. Such a demand will never—can never—be met, certainly not within the time-and-space boundaries God has set for this life, for this "faith test" He designed for us.

German logician Kurt Gödel proved that absolute proof lies beyond human reach.[3] Absolute proof of anything requires complete knowledge, and we do not—cannot—have complete knowledge of anything in this universe because we are merely part of it. What scientists demand, and rightly so, is practical proof. Scientists and the rest of us accept the truth of gravity, for example, based on practical, not absolute, proof. We observe this phenomenon we call gravity to operate so consistently and predictably in all circumstances through all observable time that we do not doubt its reality or reliability.

According to the book of Romans, God holds every human being accountable to discern fact from fiction, truth from tale, in the stories we are taught from childhood. Each of us recognizes, at some point in growing up, where a story like that of Santa Claus departs from the realm of plausibility, or even possibility, and enters the realm of fantasy. Some question earlier, some question later, but eventually we all question the tales with which we have been raised. God expects us to test them; God wants us to test them; God even commands us to test them ("prove" them, in the *King James Version*).[4]

All through Scripture we see examples of God giving people the "proof" they needed to believe His words. Adam, Eve, and others heard from God directly, audibly. Others heard from Him through special messengers, called angels. Some heard from Him through prophets, whose authenticity could be established via the accuracy of their predictions. Some walked and talked with God in human form, Jesus Christ, whose words also were subject to verification by His fulfillment of Old Testament prophecies and by observable supernatural wonders beyond the scope of "magic." Some of us, in the era since Christ, have access to His written Word, while many others have examined "the word written on their hearts." According to Romans 1, nature itself provides a testing tool available to all people everywhere and in all eras.[5]

Two of the many dramatic changes that have occurred in human history since the time of Christ include the increasing availability of the Bible, in written and audio (and now video!) form, and the exponential increase in human knowledge about the natural realm. Testing of God's revelation, in other words, has become at the same time easier and more difficult. We have more biblical material to test—sixty-six books in both ancient and modern languages, more manuscripts to examine, and greater understanding of ancient languages through archeological research—and more knowledge of nature, human history, and natural history with which to compare it. The quantity and complexity of the testing tools can be daunting.

Scientific testing proved especially frightening in the early days of scientific advance. Scientific "truth" seemed to change from year to year, discovery to discovery, and that truth sometimes clashed with people's understanding of biblical truth, particularly with

Genesis 1–11. As I described in chapters two, ten, and eleven, this development seemed to heighten dogmatism on all sides. One group said, "Science is true; the Bible is false." Another group said, "The Bible is true; science is false." Others said, "The Bible is true in parts, mythical or legendary in parts, and science can help us sift." Others said, "The Bible is true, and the parts that clash with science must be allegorical." At least this latter group kept the baby *and* the bathwater. A group that has grown large in the last decade of the twentieth century says, "The Bible (and all religions) teach one kind of truth, science teaches another, and never the twain shall meet." In other words, we can forget testing; it's irrelevant. We can believe whatever we want, "create our own reality." But whose mind really buys this notion?

One group of people, whose voice was and still is seldom heard in either the church or the media worldwide, says, "The Bible reveals truth, and science reveals truth, and wherever the twain meet they agree." This group, whom I meet wherever I travel on the planet and to whom I belong, says that truth never contradicts truth. If God's Word in the Bible and God's expression of Himself in nature seem to clash, we must dig deeper to understand each. It is our understanding of the data, and not the data themselves, which presents the problem. Increasing our understanding constitutes a large part of our assignment here on Earth. The first commandment is clear: "Love the Lord your God with all your heart and with all your soul *and with all your mind* and with all your strength" (emphasis added). Living by that commandment enables us to obey the rest, which Jesus summarized as "Love your neighbor as yourselves" (Mark 12:30-31).

Testing Genesis 1–11 holds the potential to increase our understanding of both God and humanity—and the rest of God's creation, as well. If people can embrace the truth of these chapters, they can embrace the truth of all Scripture and of all the divine interventions or "miracles" it describes, including the miracle of our salvation. We can begin to grasp the point of all God's creation: to bring us to the new creation God has promised. In that new creation, "the dwelling of God is with men, . . . and God himself will be with them and be their God" (Revelation 21:3). To be with us personally and to be our God is His ultimate goal.

A Look to the Future

As scientists discover more and more about the creation, including human origins, we can be certain that the case for the divine inspiration of Scripture will grow stronger and stronger. The basis for this certainty lies in the pattern observable over the centuries, decades, years, and days right up to the writing of this book: advancing scientific research brings an accumulation of reasons to believe. We owe it to ourselves and to those around us who still struggle with questions and doubts, or who hide behind excuses, to keep informed and enthusiastic about new developments in research and the added support they provide. We may need to remind someone that choosing *not* to test the Book that claims to be truth about our past, present, and future means choosing to gamble recklessly with the invaluable gift of eternal life.

BIBLICAL ORIGINS OF THE SCIENTIFIC METHOD

Arguably the most famous example of misapplication of the scientific method was the Roman Catholic Church's rejection of Galileo's heliocentric (sun-centered) theory of the solar system. What is missed by most accounts of the incident, however, is that Galileo defended his interpretation by pointing out that the Roman Catholic Church leaders were guilty of misapplying the scientific method both in their treatment of observations of solar-system dynamics and of the words of the Bible.

Scientifically, the movement of the sun across the sky could be the result of the sun moving relative to the earth or the earth relative to the sun. Biblically, the "foundations of the earth" indeed are "immovable" in spite of any revolution of the earth about the sun or rotation of the earth about its axis because the Bible verses making such statements always are from the perspective, or point of view, of an observer on the surface of the earth.[1-4] Because that observer is revolving and rotating at the same rate as the foundations of the earth, the earth's foundations never appear to move with respect to that observer.

The heart of Galileo's rebuke is that certain Roman Catholic theologians began to interpret scientific observations and Bible passages on the movement of the sun and planets before they had properly established the frame of reference, or point of view, and the initial conditions. Failure to do either, Galileo warned, was bound to lead to serious misinterpretations.[5]

Today very few doubt that Galileo was on target in rebuking the Roman Catholic Church leaders on their misapplication of the scientific method as it pertains to the astronomical observations. But was he right to say they had misapplied the method in their understanding of the biblical texts? He definitely was in the sense that the scientific method arose from the Bible texts and Christian theology.

The Bible alone among the scriptures or "holy books" of the religions of the world strongly exhorts readers to test before they believe. In his first letter to the Thessalonians, the apostle Paul commanded:

Test everything. Hold on to the good.[6]

In his first epistle John echoed Paul's sentiments:

Dear friends, do not believe every spirit, but test the spirits to see whether they are from God.[7]

Such diligent and thorough testing was commended by Luke and Jesus:

Now the Bereans were of more noble character than the Thessalonians, for they received the message with great eagerness and examined the Scriptures every day to see if what Paul said was true.[8]

"You have tested those who claim to be apostles but are not, and have found them false."[9]

Paul exhorted us that such testing, to be effective, requires education and training:

Do not conform any longer to the pattern of this world, but be transformed by the renewing of your mind. Then you will be able to test and approve what God's will is.[10]

In the Old Testament, Job foreshadowed Paul's exhortation:

Let us discern for ourselves what is right; let us learn together what is good.[11]

This theme of testing before believing pervades both the Old and New Testaments and forms the very heart of the biblical concept of faith. The Hebrew word for faith, *'emûna*, means a strongly held conviction that something or someone is certainly existing, firmly established, constant, and dependable.[12] The Greek word for faith, *pistis*, means a strong and welcome conviction of the truth of anything or anyone to the degree that one places complete trust and confidence in that thing or person.[13] In every instance in the Bible, faith connotes the acting upon specific established truth. Just as there is no faith without action,[14] neither is there any faith unless certain truth(s) have been established.

Christian scholars throughout church history, from the early church fathers, to Renaissance naturalists, to Reformation theologians, to present-day evangelical scientists, philosophers, and theologians, have all noted that wherever the Bible describes a sequence of physical events, it always prefaces that description with statements of the frame(s) of reference (points of view) and the initial conditions and closes it with statements of the final conditions and conclusions about the physical events. The Scottish theologian Thomas Torrance has both authored and edited book-length discussions on how Christian theology, and Reformed theology in particular, played a critical role in the development of the scientific method and the amazing advances achieved by Western science.[15-17] I recommend his books and others like them for anyone who wants to study further the biblical roots of the scientific method.

WORD STUDIES IN GENESIS 1

The English translation of Genesis 1 presented below is taken from the *New International Version*. Superscripts to the right of certain words key to the list of definitions that follows. Lexical definitions are taken from four different sources.[1-4]

1. In the beginning God[1] created[2] the heavens[5] and the earth.[20]

2. Now the earth[20] was formless[6] and empty,[7] darkness was over the surface of the deep,[8] and the Spirit[9] of God[1] was hovering[21] over the waters.

3. And God[1] said, "Let there be[3] light," and there was light.

4. God[1] saw that the light was good, and he separated the light from the darkness.

5. God[1] called the light "day"[19] and the darkness he called "night." And there was evening,[22] and there was morning[23]—the first day.[19]

6. And God[1] said, "Let there be[3] an expanse[10] between the waters to separate water from water."

7. So God[1] made[4] the expanse[10] and separated the water under the expanse[10] from the water above it. And it was so.

8. God[1] called the expanse[10] "sky."[5] And there was evening,[22] and there was morning[23]—the second day.[19]

9. And God[1] said, "Let the water under the sky[5] be[3] gathered to one place, and let dry ground appear."[24] And it was so.

10. God[1] called the dry ground "land" and the gathered waters he called "seas." And God[1] saw that it was good.

11. Then God[1] said, "Let the land produce[25] vegetation:[26] seed[11]-bearing plants[29] and trees[12] on the land that bear fruit[13] with seed[11] in it, according to their various kinds."[27] And it was so.

12. The land produced[28] vegetation:[26] plants[29] bearing seed[11] according to their kinds[27] and trees[12] bearing fruit[13] with seed[11] in it according to their kinds.[27] And God[1] saw that it was good.

13. And there was evening,[22] and there was morning[23]—the third day.[19]

14. And God[1] said, "Let there be [3] lights[30] in the expanse[10] of the sky[5] to separate the day[19] from the night, and let them serve as signs[31] to mark seasons and days[19] and years.

15. And let there be[3] lights[30] in the expanse[10] of the sky[5] to give light on the earth."[20] And it was so.

16. God[1] made[4] two great lights[30]—the greater light[30] to govern the day[19] and the lesser light[30] to govern the night. He also made[4] the stars.

17. God[1] set[14] them in the expanse[10] of the sky[5] to give light on the earth,[20]

18. to govern the day[19] and the night, and to separate light from darkness. And God[1] saw that it was good.

19. And there was evening,[22] and there was morning[23]—the fourth day.[19]

20. And God[1] said, "Let the water teem with living creatures,[15] and let birds fly above the earth[20] across the expanse[10] of the sky."[5]

21. So God[1] created[2] the great creatures[16] of the sea and every living[17] and moving thing[17] with which the water teems, according to their kinds,[27] and every winged bird according to its kind.[27] And God[1] saw that it was good.

22. God[1] blessed them and said, "Be[3] fruitful and increase in number and fill the water in the seas, and let the birds increase on the earth."[20]

23. And there was evening,[22] and there was morning [23]—the fifth day.[19]

24. And God[1] said, "Let the land produce[28] living creatures[17] according to their kinds:[27] livestock,[32] creatures that move[33] that move along the ground, and wild animals,[34] each according to its kind."[27] And it was so.

25. God[1] made[4] the wild animals[34] according to their kinds,[27] the livestock[32] according to their kinds,[27] and all the creatures that move [33] along the ground according to their kinds.[27] And God[1] saw that it was good.

26. Then God[1] said, "Let us make[4] man[18] in our image, in our likeness, and let them rule over the fish of the sea and the birds of the air, over the livestock,[32] over all the earth, and over all the creatures that move[33] along the ground."

27. So God[1] created[2] man[18] in his own image, in the image of God[1] he created[2] him; male and female he created them.

28. God[1] blessed them and said to them, "Be[3] fruitful and increase in number; fill the earth[20] and subdue[35] it. Rule over the fish of the sea and the birds of the air and over every living creature[34] that moves on the ground."

29. Then God[1] said, "I give you every seed[11]-bearing plant[29] of the face of the

whole earth[20] and every tree that has fruit with seed[11] in it. They will be yours for food.

30. And to all the beasts[34] of the earth[20] and all the birds of the air and all the creatures that move[33] on the ground—everything that has the breath of life in it—I give every green plant[29] for food." And it was so.

31. God[1] saw all that He had made,[4] and it was very good. And there was evening,[22] and there was morning[23]—the sixth day.[19] Thus the heavens[5] and the earth[20] were completed in all their vast array.

Definitions

1. **'elohim** (plural of 'eloah): the deity; the supreme Being; the true God—a compound word composed of El (the strong one), and Alah (to bind oneself by an oath); hence, Elohiym = the mighty and faithful one—a uni-plural noun; thus, Elohiym latently implies the Trinity—the only name used for God in Genesis 1; this name is used about 2,500 times in the Old Testament.

2. **bara'**: bring forth something that is radically new; produce that which is new, extraordinary, and/or epochal; produce through supernatural activity. God is always the subject of this verb.

3. **haya**: become (when coupled with the Hebrew preposition *l*); cause to appear or arise; cause to be made or done; come into existence; come to pass; make into something.

4. **'asa**: produce; manufacture; fabricate.

5. **shamayim** (pl), **shameh** (sing): visible dome of the sky above and in which the clouds move; the realm in which the celestial bodies move; the spiritual realm in which God and the angels dwell and operate—with respect to the above definitions, the Hebrews referred to the three heavens (cf. II Cor. 12:2); whenever shamayim is used with the erets (earth), as in 1:1, the combination refers to the entire physical universe.

6. **tohu**: desolate; worthless; wasteness; useless; incapable of being utilized; unformed.

7. **bohu**: empty; void; devoid of existence.

8. **tehom**: a great mass of water; the oceans and the seas.

9. **ruah**: spirit; breath; wind—in conjunction with Elohim refers to the Holy Spirit.

10. **raqia'**: (apparently) visible dome of the sky; (technically, the atmosphere immediately above the surface of the earth).

11. **zera'**: embryos of plants, trees, grasses, etc., i.e., the embryos of any plant species.

12. **'es**: any large plant containing woody fiber.

13. **peri**: food and/or embryos produced by any living thing.

14. **natan**: set; put; place; appoint; bring forth; apply; ascribe; set forth; send out; show; trust; bestow; cause to appear; charge; commit; deliver.

15. **sheres**: swarm of small or minute animals.

16. **tanniym**: great or large sea animal; monster.

17. **nepesh**: vital animals, i.e. animals that clearly manifest the soulish attributes of mind, will, and emotion.

18. **'adam**: human being; the human race; i.e., animals that clearly manifest spirit attributes. NOTE: there is no evidence for a spirit dimension for the pre-Adamic hominids.

19. **yôm**: sunrise to sunset; sunset to sunset; a space of time (defined by an associated term); an age; time or period (without any reference to solar days).

20. **'eres**: the planet Earth; a land, a country, or a continent; lands, countries, kingdoms, or regions.

21. **rahap**: to brood over, cherishing and vivifying; to be tenderly affected; to be moved.

22. **'ereb**: the beginning of darkness; dusk, twilight, or nightfall; closing, ending, or completion.

23. **boqer**: the breaking forth of light; dawn, daybreak, or morning; dawning, beginning, or origin.

24. **ra' a**: be seen; appear; show forth, cause one to see; to be perceived or beheld; to be considered.

25. **dasha'**: to bring forth herbage; to sprout; to bring forth.

26. **deshe'**: new vegetation; young plants.

27. **min**: species; life-form.

28. **yasa'**: germinate, bring forth; produce; spring forth; promulgate; to cause to come forth; issue out; proceed.

29. **'eseb**: green plant(s).

30. **ma'or**: a luminous body; brightness; light.

31. **'ot**: signal; sign, measuring mark; token, omen; evidence.

32. **behemot**: large land quadruped.

33. **remes**: rapidly moving vertebrates; rodents and/or reptiles.

34. **hay**: wild animals; a multitude or mob; that which is lively or fresh.

35. **kabash**: subject; subdue; subjugate.

SONS OF GOD AND SONS OF MEN

As noted in chapter sixteen, the biblical phrases translated as "sons of God" and "sons of men," or the equivalent "children of God" and "children of men," play a critical role in the identification of the source and attributes of the Nephilim. What follows are complete lists of all the Bible references to these terms.

Table C.1: Biblical References to "sons of God"

Old Testament	New Testament
Genesis 6:2	Matthew 5:9
Genesis 6:4	John 1:12
Job 1:6	Romans 8:14
Job 2:1	Romans 8:19
Job 38:7	Galatians 3:26
	Philippians 2:15
	1 John 3:1
	1 John 3:2

Table C.2: Biblical References to "children of God"
(based on original language phrase translated as "sons of men")

Old Testament	New Testament
None	John 11:52
	Romans 8:16
	Romans 8:21
	Romans 9:8
	1 John 3:10
	1 John 5:2

Table C.3: Biblical References to "sons [or daughters] of men"

Old Testament	New Testament
Psalm 4:2	Mark 3:28
Psalm 31:19	Ephesians 3:5

Old Testament (cont.)　**New Testament** (cont.)
Psalm 33:13
Psalm 57:4
Psalm 58:1
Psalm 145:12
Proverbs 8:31
Ecclesiastes 2:3
Ecclesiastes 2:8
Ecclesiastes 3:10
Ecclesiastes 3:18
Ecclesiastes 3:19
Ecclesiastes 8:11
Ecclesiastes 9:3
Ecclesiastes 9:12
Isaiah 52:14
Jeremiah 32:19
Daniel 5:21
Daniel 10:16
Joel 1:12
Micah 5:7

Table C.4: Biblical References to "children of men"
(based on original language phrase translated as "sons of men")

Old Testament	New Testament
2 Chronicles 6:30	None
Psalm 11:4	
Psalm 12:1	
Psalm 14:2	
Psalm 21:10	
Psalm 36:7	
Psalm 45:2	
Psalm 53:2	
Psalm 66:5	
Psalm 90:3	
Psalm 107:8	
Psalm 107:15	
Psalm 107:21	
Psalm 107:31	
Psalm 115:16	
Proverbs 15:11	
Lamentations 3:33	
Ezekiel 31:14	
Daniel 2:38	

SCIENTIFIC DISCOVERIES SUPPORTING GENESIS 1–11

A summary list of new scientific discoveries affirming the far-beyond accuracy of Genesis 1–11, plus Scripture references and page references to their discussion in this book, appear in the following table. It is included for the sake of anyone who cares to test or retest these Genesis chapters and to share the testing process, as well as the understanding and faith to which it leads, with others.

Table D: Summary of New Scientific Discoveries Substantiating Divine Inspiration of Genesis 1–11.

Scientific discovery	Scripture reference	Page reference
1. evidences for a big-bang creation event	Genesis 1:1	8, 9, 18-19
2. evidences for a beginning of all matter, energy, space, and time	Genesis 1:1	9, 18-19
3. evidence for the fixity of physical constants and laws	Genesis 1–9; Job; Psalms; Jeremiah 33:25	10, 18-19
4. evidence for primordial darkness on Earth's surface	Genesis 1:2	24-25
5. evidence for a global primordial ocean	Genesis 1:2	25, 27
6. evidence for ancient life in the oceans	Genesis 1:2	27-28
7. evidence for transformation of Earth's atmosphere from opaque to translucent	Genesis 1:3-5	29-31
8. evidence for transformation of Earth's atmosphere from toxic to life-supporting	Genesis 1:3-19	29-31 ·
9. evidences for fine-tuning of solar luminosity, Earth's gravitational pull, plate tectonics, vulcanism, cometary infall, and life quantity and diversity to maintain adequate-for-life water quantities in all three states: vapor, liquid, ice	Genesis 1:6-22	29-34

Scientific discovery	Scripture reference	Page reference
10. evidence that early high levels of tectonics and vulcanism yielded rapid continental development	Genesis 1:9-11	36
11. evidence that carbon-13 to carbon-12 ratios for all kerogen tars are biological in origin, implying that life cannot have emerged naturally	Genesis 1:2-13	38
12. evidence for life's abundance on Earth throughout the past 3.86 billion years, implying life originated in a span much briefer than five million years	Genesis 1:2-13	38-39
13. calculations demonstrating the impossibility of the molecular complexity of even the simplest life could develop by chance processes	Genesis 1:2-13	39
14. evidence for the improbability of homochirality's origin outside living organisms	Genesis 1:2-13	39
15. demonstration that the different nucleotides necessary for building DNA and RNA molecules cannot be constructed in the same environment	Genesis 1:2-13	39
16. demonstration that RNA molecules and their nucleotides will chemically degrade quickly anywhere outside the cell	Genesis 1:2-13	39-40
17. evidence against the panspermia hypothesis, the belief that life or life remains can be transported across interstellar distances	Genesis 1:2-13	40
18. evidence for fine-tuning of both the amount and the location of several forms of radiation to make life possible	Genesis 1:2-13	40
19. evidence that the building blocks for life molecules cannot possibly exist without radiation but that to assemble and maintain, under natural conditions alone, the building blocks into life molecules under the exposure to radiation is impossible	Genesis 1:2-13	40
20. evidence that the decay of radiometric elements in the earth's crust released enough oxygen into the atmosphere so as to shutdown any possibility of a naturalistic assembly of molecules into an organism	Genesis 1:2-13	40-41
21. evidence that trees date as early as 370 million years ago and flowering plants as early as 290 million years ago	Genesis 1:11-12	37-38
22. evidence for limits on natural plant and animal speciation	Genesis 1:2-27	41
23. evidence that sea-salt aerosols help explain fourth creation day events since they play the most significant role in cloud nuclei and that the formation of such aerosols depends on the planet's rotation and continent distribution	Genesis 1:9-27	41-42

Scientific discovery	Scripture reference	Page reference
24. evidence for fine-tuning of vulcanism, plate tectonics, and crustal composition to avoid a carbonate doomsday	Genesis 1:9-27	42
25. evidence for exquisite balance and delicacy of Earth's three ozone layers for the survival of advanced life	Genesis 1:14-27	44-46
26. evidence that sea mammals date earlier in the fossil record than previously thought	Genesis 1:21-22	50-51
27. evidence that the earliest sea mammals changed far too rapidly for either Darwinism or punctuated equilibria to explain	Genesis 1:21-22	50-51
28. evidence for the size of the cosmos and diameter of stars, implying a lower limit for the creation date	Genesis 1:3–2:3	66, 97
29. evidence of splash patterns from falling rain in ancient sandstone deposits	Genesis 2:4-6	73
30. discovery that matter, energy, and the space-time manifold of the universe interrelate	Genesis 1:1; 2:15–3:24; Romans 8:18-23	97
31. evidence for extremely high cosmic entropy and high homogeneity	Genesis 1:1–3:24; Romans 8:18-23	97
32. evidence for and dating of earliest spirit expression	Genesis 1:26-27; 5; 11	110
33. Y-chromosome date for the most recent common ancestor of all men	Genesis 1:26-27; 5; 11	111
34. mitochondrial DNA date for the most recent common ancestor of all women	Genesis 1:26-27; 5; 11	111-112
35. morphological evidence that Neandertals are not biologically linked to any other species	Genesis 1:25-27	112-113
36. mitochondrial DNA evidence that Neandertals are unrelated to humans	Genesis 1:25-27	114-115
37. discovery that most of the harmful cosmic rays striking Earth come from the Vela supernova	Genesis 5:1–6:3	121
38. evidence for the date of the Vela supernova eruption	Genesis 5:1–6:3	122-123
39. evidence that a lower level of telomerase activity protects against cancer's advance	Genesis 5:1–6:3	124-125
40. evidence for limitation on human height	Genesis 6:2-4	129-130
41. evidence against extreme tectonics, vulcanism, or erosion during the Genesis Flood	Genesis 7–8	152-154
42. evidence that evolutionary processes do not proceed rapidly in animals	Genesis 7–9	154-155

Scientific discovery	Scripture reference	Page reference
43. determination of the limits on the number of species Earth can support at one time	Genesis 7–9	156
44. evidence for high speciation rate before the creation of humanity compared to the zero or near-zero rate afterward	Genesis 1:11–9:17	155-156
45. evidence that Earth's biodeposits vastly exceed what could have been laid down during a single year	Genesis 7–9	156-159
46. demonstration of the impossibility of a water "canopy"	Genesis 2–9	157
47. evidence that marine fossils and marine deposits on the continental land masses are of ancient rather than recent origin	Genesis 7–8	158-159
48. comparative evidence that the Genesis Flood event would not be expected to leave behind a discoverable deposit	Genesis 7–8	159-160
49. evidence for the formation and subsequent destruction of a warm land bridge between Siberia and Alaska during the post-Flood era	Genesis 10:25	177-178
50. evidence for the formation and subsequent destruction of a land bridge between the Queen Charlotte Islands and the North American mainland during the post-Flood era	Genesis 10:25	178-179
51. evidence that human racial diversity and racial separation likely developed through more than natural means	Genesis 11:1-9	181-182
52. measurements from DNA analysis of the dates and locations for the origin and spread of domesticated wheat	Genesis 10 Genesis 11:1-9	185-186
53. measurements from the skeletal sizes of female and male goats for the origin and spread of goat husbandry	Genesis 10 Genesis 11:1-9	186-187

NOTES

One: A Personal Journey
1. 2 Timothy 3:16.
2. 1 Thessalonians 5:21.
3. Hugh Ross, *My Search for Truth* (Pasadena, CA: Reasons to Believe, 1990).
4. Hugh Ross, *An Astronomer's Quest*, sixty-minute audiocassette (Forest, VA: Life Story Foundation, 1995).

Two: Reasons for Resistance
1. Hugh Ross, *The Fingerprint of God*, 2d ed. (Orange, CA: Promise Publishing, 1991), pages 119-138.
2. Hugh Ross, *The Creator and the Cosmos*, 2d ed. (Colorado Springs, CO: NavPress, 1995), pages 105-156.
3. Hugh Ross, *Beyond the Cosmos* (Colorado Springs, CO: NavPress, 1996), pages 21-33.
4. Hugh Ross, *Big Bang Model Refined by Fire* (Pasadena, CA: Reasons to Believe, 1998), pages 1-18.
5. David Briggs, "Science, Religion Are Discovering Commonality in Big Bang Theory," *Los Angeles Times*, 2 May 1992, pages B6-B7.
6. Isaac Asimov, *Asimov's Guide to the Bible: The Old and New Testaments* (New York: Random House Value Publishing, 1988).
7. Isaac Asimov, "Notes on Genesis 1:1-19," in *Creations: The Quest for Origins in Story and Science*, eds. Isaac Asimov, George Zebrowski, and Martin Greenberg (London, U.K.: Harrap, 1984), page 6.
8. Asimov, *Asimov's Guide*, page 195.
9. Steve Allen, *Steve Allen on the Bible, Religion, and Morality* (Buffalo, NY: Prometheus Books, 1990), page 152.
10. Allen, *Bible, Religion, and Morality*, page 154.
11. Allen, *Bible, Religion, and Morality*, page 155.
12. Franz Delitzsch, *Babel und Bible*, trans. by Thomas J. McCormack and W. H. Carruth (Chicago: The Open Court Publishing, 1903), page 45.
13. Frank Press, *Science and Creationism: A View from the National Academy of Sciences* (Washington, DC: National Academy Press, 1984), page 6.

14. This often-repeated assertion was first uttered by Cardinal Cesare Baronio and Galileo Galilei.

15. Frank J. Tipler, *The Physics of Immortality* (New York: Doubleday, 1994), page 7.

16. Tipler, *Physics of Immortality*, page 5.

17. Michael Ruse, "Naturalistic Fallacy," *Reason* (October 1996), page 56.

18. 2 Corinthians 5:7.

19. Proverbs 12:1.

Three: Creation of the Cosmos
1. Bruce Waltke, *Creation and Chaos: An Exegetical and Theological Study of Biblical Cosmogony* (Portland, OR: Western Conservative Baptist Seminary, 1974). Waltke has since prepared a nine-hundred-page manuscript on the first three verses of Genesis 1.

2. Hugh Ross, *The Fingerprint of God*, 2d ed. (Orange, CA: Promise, 1991), pages 27-35.

3. Herman Bondi and T. Gold, "The Steady-State Theory of the Expanding Universe," *Monthly Notices of the Royal Astronomical Society* 108 (1948), pages 252-270.

4. Fred Hoyle, "A New Model for the Expanding Universe," *Monthly Notices of the Royal Astronomical Society* 108 (1948), pages 372-382.

5. Ross, *Fingerprint of God*, pages 53-105.

6. Robert H. Dicke, "Cosmic Black-Body Radiation," *Astrophysical Journal Letters* 142 (1965), pages 414-419.

7. John Gribbin, "Oscillating Universe Bounces Back," *Nature* 259 (1976), pages 15-16.

8. Genesis 1:1; Psalm 33:6-9; Psalm 90:2; John 17:24; 2 Timothy 1:9; Titus 1:2; Revelation 21:1.

9. Job 37:23; John 1:3; Ephesians 1:4; Colossians 1:15-16; 2 Timothy 1:9; Titus 1:2; Hebrews 11:3.

10. R. Laird Harris, Gleason L. Archer, and Bruce K. Waltke, *Theological Wordbook of the Old Testament*, vol. 1 (Chicago: Moody Press, 1980), page 127.

11. R. Laird Harris, Gleason L. Archer, and Bruce K. Waltke, *Theological Wordbook of the Old Testament*, vols. 1 & 2 (Chicago: Moody, 1980). There were no vowels in the oldest Hebrew biblical manuscripts. The later insertion of vowel sounds multiplied the 3,067 biblical Hebrew words (not including seldom used proper nouns) to 8,674 (including all proper nouns used in the Old Testament).

12. Harris, Archer, and Waltke, *Theological Wordbook*, vol. 1, pages 74-75.

13. Harris, Archer, and Waltke, *Theological Wordbook*, vol. 2, pages 935-936.

14. 2 Corinthians 12:2.

15. Waltke, *Creation and Chaos*, pages 20, 25-26. This point was also one of Waltke's central themes in his Kenneth S. Kantzer Lectures in Systematic Theology given 8-10 January 1991 at Trinity Evangelical Divinity School, Deerfield, IL.

16. Allen P. Ross, *Creation & Blessing: A Guide to the Study and Exposition of Genesis* (Grand Rapids, MI: Baker, 1988), pages 721, 725-726.

17. Genesis 1:1; Psalm 33:6-9; Isaiah 40:26-28; 42:5; John 1:3; 17:24; Ephesians 1:4; Colossians 1:15-16; 2 Timothy 1:9; Titus 1:2; Hebrews 11:3; 1 Peter 1:20; Revelation 4:11.

18. Hugh Ross, *The Creator and the Cosmos,* 2d ed. (Colorado Springs, CO: NavPress, 1995), pages 19-103.

19. Hugh Ross, *Beyond the Cosmos* (Colorado Springs, CO: NavPress, 1996), pages 21-33.

20. Psalm 119:160; Ecclesiastes 7:1-25; Acts 17:11; Romans 12:2; 1 Thessalonians 5:21; Hebrews 6:18; 1 John 4:1.

21. Isaiah 41:5-7; 44:9-20; Jeremiah 23:9-40; Colossians 2:4,8.

22. Herbert W. Morris, *Work-Days of God, or Science and the Bible,* enlarged ed. (London: W. Nicholson and Sons, ~1915), pages 21-106.

23. Cunningham Geikie, *Hours with the Bible,* vol. 1 (New York: James Pott, 1905), pages 40-42.

24. C. I. Scofield, *The Scofield Reference Bible* (New York: Oxford University Press, 1945), pages 3-4.

25. James Buswell, Hugh Ross, Robert Saucy, and Dallas Willard, *Round Table on Genesis One,* 120-minute video cassette (Pasadena, CA: Reasons to Believe, 1992). Four scholars, including gap theorist Robert Saucy, interact on their differing interpretations of Genesis 1.

26. 1 Samuel 2:8; 1 Chronicles 16:26; Job 9:8; Psalms 24:1; 89:11-12; 146:5-6; 148:5-6; Isaiah 37:16; 44:24; 45:7-18; Romans 11:36; 1 Corinthians 8:6; Ephesians 3:9; Hebrews 1:1-14; Revelation 4:11; 10:6.

27. Ross, *Creator and the Cosmos,* pages 112-121.

28. Hugh Ross, *Creation and Time* (Colorado Springs, CO: NavPress, 1994), pages 65-69, 91-100.

29. The continued existence of stars, planets, and physical plant and animal life demands the ongoing and constant operation of the laws of gravity, electromagnetism, and thermodynamics.

30. Harris, Archer, and Waltke, *Theological Wordbook,* vol. 2, pages 964-965.

31. Ross, *Creation and Time,* pages 45-72.

32. Job 10:8-14; 12:7; 34:14-15; 35:10-12; 37:5-7; 38-41; Psalms 8; 19:1-6; 50:6; 85:11; 97:6; 98:2-3; 104; 139; Proverbs 8:22-31; Ecclesiastes 3:11; Habakkuk 3:3; Acts 14:17; 17:23-31; Romans 1:18-25; 2:14-15; 10:16-18; Colossians 1:23; 1 Thessalonians 5:21.

33. Bernard Ramm, *The Christian View of Science and Scripture* (Grand Rapids, MI: Eerdmans, 1955), pages 195-210.

34. Steven V. W. Beckwith and Anneila I. Sargent, "Circumstellar Disks and the Search for Neighboring Planetary Systems," *Nature* 383 (1996), page 141.

35. David Arnett and Grant Bazan, "Nucleosynthesis in Stars: Recent Developments," *Science* 276 (1997), pages 1359-1362.

36. Ralph Neuhäuser, "Low-Mass Pre-Main Sequence Stars and Their X-Ray Emission," *Science* 276 (1997), pages 1363-1370.

37. J. H. Kastner, B. Zuckerman, D. A. Weintraub, and T. Forveille, "X-Ray and Molecular Emission from the Nearest Region of Recent Star Formation," *Science* 277 (1997), pages 67-71.

38. C. Robert O'Dell and Stephen V. W. Beckwith, "Young Stars and Their Surroundings," *Science* 276 (1997), pages 1355-1359.

39. Frank H. Shu, Hsien Shang, Alfred E. Glassgold, and Typhoon Lee, "X-Rays and Fluctuating X-Winds from Protostars," *Science* 277 (1997), pages 1475-1479.
40. V. Mannings, D. W. Koerner, and A. I. Sargent, "A Rotating Disk of Gas and Dust Around a Young Counterpart to β Pictoris," *Nature* 388 (1997), pages 555-557.
41. Jack J. Lissauer, "Growing Up in a Two-Parent Family?" *Nature* 386 (1997), pages 18-19.
42. Govert Schilling, "Spying on Solar Systems in the Making," *Science* 280 (1998), pages 523-524.
43. Wayne S. Holland et al., "Submillimeter Images of Dusty Debris Around Nearby Stars," *Nature* 392 (1998), pages 788-791.
44. S. E. Thorsett, "The Times They Are A-Changing," *Nature* 367 (1994), pages 684-685.
45. James Glanz, "Worlds Around Other Stars Shake Planet Birth Theory," *Science* 276 (1997), page 1336.
46. The latest data and research papers on extrasolar planets are available on the website http://wwwusr.obspm.fr/departement/ darc/planets/encycl.html
47. P. Jonathan Patchett, "Scum of the Earth After All," *Nature* 382 (1996), page 758.
48. R. Monastersky, "Speedy Spin Kept Early Earth from Freezing," *Science News* 143 (1993), page 373.
49. W. R. Kuhn, J. C. G. Walker, and H. G. Marshall, "The Effect on Earth's Surface Temperature from Variations in Rotation Rate, Continent Formation, Solar Luminosity, and Carbon Dioxide," *Journal of Geophysical Research* 94 (1989), pages 11, 129-131, 136.
50. Hubert P. Yockey, *Information Theory and Molecular Biology* (Cambridge, UK: Cambridge University Press, 1992), pages 222-223.
51. Richard A. Kerr, "Fiery Io Models Earth's First Days," *Science* 280 (1998), page 382.
52. John M. Hayes, "The Earliest Memories of Life on Earth," *Nature* 384 (1996), page 21.
53. S. J. Mojzsis et al., "Evidence for Life on Earth Before 3,800 Million Years Ago," *Nature* 384 (1996), pages 55-59.

Four: Creation Events: Days One and Two

1. R. Laird Harris, Gleason L. Archer, and Bruce K. Waltke, *Theological Wordbook of the Old Testament*, vol. 2 (Chicago: Moody Press, 1980), page 843.
2. William Gesenius, *Gesenius' Hebrew-Chaldee Lexicon to the Old Testament* (Grand Rapids, MI: Baker, 1979), page 766.
3. S. J. Mojzsis et al., "Evidence for Life on Earth Before 3,800 Million Years Ago," *Nature* 384 (1996), page 56.
4. Mojzsis et al., "Evidence for Life," pages 55-59.
5. John M. Hayes, "The Earliest Memories of Life on Earth," *Nature* 384 (1996), pages 21-22.
6. Charles B. Thaxton, Walter L. Bradley, and Roger L. Olsen, *The Mystery of Life's Origin* (Dallas, TX: Lewis and Stanley, 1984), pages 69-98.

7. Job 36:25–37:23.
8. R. Laird Harris, Gleason L. Archer, and Bruce K. Waltke, *Theological Wordbook of the Old Testament*, vol. 1 (Chicago: Moody Press, 1980), pages 213-214.
9. Neil F. Comins, *What If the Moon Didn't Exist?* (New York: HarperCollins, 1993), pages 53-65.
10. Comins, *Moon Didn't Exist*, pages 4-5, 58.
11. W. R. Kuhn, J. C. G. Walker, and H. G. Marshall, "The Effect on Earth's Surface Temperature from Variations in Rotation Rate, Continent Formation, Solar Luminosity, and Carbon Dioxide," *Journal of Geophysical Research* 94 (1989), pages 11, 129-131, 136.
12. Neil F. Comins, pages 2-8.
13. H. E. Newsom and S. R. Taylor, "Geochemical Implications of the Formation of the Moon by a Single Giant Impact," *Nature* 338 (1989), pages 29-34.
14. Hugh Ross, "Lunar Origin Update," *Facts & Faith*, vol. 9, no. 1 (1995), pages 1-3.
15. Jack J. Lissauer, "It's Not Easy to Make the Moon," *Nature* 389 (1997), pages 327-328.
16. Sigeru Ida, Robin M. Canup, and Glen R. Stewart, "Lunar Accretion from an Impact-Generated Disk," *Nature* 389 (1997), pages 353-357.
17. Louis A. Codispoti, "The Limits to Growth," *Nature* 387 (1997), page 237.
18. Kenneth H. Coale, "A Massive PhytoPlankton Bloom Induced by an Ecosystem-Scale Iron Fertilization Experiment in the Equatorial Pacific Ocean," *Nature* 383 (1996), pages 495-499.
19. P. Jonathan Patchett, "Scum of the Earth After All," *Nature* 382 (1996), page 758.
20. William R. Ward, "Comments on the Long-Term Stability of the Earth's Obliquity," *Icarus* 50 (1982), pages 444-448.
21. Carl D. Murray, "Seasoned Travellers," *Nature* 361 (1993), pages 586-587.
22. Jacques Laskar and P. Robutel, "The Chaotic Obliquity of the Planets," *Nature* 361 (1993), pages 608-612.
23. Jacques Laskar, F. Joutel, and P. Robutel, "Stabilization of the Earth's Obliquity by the Moon," *Nature* 361 (1993), pages 615-617.
24. Hugh Ross, *The Creator and the Cosmos*, 2d. ed. (Colorado Springs, CO: NavPress, 1995), pages 137-144.
25. Hugh Ross, *Big Bang Model Refined by Fire* (Pasadena, CA: Reasons to Believe, 1998), pages 6-14.
26. F. M. Walter and D. C. Barry, "Evolution of Solar Activity," in *The Sun in Time*, eds. C. P. Sonnett, M. S. Giampapa, and M. S. Matthews (Tucson, AZ: University of Arizona, 1991), pages 651-652.
27. James F. Kasting and David H. Grinspoon, "The Faint Young Sun Problem," in *The Sun in Time*, eds. C. P. Sonnett, M. S. Giampapa, and M. S. Matthews (Tucson, AZ: University of Arizona, 1991), pages 447-450.
28. Ken Caldeira and James F. Kasting, "Susceptibility of the Early Earth to Irreversible Glaciation Caused by Carbon Dioxide Clouds," *Nature* 359 (1992), pages 226-228.
29. Guillermo Gonzalez, "Mini-Comets Write New Chapter in Earth-Science," *Facts & Faith*, vol. 11, no. 3 (1997), page 7.

30. Gonzalez, "Mini-Comets Write New Chapter," pages 6-7.
31. David Deming, "Extraterrestrial Accretion and Earth's Climate," *Geology* (1998), in press.
32. R. A. Kerr, "Spots Confirmed, Tiny Comets Spurned," *Science* 276 (1997), pages 1333-1334.
33. The latest data and research papers on minicomets are available on the website http://smallcomets.physics.uiowa.edu/
34. Susan Taylor, James H. Lever, and Ralph P. Harvey, "Accretion Rate of Cosmic Spherules Measured at the South Pole," *Nature* 392 (1998), pages 899-903.
35. Harris, Archer, and Waltke, *Theological Wordbook*, vol. 2, page 862.
36. Harris, Archer, and Waltke, *Theological Wordbook*, vol. 2, page 935.
37. Harris, Archer, and Waltke, *Theological Wordbook*, vol. 2, pages 701-702.
38. William Gesenius, *Gesenius' Hebrew-Chaldee Lexicon to the Old Testament* (Grand Rapids, MI: Baker, 1979), page 657.

Five: Creation Events: Days Three and Four

1. Psalm 33:7.
2. Psalm 104:6.
3. Psalm 104:7-8.
4. Psalm 104:9.
5. R. Laird Harris, Gleason L. Archer, and Bruce K. Waltke, *Theological Wordbook of the Old Testament*, vol. 1 (Chicago: Moody Press, 1980), pages 252-253.
6. R. Laird Harris, Gleason L. Archer, and Bruce K. Waltke, *Theological Wordbook of the Old Testament*, vol. 2 (Chicago: Moody Press, 1980), pages 688-689.
7. Harris, Archer, and Waltke, *Theological Wordbook*, vol. 2, page 734.
8. Brigitte Meyer-Berthaud, Stephen E. Scheckler, and Jobst Wendt, "Archaeopteris is the Earliest Known Modern Tree." *Nature* 398 (1999), pages 700-701.
9. Paul Kenrick, "The Family Tree Flowers," *Nature* 402 (1999), pages 358-359.
10. Yin-Long Qiu, et al., "The Earliest Angiosperms: Evidence from Mitochondrial, Plastid and Nuclear Genomes," *Nature* 402 (1999), pages 404-407.
11. Hubert P. Yockey, "The Soup's *Not* On," *Facts & Faith*, vol. 10, no. 4 (1996), pages 10-11.
12. S. J. Mojzsis et al., "Evidence for Life on Earth Before 3,800 Million Years Ago," *Nature* 384 (1996), pages 55-59.
13. John M. Hayes, "The Earliest Memories of Life on Earth," *Nature 384* (1996), pages 21-22.
14. Verne R. Oberbeck and Guy Fogleman, "Impacts and the Origin of Life," *Nature* 339 (1989), page 434.
15. Christopher Chyba and Carl Sagan, "Endogenous Production, Exogenous Delivery and Impact-Shock Synthesis of Organic Molecules: An Inventory for the Origins of Life," *Nature* 355 (1992), pages 125-132.
16. Robert Shapiro, *Origins: A Skeptic's Guide to the Creation of Life on Earth* (New York: Summit Books, 1986), pages 52-224.
17. Hubert P. Yockey, *Information Theory and Molecular Biology* (Cambridge, U.K.: Cambridge University Press, 1992), pages 231-309.

18. Robert Shapiro, "Prebiotic Ribose Synthesis: A Critical Analysis," *Origin of Life and Evolution of the Biosphere* 18 (1988), pages 71-85.
19. Robert Shapiro, "Protometabolism: A Scenario for the Origin of Life," *The American Scientist* (July-August 1992), page 387.
20. Shapiro, *Origins*, page 128.
21. Michael H. Hart, "Atmospheric Evolution, the Drake Equation, and DNA: Sparse Life in an Infinite Universe," *Physical Cosmology and Philosophy*, ed. John Leslie (New York: Macmillan, 1990), pages 263-264.
22. Shapiro, *Origins*, pages 52-224.
23. Yockey, *Information Theory*, pages 231-309.
24. Charles B. Thaxton, Walter L. Bradley, and Roger L. Olsen, *The Mystery of Life's Origin: Reassessing Current Theories* (New York: Philosophical Library, 1984), pages 73-76.
25. Hugh Ross, "Molecular Mystery Fuels Faith," *Facts & Faith*, vol. 9, no. 2 (1995), pages 3-5.
26. Jon Cohen, "Getting All Turned Around over the Origin of Life on Earth," *Science* 267 (1994), pages 1265-1266.
27. Jeffrey L. Bada, "Origins of Homochirality," *Nature* 374 (1995), pages 594-595.
28. Michael P. Robertson and Stanley L. Miller, "An Efficient Prebiotic Synthesis of Cytosine and Uracil," *Nature* 375 (1995), pages 772-773.
29. Robert Irion, "Ocean Scientists Find Life, Warmth in the Seas," *Science* 279 (1998), page 1303.
30. Paul Parsons, "Dusting Off Panspermia," *Nature* 383 (1996), pages 221-222.
31. Hugh Ross, "New Developments in Martian Meteorite," *Facts & Faith*, vol. 10, no. 4 (1996), page 2.
32. Hugh Ross, *The Creator and the Cosmos*, 2d ed. (Colorado Springs, CO: NavPress, 1995), pages 134-135, 139-140.
33. Ross, *Creator and the Cosmos*, pages 113-115, 118-120, 134-135, 139-141.
34. Ivan G. Dragonic, "Oxygen and Oxidizing Free-Radicals in the Hydrosphere of Early Earth," *9th Meeting of the International Society for the Study of the Origin of Life*, University of California, San Diego, July 11-16, 1999, #cA1.3, Book of Abstracts, page 34.
35. Jared M. Diamond, "Daisy Gives an Evolutionary Answer," *Nature* 380 (1996), pages 103-104.
36. Paul R. and Anne H. Ehrlich, *Extinction: The Causes and Consequences of the Disappearance of Species* (New York: Ballantine, 1981), pages 22-23.
37. Ehrlich, *Extinction*, pages 166-169.
38. Robert M. May, John H. Lawton, and Nigel E. Stork, "Assessing Extinction Rates," in *Extinction Rates*, eds. John H. Lawton and Robert M. May (New York: Oxford University Press, 1995), pages 2-16.
39. D. M. Murphy, et al., "Influence of Sea-Salt on Aerosol Radiative Properties in the Southern Ocean Marine Boundary Layer," *Nature* 392 (1998), pages 62-65.
40. P. Jonathan Patchett, "Scum of the Earth After All," *Nature* 382 (1996), page 758.
41. Henri Blocher, *In the Beginning* (Downers Grove, IL: InterVarsity Press, 1984), pages 45-46, 51-53.

42. John C. Whitcomb, Jr., *The Early Earth* (Grand Rapids, MI: Baker Book House, 1972), pages 47-60.

43. Scott M. Huse, *The Collapse of Evolution, third edition* (Grand Rapids, MI: Baker Book House, 1997), page 77.

44. Douglas F. Kelly, *Creation and Change* (Fearn, Ross-shire, UK: Mentor, 1997), pages 201-204.

45. D. Russell Humphreys, *Starlight and Time* (Colorado Springs, CO: Master Books, 1994), pages 78, 126.

46. Exodus 34:29-35.

47. D. J. Hofmann, "Recovery of Antarctic Ozone Hole," *Nature* 384 (1996), pages 222-223.

48. R. Monastersky, "Ozone Hysteria?" *Science News* 138 (1990), page 307.

49. Constance Holden, "Antarctic Ozone Hole Hits Record Depth," *Science* 254 (1991), page 373.

50. R. Monastersky, "Antarctic Ozone Hole Sinks to a Record Low," *Science News* 140 (1991), pages 244-245.

51. R. Monastersky, "Summer Ozone Loss Detected for the First Time," *Science News* 140 (1991), page 278.

52. Harry Slaper et al., "Estimates of Ozone Depletion and Skin Cancer Incidence to Examine the Vienna Convention Achievements," *Nature* 384 (1996), pages 256-258.

53. Eds., "UV Pours Through the Ozone Hole," *Science News* 140 (1991), page 214.

54. W. L. Chameides, P. S. Kasibhatla, J. Yienger, and H. Levy II, "Growth of Continental Scale Metro-Agro-Plexes, Regional Ozone Pollution and World Food Production," *Science* 264 (1994), pages 74-77.

55. Paul Crutzen and Mark Lawrence, "Ozone Clouds over the Atlantic," *Nature* 388 (1997), page 625.

56. Paul Crutzen, "Mesospheric Mysteries," *Science* 277 (1997), pages 1951-1952.

57. M. E. Summers et al., "Implications of Satellite OH Observations for Middle Atmospheric H_2O and Ozone," *Science* 277 (1997), pages 1967-1970.

58. Crutzen and Lawrence, "Ozone Clouds," page 625.

59. K. Suhre et al., "Ozone-Rich Transients in the Upper Equatorial Atlantic Troposphere," *Nature* 388 (1997), pages 661-663.

Six: Creation Events: Days Five and Six

1. Hugh Ross, *Creation and Time* (Colorado Springs, CO: NavPress, 1994), pages 114-115.

2. R. Laird Harris, Gleason L. Archer, and Bruce K. Waltke, *Theological Wordbook of the Old Testament*, vol. 2 (Chicago: Moody Press, 1980), pages 587-591.

3. J. G. M. Thewissen et al., "Evolution of Cetacean Osmoregulation," *Nature* 381 (1996), pages 379-380.

4. Carl Zimmer, *At the Water's Edge: Macroevolution and the Transformation of Life* (New York: The Free Press, 1998).

5. Michael Behe, David Berlinkski, William F. Buckley, Jr., Philip Johnson, Barry Lynn, Kenneth Miller, Michael Ruse, Eugenie Scott, *Firing Line*, PBS Debate on Creation and Evolution, 19 December 1997.

6. Annalisa Berta, "What Is a Whale?" *Science* 263 (1994), pages 180-181.
7. J. G. M. Thewissen, S. I. Madar, and S. T. Hussain, "Whale Ankles and Evolutionary Relationships," *Nature* 395 (1998), page 452.
8. Daniel 5:9-11,18-22.
9. Luke 3:35-36.
10. Bernard Wood, "The Oldest Hominid Yet," *Nature* 371 (1994), pages 280-281.
11. Bruce Bower, "Retooled Ancestor," *Science News* 133 (1988), pages 344-345.
12. Bruce Bower, "Early Human Skeleton Apes Its Ancestors," *Science News* 131 (1987), page 340.
13. Bruce Bower, "Family Feud: Enter the 'Black Skull,'" *Science News* 131 (1987), pages 58-59.
14. C. Simon, "Stone-Age Sanctuary, Oldest Known Shrine, Discovered in Spain," *Science News* 120 (1981), page 357.
15. Bruce Bower, "When the Human Spirit Soared," *Science News* 130 (1986), pages 378-379.
16. J. S. Jones and S. Rouhani, "Human Evolution: How Small Was the Bottleneck?" *Nature* 319 (1986), pages 449-450.
17. Bower, "Retooled Ancestor," pages 344-345.
18. Jean-Jacques Hublin et al., "A Late Neanderthal Associated with Upper Paleolithic Artifacts," *Nature* 381 (1996), pages 224-226.
19. Jeffrey H. Schwartz and Ian Tattersall, "Significance of Some Previously Unrecognized Apomorphies in the Nasal Region of *Homo neanderthalensis*," *Proceedings of the National Academy of Sciences USA,* vol. 93 (1996), pages 10852-10854.
20. Ryk Ward and Chris Stringer, "A Molecular Handle on the Neanderthals," *Nature* 388 (1997), pages 225-226.
21. Hugh Ross, *Beyond the Cosmos* (Colorado Springs, CO: NavPress, 1996), pages 181-184, 186-187, 196-198.
22. Ross, *Beyond the Cosmos*, pages 196-200.
23. Hugh Ross, *The Creator and the Cosmos,* 2d ed. (Colorado Springs, CO: NavPress, 1995), pages 132-144.
24. Hugh Ross, *Big Bang Model Refined by Fire* (Pasadena, CA: Reasons to Believe, 1998), pages 7-14.
25. Ross, *Creator and the Cosmos,* pages 105-156.

Seven: The Source Controversy
1. Allen P. Ross, *Creation and Blessing: A Guide to the Study and Exposition of Genesis* (Grand Rapids, MI: Baker Book House, 1988), pages 24-35.
2. Ronald Youngblood, *How It All Began* (Ventura, CA: Regal, 1980), pages 13-15.
3. Josh McDowell, *More Evidence That Demands a Verdict* (San Bernardino, CA: Campus Crusade for Christ, 1975), pages 91-116.
4. Ellen Van Wolde, *Stories of the Beginning: Genesis 1–11 and Other Creation Stories,* translated by John Bowden (Ridgefield, CT: Morehouse Publishing, 1996), pages 188-194.
5. Don J. Wiseman, "Babylonia," *International Standard Bible Encyclopedia, revised,* edited by G. W. Bromiley, vol. 1 (A-D) (Grand Rapids, MI: Eerdmans, 1979), page 398.

6. Edith Hamilton, *Mythology* (New York: Mentor, 1969), page 312.
7. Marie-Louise Franz, *Patterns of Creativity Mirrored in Creation Myths* (Zurich: Spring 1972), page 6.
8. Albert R. Kilzhaber, *Myths, Fables, and Folktales* (New York: Holt, 1974), pages 113-114.
9. Cunningham Geikie, pages 26-32.
10. Alexander Heidel, *The Babylonian Genesis* (Chicago: University of Chicago Press, 1951), pages 1-140.
11. Howard F. Vos, *Genesis and Archeology* (Chicago: Moody, 1963), chapters 2–4.
12. Exodus 19:3-25; 24:9-18; 32:1; 33:11; 34:28.
13. Hugh Ross, *The Fingerprint of God,* 2d ed. (Orange, CA: Promise Publishing, 1991), pages 107-118.
14. Hugh Ross, *Beyond the Cosmos* (Colorado Springs, CO: NavPress, 1996), pages 24-32.
15. Hebrews 11:3.
16. Heidel, *Babylonian Genesis,* pages 1-140.

Eight: Rest: Day Seven

1. Exodus 20:8-10; Deuteronomy 5:12-15.
2. Leviticus 25:1-7.
3. Revelation 21:1–22:5. See also Hugh Ross, *Beyond the Cosmos,* pages 217-232.
4. Paul R. and Anne H. Ehrlich, *Extinction: The Causes and Consequences of the Disappearance of Species* (New York: Ballantine, 1981), pages 19-38, 123-247.
5. Robert M. May, John H. Lawton, and Nigel E. Stork, "Assessing Extinction Rates," in *Extinction Rates,* eds. John H. Lawton and Robert M. May (New York: Oxford University Press, 1995), pages 10-21.
6. Paul R. Ehrlich, "The Scale of the Human Enterprise and Biodiversity Loss," pages 214-224.
7. David W. Steadman, "Human-Caused Extinction of Birds," in *Biodiversity II: Understanding and Protecting Our Biological Resources,* eds. Marjorie L. Reaka-Kudla, Don E. Wilson, and Edward O. Wilson (Washington, DC: Joseph Henry Press, 1997), pages 139-158.
8. Ehrlich, *Extinction,* page 23.
9. Jared M. Diamond, "Daisy Gives an Evolutionary Answer," *Nature* 380 (1996), pages 103-104.
10. Ehrlich, *Extinction,* page 23.
11. R. Laird Harris, Gleason L. Archer, and Bruce K. Waltke, *Theological Wordbook of the Old Testament,* vol. 1 (Chicago: Moody, 1980), pages 370-371.
12. William Wilson, *Old Testament Word Studies* (Grand Rapids, MI: Kregel Publications, 1978), page 109.
13. Hugh Ross, *Creation and Time* (Colorado Springs, CO: NavPress, 1994), pages 46-47.
14. Harris, Archer, and Waltke, *Theological Wordbook,* vol. 1, pages 370-371, vol. 2, pages 672-673.
15. Samuel P. Tregelles, *Gesenius' Hebrew-Chaldee Lexicon to the Old Testament* (Grand Rapids, MI: Baker, 1979), pages 612-613.
16. Ross, *Creation and Time,* pages 25-27, 48.

17. Ross, *Creation and Time*, pages 27-28, 91-118.
18. Ross, *Creation and Time*, pages 17-23.

Nine: A Spiritual Perspective on Creation—Genesis 2
1. R. Laird Harris, Gleason L. Archer, and Bruce K. Waltke, *Theological Wordbook of the Old Testament*, vol. 1 (Chicago: Moody, 1980), pages 500-501.
2. Harris, Archer, and Waltke, *Theological Wordbook*, vol. 1, page 17.
3. Harris, Archer, and Waltke, *Theological Wordbook*, vol. 1, pages 92-93, 281.
4. R. Laird Harris, Gleason L. Archer, and Bruce K. Waltke, *Theological Wordbook of the Old Testament*, vol. 2 (Chicago: Moody, 1980), page 655.
5. Robert M. May, John H. Lawton, and Nigel E. Stork, "Assessing Extinction Rates," in *Extinction Rates*, eds. John H. Lawton and Robert M. May (New York: Oxford University Press, 1995), page 11.
6. Gary K. Meffe, C. Ronald Carroll, and Contributors, *Principles of Conservation Biology*, 2d ed. (Sunderland, MA: Sinauer Associates, 1997), pages 90-112, 131-139.
7. Henry M. Morris, "Adam and the Animals," *Impact*, No. 212 (February 1991), page ii.
8. Ken Ham, "Revelation: Key to the Past," *Back to Genesis*, No. 39, March 1992, page b.
9. William J. Spear, Jr., "Could Adam Really Name All Those Animals?" *Impact*, No. 265 (July 1995), pages i-iv.
10. Henry M. Morris, *Biblical Creationism* (Grand Rapids, MI: Baker, 1993), page 25.
11. Hugh Ross, *Creation and Time* (Colorado Springs, CO: NavPress, 1994), page 51.
12. 1 Corinthians 11:11-12.
13. Harris, Archer, and Waltke, *Theological Wordbook*, vol. 2, pages 660-661.
14. Doug Phillips, "An Urgent Appeal to Pastors," *Back to Genesis*, no. 119, November 1998, page c.
15. Henry M. Morris, "The Wolf and the Lamb," *Back to Genesis*, no. 69, September 1994, pages a-c.
16. John C. Whitcomb, Jr., *The Early Earth* (Grand Rapids, MI: Baker Book House, 1972), pages 65, 116, 131.
17. John D. Morris, "Evolution and the Wages of Sin," *Impact*, no. 209, November 1990, pages ii-iii.
18. Genesis 2:8.
19. Genesis 2:10.
20. Genesis 2:11-14.
21. Genesis 2:9, 3:22.
22. Hugh Ross, *Beyond the Cosmos* (Colorado Springs, CO: NavPress, 1996), pages 176-184.
23. Revelation 21:1-22:5.
24. Hugh Ross, *Beyond the Cosmos*, pages 195-205.

Ten: Modern Criticism Arises

1. D. C. Simpson, *Pentateuchal Criticism* (London: Oxford University Press, Humphrey Milford, 1924), pages 23-24.
2. William Henry Green, *The Higher Criticism of the Pentateuch* (New York: Charles Scribner's Sons, 1895), page 61.
3. Howard Osgood, "Jean Astruc," *Presbyterian and Reformed Review,* 3 (1892), pages 97-101.
4. Osgood, "Jean Astruc," page 87.
5. Jean Astruc, *Conjectures sur les mémoirs originaux dont il parait que Moise s'est servi pour composer la Genèse, avec des remarques qui appuient ou éclaircissens ces conjectures* (Bruxelles, Fricx, 1753), pages 378, 439.
6. Eamonn O'Doherty. "The Conjectures of Jean Astruc, 1753," *Catholic Biblical Quarterly,* 15 (1953), pages 300-304.
7. Johann Gottfried Eichhorn, *Einleitung in das Alte Testament,* vols. 1–5. (Göttingen, Netherlands: C. E. Rosenbusch, 1823-24). Most of the relevant material is in the first volume.
8. S. R. Driver, *The Book of Genesis,* 3d ed. (London: Methuen and Co., 1904), pages 3-43.
9. George A. Buttrick, Walter R. Bowie, Paul Scherer, John Knox, Samuel Terrien, and Nolan B. Harmon, eds., *The Interpreter's Bible,* vol. 1 (New York: Abingdon Press, 1952), pages 462-500.
10. L. Berkhof, *Systematic Theology,* 4th ed. (Grand Rapids, MI: Eerdmans, 1941), pages 150-160.
11. David N. Livingstone, *Darwin's Forgotten Defenders* (Grand Rapids, MI: Eerdmans, 1987), pages 57-145.
12. Gleason L. Archer, *A Survey of Old Testament Introduction* (Chicago: Moody, 1974).
13. Walter C. Kaiser, Jr., "The Literary Form of Genesis 1–11," in *New Perspectives on the Old Testament* (Waco, TX: Word, 1970).
14. Josh McDowell, *More Evidence That Demands a Verdict* (San Bernardino, CA: Campus Crusade for Christ, 1975).

Eleven: Genesis and "Creation Science"

1. George McCready Price, *The New Geology* (Mountain View, CA: Pacific Press, 1923).
2. Ronald L. Numbers, *The Creationists: The Evolution of Scientific Creationism* (New York: Alfred A. Knopf, 1992), page 90.
3. Numbers, *Creationists,* page 87.
4. Numbers, *Creationists,* page 111.
5. Numbers, *Creationists,* page 75.
6. Bernard Ramm, *The Christian View of Science and Scripture* (Grand Rapids, MI: Eerdmans, 1955).
7. Ramm, *Christian View,* page 180.
8. Ramm, *Christian View,* page 9. The phrase "narrow bibliolatry" appeared only in the paperback edition. In the cloth editions, page 9, Ramm used the phrase "narrow evangelical Biblicism."
9. Ramm, *Christian View,* pages 115-117, 271-280.

10. Ramm, *Christian View,* pages 220-222.
11. Ramm, *Christian View,* pages 308-328.
12. Ramm, *Christian View,* pages 220-221.
13. Ramm, *Christian View,* pages 221-222.
14. Numbers, *Creationists,* pages 187-189, 196-197.
15. John C. Whitcomb, Jr., and Henry M. Morris, *The Genesis Flood* (Philadelphia: Presbyterian and Reformed Publishing, 1961).
16. Ronald L. Numbers, "Creating Creationism: Meanings and Usage Since the Age of Agassiz—Part Three," *Facts & Faith,* vol. 10, no. 2 (1996), page 13.
17 James S. Stambaugh, "Death Before Sin," *Impact,* No. 191 (May 1989), pages i-iv.
18. John C. Whitcomb, Jr. and Henry M. Morris, *The Genesis Flood* (Phillipsburg, NJ: Presbyterian and Reformed Publishing, 1961), pages 461-466.
19. John D. Morris, "If All Animals Were Created As Plant Eaters, Why Do Some Have Sharp Teeth?" *Back to Genesis,* No. 100, April 1997, page d.
20. John C. Whitcomb, Jr. and Henry M. Morris, *The Genesis Flood* (Grand Rapids, MI: Baker, 1961), pages 66-69.
21. Paul R. and Anne H. Ehrlich, *Extinction: The Causes and Consequences of the Disappearance of Species* (New York: Ballantine, 1981), page 33.
22. Gary K. Meffe, C. Ronald Carroll, and Contributors, *Principles of Conservation Biology,* 2d ed. (Sunderland, MA: Sinauer Associates, 1997), pages 91-93.
23. Whitcomb and Morris, *Genesis Flood,* pages 66-69 (in particular, Figure 4 on page 67 shows, for example, zebras and horses evolving from a single horselike pair on board Noah's ark) and pages 80-87.
24. Henry M. Morris and John D. Morris, *Science, Scripture, and the Young Earth* (El Cajon, CA: Institute for Creation Research, 1989), page 67.
25. Ken Ham, "What Is a Creationist?" *Back to Genesis* 30 (June 1991), page b.
26. Hugh Ross, *Creation and Time* (Colorado Springs, CO: NavPress, 1994), pages 81-125.

Twelve: How Far the Fall—Genesis 3

1. Job 38:4-7.
2. Revelation 1:20; 12:3-4.
3. Revelation 21:1–22:5.
4. 1 Corinthians 2:9.
5. Revelation 20:11-15; 21:8,27; 22:3-5,11-17.
6. Romans 12:1-2; Hebrews 12:1-28.
7. Genesis 2:17.
8. Numbers 22:21-33.
9. Genesis 3:22-24; Romans 5:12–6:14.
10. Mark W. Zemansky, *Heat and Thermodynamics* (New York: McGraw-Hill, 1957), pages 42-60, 157-194.
11. Romans 8:20-22.
12. J. H. Taylor et al., "Experimental Constraints on Strong-Field Relativistic Gravity," *Nature* 355 (1992), pages 132-136.
13. Roger Penrose, *Shadows of the Mind* (New York: Oxford University Press, 1994), pages 229-231.

14. Roger Penrose, "An Analysis of the Structure of Space-Time," *Adam Prize Essay*, Cambridge University (1966).
15. Stephen W. Hawking, "Singularities and the Geometry of Space-Time," *Adam Prize Essay*, Cambridge University (1966).
16. Stephen W. Hawking and George F. R. Ellis, "The Cosmic Black-Body Radiation and the Existence of Singularities in Our Universe," *Astrophysical Journal* 152 (1968), pages 25-36.
17. Stephen W. Hawking and Roger Penrose, "The Singularities of Gravitational Collapse and Cosmology," *Proceedings of the Royal Society of London*, series A, 314 (1970), pages 529-548.
18. Hugh Ross, *Beyond the Cosmos* (Colorado Springs, CO: NavPress, 1996), pages 21-23.
19. Hugh Ross, *Big Bang Model Refined by Fire* (Pasadena, CA: Reasons to Believe, 1998), pages 7-9.
20. Hugh Ross, *The Fingerprint of God*, 2d ed. (Orange, CA: Promise Publishing, 1991), page 124.
21. Revelation 21:1–22:5.
22. Ross, *Beyond the Cosmos*, pages 195-205.
23. Ross, *Beyond the Cosmos*, pages 175-184.
24. John 16:8-11.
25. Hebrews 9:27.
26. Exodus 10:12-17; Job 14:8-10; Psalm 37:2; Matthew 6:28,30; John 15:6.
27. Hugh Ross, *Scriptural Evidences for Plants and Primitive Animals Experiencing Life and Death* (Pasadena, CA: Reasons to Believe, 1996).
28. John M. Hayes, "The Earliest Memories of Life on Earth," *Nature* 384 (1996), page 21.
29. S. J. Mojzsis et al., "Evidence for Life on Earth Before 3,800 Million Years Ago," *Nature* 384 (1996), pages 55-59.
30. Hugh Ross, *Creation and Time* (Colorado Springs, CO: NavPress, 1994), pages 53-55.

Thirteen: Cain's Wife and City—Genesis 4

1. Genesis 4:16.
2. Genesis 4:25.
3. William Whiston, translator, *The Works of Josephus, new updated edition*, Antiquities, Book I, Chapter 2, ¶ 2, subsection 66 (Peabody, MA: Hendrickson Publications, 1987), page 31.
4. Genesis 20:2-16.
5. Thomas Virgil Peterson, *Ham & Japheth: The Mythic World of Whites in the Antebellum South*, American Theological Library Association Monograph 12 (Metuchen, NJ: Scarecrow/American Theological Library Association, 1978).

Fourteen: Dating the Origin of Humanity—Genesis 5

1. James Ussher, Archbishop of Armagh, *Annalis Veteris Testamenti* (Londini: J. Flesher, 1650–1654). For the same book in English, see James Ussher, Archbishop of Armagh, *The Annals of the World* (London: E. Tyler for J. Crook and G. Bedell, 1658).

2. E. T. Brewater, *Creation: A History of Non-Evolutionary Theories* (1927), page 109. Quoted in Bernard Ramm, *The Christian View of Science and Scripture* (Grand Rapids, MI: Eerdmans, 1955), page 174.

3. Paul Johnson, *A History of Christianity* (New York: Atheneum, 1976), page 413.

4. R. Laird Harris, Gleason L. Archer, and Bruce K. Waltke, *Theological Wordbook of the Old Testament*, vol. 1 (Chicago: Moody, 1980), pages 5-6, 113-114.

5. Bruce Bower, "Retooled Ancestor," *Science News* 133 (1988), pages 344-345.

6. Bruce Bower, "Early Human Skeleton Apes Its Ancestors," *Science News* 131 (1987), page 340.

7. Bruce Bower, "Family Feud: Enter the 'Black Skull,'" *Science News* 131 (1987), pages 58-59.

8. C. Simon, "Stone-Age Sanctuary, Oldest Known Shrine, Discovered in Spain," *Science News* 120 (1981), page 357.

9. Bruce Bower, "When the Human Spirit Soared," *Science News* 130 (1986), pages 378-379.

10. Bruce Bower, "Visions on the Rocks," *Science News* 150 (1996), pages 216-217.

11. Antti Sajantila et al., "Paternal and Maternal DNA Lineages Reveal a Bottleneck in the Founding of the Finnish Population," *Proceedings of the National Academy of Sciences USA*, vol. 93 (1996), pages 12035-12039.

12. John Travis, "Jomon Genes: Using DNA, Researchers Probe the Genetic Origins of Modern Japanese," *Science News* 151 (1997), pages 106-107.

13. Karl Skorecki et al., "Y Chromosomes of Jewish Priests," *Nature* 385 (1997), page 32.

14. Travis, "Jomon Genes," pages 106-107.

15. Sajantila et al., "Paternal and Maternal DNA Lineages," pages 12035-12039.

16. Michael F. Hammer, "A Recent Common Ancestry for Human Y Chromosomes," *Nature* 378 (1995), pages 376-378.

17. Simon I. Whitfield, John E. Sulston, and Peter N. Goodfellow, "Sequence Variation of the Human Y Chromosome," *Nature* 378 (1995), pages 379-380.

18. John D. Morris, "Is Neanderthal in Our Family Tree?" *Back to Genesis*, No. 105 (September 1997), page d.

19. Eds., "An Unusual 'Case for Creation' Seminar," *Acts & Facts*, vol. 24, no. 7 (July 1995), pages 1-2.

20. Hugh Ross, "The Meaning of Art and Music," *Facts & Faith*, vol. 10, no. 4 (1996), pages 6, 11.

21. Bruce Bower, "Neandertal Tot Enters Human-Origins Debate," *Science News* 145 (1994), page 5.

22. Hugh Ross, "Neandertal Tot Discovery," *Facts & Faith*, vol. 8, no. 1 (1994), page 4.

23. Jeffrey H. Schwartz and Ian Tattersall, "Significance of Some Previously Unrecognized Apomorphies in the Nasal Region of Homo neanderthalensis," *Proceedings of the National Academy of Sciences USA*, vol. 93 (1996), pages 10852-10854.

24. Jeffrey T. Laitman et al., "What the Nose Knows: New Understandings of Neanderthal Upper Respiratory Tract Specializations," *Proceedings of the National Academy of Sciences USA*, vol. 93 (1996), pages 10543-10545.

25. Patricia Kahn and Ann Gibbons, "DNA from an Extinct Human," *Science* 277 (1997), pages 176-178.
26. Kahn and Gibbons, "DNA from an Extinct Human," page 176.
27. Kahn and Gibbons, "DNA from an Extinct Human," page 177.
28. Matthias Krings, et al., "Neandertal DNA Sequences and the Origin of Modern Humans," *Cell* 90 (1997), pages 19-30.
29. Matthias Krings, et al., "DNA Sequence of the Mitochondrial Hypervariable Region II from the Neandertal Type Specimen," *Proceedings of the National Academy of Sciences USA,* vol. 96 (2000), pages 5581-5585.
30. Matthias Krings, et al., page 5584.
31. Matthias Höss, "Neanderthal Population Genetics," *Nature* 404 (2000), pages 453-454.
32. Igor V. Ovchinnikov, et al., "Molecular Analysis of Neanderthal DNA from the Northern Caucasus," *Nature* 404 (2000), pages 490-493.
33. Matthias Krings, et al., "A View of Neandertal Genetic Diversity," *Nature Genetics* 26 (2000), pages 144-146.
34. Matthias Krings, et al., page 145.
35. Matthias Krings, et al., pages 144-146.

Fifteen: The Possibility of Long Life Spans—Genesis 5–6

1. Genesis 4:19-22.
2. Judith Campisi, "Aging, Chromatin, and Food Restriction—Connecting the Dots," *Science* 289 (2000), pages 2062-2063.
3. Su-ju Lin, Pierre-Antoine Defossez, and Leonard Guarente, "Requirement of NAD and SIR2 for Life-Span Extension by Calorie Restriction in Saccharomyces cerevisiae," *Science* 289 (2000), pages 2126-2128.
4. Simon Melov, et al., "Extension of Life-Span with Superoxide Dismutase/Catalase Mimetics," *Science* 289 (2000), pages 1567-1569.
5. A. Erlykin and A. Wolfendale, "High Energy Cosmic Ray Spectroscopy: I. Status and Prospects," *Astroparticle Physics* 7 (1997), pages 1-13.
6. Peter L. Biermann, "Not-So-Cosmic Rays," *Nature* 388 (1997), page 25.
7. Robert G. Brakenridge, "Terrestrial Paleoenvironmental Effects of a Late Quaternary-Age Supernova," *Icarus* 46 (1981), pages 81-93.
8. B. Aschenback, R. Egger, and J. Trümper, "Discovery of Explosion Fragments Outside the Vela Supernova Remnant Shock-Wave Boundary," *Nature* 373 (1995), page 588.
9. A. G. Lyne, R. S. Pritchard, F. Graham-Smith, and F. Camilo, "Very Low Braking Index for the Vela Pulsar," *Nature* 381 (1996), pages 497-498.
10. Douglas Hanahan, "Benefits of Bad Telomerase," *Nature* 406 (2000), pages 573-574.
11. Steven E. Artandi, et al., "Telomere Dysfunction Promotes Non-Reciprocal Translocations and Epithelial Cancers in Mice," *Nature* 406 (2000), pages 641-645.
12. Elizabeth H. Blackburn, "Telomere States and Cell Fates," *Nature* 408 (2000), pages 53-56.
13. Su-ju Lin, Pierre-Antoine Defossez, and Leonard Guarente, pages 2126-2128.

14. Simon Melov, et al., "Extension . . . " pages 1567-1569.
15. Genesis 9:29; 11:10-25.

Sixteen: Sons of God and the Nephilim—Genesis 6
1. Genesis 6:4.
2. Numbers 13:28,33; Deuteronomy 2:10-11; 3:11; 2 Samuel 21:16-22.
3. Gleason L. Archer, *Encyclopedia of Bible Difficulties* (Grand Rapids, MI: Zondervan, 1982), pages 79-80.
4. J. Sidlow Baxter, "Who Were Those 'Sons of God?'" *Studies in Problem Texts* (Grand Rapids, MI: Zondervan, 1960), pages 147-192.
5. James Boice, "The Gathering Storm: Genesis 6:1-22," *Bible Studies,* vol. 12, no. 10 (1980), pages 4-12.
6. Ellen Van Wolde, *Stories of the Beginning: Genesis 1-11 and Other Creation Stories,* trans. John Bowden (Ridgefield, CT: Morehouse Publishing, 1996), pages 112-116.
7. Ezra 9:1-10:44; 2 Corinthians 6:14-18.
8. 1 Samuel 17:4-7; 21:9; 1 Chronicles 20:5.
9. Deuteronomy 3:11.
10. James Orr, gen. ed., *The International Standard Bible Encyclopedia,* vol. 2 (Grand Rapids, MI: Eerdmans, 1956), page 765.
11. Ezekiel 40:5.
12. 1 Samuel 17:4-16,25,33; 2 Samuel 21:16,18-22.
13. 2 Samuel 21:20.
14. Norris McWhirter and Ross McWhirter, *Guinness Book of World Records, 1975* (New York: Sterling Publishing, 1975), page 13.
15. 1 Samuel 9:2.
16. J. D. Douglas, organizing ed., *The New Bible Dictionary* (Grand Rapids, MI: Eerdmans, 1962), page 1206.
17. Deuteronomy 14:1.
18. Deuteronomy 32:5.
19. Matthew 22:30.
20. Revelation 21:2-7; 22:2-5.
21. Some of the best documentation comes from the nonprofit organization Spiritual Counterfeits Projects (P.O. Box 4308, Berkeley, CA 94704, phone: 510/540-0300), which makes available for the public scholarly articles, journals, and papers on occult practices and organizations.
22. J. Sidlow Baxter, "Who Were Those 'Sons of God?'" page 152.
23. Genesis 18:1-8,16; 19:1-22; Joshua 5:13-15; 1 Kings 19:5-8; Daniel 9:21-23; 10:4-21; Luke 1:11-20; Luke 24:4-8; Acts 1:10-11; 10:2-8; 12:4-11; 27:23; Hebrews 13:2; Revelation 21:9–22:11.
24. Genesis 18:2-8; 19:3-8; Joshua 5:13-15; Daniel 3:25; 9:21-23; Luke 24:4-8; Acts 1:10-11; Hebrews 13:2.
25. Genesis 19:4-11.
26. Matthew 8:28-33; Mark 1:23-26.
27. Genesis 6:5,12.

Seventeen: The Boundaries of God's Wrath—Genesis 6

1. Matthew 5:18-20; James 2:10.
2. Romans 3:23.
3. Romans 5:12-14.
4. Job 4:8; Proverbs 5:22; 11:5; Isaiah 57:20-21; Jeremiah 5:25; Romans 7:5; Galatians 5:19-21; 6:7-8.
5. Genesis 18:20-21; 19:13; Exodus 20:4-6; Joshua 6:22–7:26; 1 Corinthian 6:12-20.
6. 1 Corinthians 6:12-20.
7. Genesis 19:4-5.
8. 2 Corinthians 1:21-22; 5:5; Ephesians 1:13-14.
9. Matthew 5:13.
10. 2 Peter 2:14,18-19.
11. 2 Timothy 2:26; 3:2-8.
12. Romans 1:32; 2 Peter 2:18-19.
13. R. Laird Harris, Gleason L. Archer, and Bruce K. Waltke, *Theological Wordbook of the Old Testament*, vol. 2 (Chicago: Moody, 1980), pages 917-918.
14. William Gesenius, *Gesenius' Hebrew-Chaldee Lexicon to the Old Testament* (Grand Rapids, MI: Baker, 1979), pages 815-816.
15. R. Laird Harris, Gleason L. Archer, and Bruce K. Waltke, *Theological Wordbook of the Old Testament*, vol. 1 (Chicago: Moody, 1980), page 297.
16. Gesenius, *Hebrew-Chaldee Lexicon*, page 288.
17. Luke 17:26-37; 2 Timothy 3:1-8.
18. Exodus 21:28-29; Leviticus 20:15-16.
19. Genesis 15:13-16; 18:16-33.
20. 1 Thessalonians 1:10; 5:9; 2 Peter 2:9; Revelation 3:10.
21. Genesis 15:13-16.

Eighteen: The Flood: Global or Local?—Genesis 7–8

1. Romans 1:8; Colossians 1:6.
2. 2 Peter 3:6.
3. Joseph H. Thayer, *Thayer's Greek-English Lexicon of the New Testament* (Grand Rapids, MI: Baker, 1977), pages 365-366.
4. Genesis 11:1-4.
5 R. Laird Harris, Gleason L. Archer, and Bruce K. Waltke, *Theological Wordbook of the Old Testament*, vol. 1 (Chicago: Moody, 1980), pages 448-449.
6. William Gesenius, *Gesenius' Hebrew-Chaldee Lexicon to the Old Testament* (Grand Rapids, MI: Baker, 1979), page 407.
7. Harris, Archer, and Waltke, *Theological Wordbook*, vol. 1, pages 224-225.
8. Harris, Archer, and Waltke, *Theological Wordbook*, vol. 1, page 146.
9. Gesenius, *Hebrew-Chaldee Lexicon*, page 153.
10. Gesenius, *Hebrew-Chaldee Lexicon*, pages 295, 733, 807-809, 821.
11. Harris, Archer, and Waltke, *Theological Wordbook*, vol. 1, page 309.
12. R. Laird Harris, Gleason L. Archer, and Bruce K. Waltke, *Theological Wordbook of the Old Testament*, vol. 2 (Chicago: Moody, 1980), pages 800, 909, 923.
13. K. E. Bullen, *An Introduction to the Theory of Seismology* (Cambridge, UK: Cambridge University Press, 1963), pages 259-262.

14. Hiroo Kanamori, "Shaking Without Quaking," *Science* 279 (1998), pages 2063-2064.
15. John C. Whitcomb, Jr. and Henry M. Morris, *The Genesis Flood* (Grand Rapids, MI: Baker, 1961), pages 66-69 (in particular Figure 4 on page 67 shows zebras and horses evolving from a single horselike pair on board Noah's ark).
16. Don Batten, "Ligers and Wholphins? What Next?" *Creation Ex Nihilo*, v. 22, n. 3 (2000), pages 23-33.
17. Paul R. and Anne H. Ehrlich, *Extinction: The Causes and Consequences of the Disappearance of Species* (New York: Ballantine, 1981), page 23.
18. Gerhard Schönknecht and Siegfried Scherer, "Too Much Coal for a Young Earth?" *Creation Ex Niholo Technical Journal*, 11 (1997), page 279. This article was written by two scientists who are proponents of both a young earth and a global Flood. While claiming to solve the problem of too much coal (by appealing to impossibly high conversion rates of solar energy to coal), the authors admit no solution exists when all the fossil fuel deposits (coal, oil, gas, peat, and kerogen) are considered. Of course, their problems are exacerbated when one adds the remainder of biodeposits, namely top soil, limestone, marble, coral reefs, etc., to the fossil fuel deposits.
19. Hubert P. Yockey, "The Soup's Not On," *Facts & Faith*, vol. 10, no. 4 (1996), pages 10-11.
20. Hugh Ross, "New Evidence of Old Life," *Facts & Faith*, vol. 11, no. 1 (1997), pages 3-4.
21. S. J. Mojzsis et al., "Evidence for Life on Earth Before 3,800 Million Years Ago," *Nature* 384 (1996), pages 55-59.
22. Gerhard Schönknecht and Siegfried Scherer, page 281.
23. Harris, Archer, and Waltke, *Theological Wordbook*, vol. 1, page 453.
24. Roger Osborne and Donald Tarling, gen. eds., *The Historical Atlas of the Earth* (New York: Henry Holt, 1996), pages 130-131.
25. Genesis 7:19-20, 24.
26. T. C. Mitchell, "Geology and the Flood," in *New Bible Dictionary*, 2d ed., eds. J. D. Douglas, et al. (Wheaton, IL: Tyndale, 1982), pages 382-383.

Nineteen: The Ark and Its Passengers—Genesis 6–9

1. Robert A. Moore, "The Impossible Voyage of Noah's Ark," *Creation/Evolution*, Issue XI (1983), pages 3-36.
2. Moore, "Impossible Voyage," pages 29-31.
3. Moore, "Impossible Voyage," pages 1-5.
4. R. G. Elmendorf et al., "The Voyage of Noah's Ark—An Epilogue," *Creation/Evolution*, Issue XIII (1984), pages 39-48.
5. Genesis 19:12-29.
6. 2 Peter 2:5.
7. Hebrews 11:7.
8. 1 Peter 3:20.
9. Genesis 19:1,6-9.
10. R. Laird Harris, Gleason L. Archer, and Bruce K. Waltke, *Theological Wordbook of the Old Testament*, vol. 1 (Chicago: Moody, 1980), pages 135-136.

11. Harris, Archer, and Waltke, *Theological Wordbook,* vol. 1, pages 92-93.
12. Harris, Archer, and Waltke, *Theological Wordbook,* vol. 1, page 281.
13. R. Laird Harris, Gleason L. Archer, and Bruce K. Waltke, *Theological Wordbook of the Old Testament,* vol. 2 (Chicago: Moody, 1980), pages 587-591.
14. Harris, Archer, and Waltke, *Theological Wordbook,* vol. 2, pages 654-655.
15. Harris, Archer, and Waltke, *Theological Wordbook,* vol. 2, pages 850-851.
16. Harris, Archer, and Waltke, *Theological Wordbook,* vol. 2, page 775.
17. Harris, Archer, and Waltke, *Theological Wordbook,* vol. 2, pages 956-957.
18. Harris, Archer, and Waltke, *Theological Wordbook,* vol. 2, page 793.
19. Genesis 6:21.
20. Genesis 6:16.
21. Richard A. Fox, "'The Incredible Discovery of Noah's Ark: An Archaeological Quest?" *Free Inquiry,* vol. 13, no. 3 (1993), pages 43-48.
22. Gerald A. Larue, "More on 'The Incredible Discovery of Noah's Ark,'" *Free Inquiry,* vol. 13, no. 4 (1993), pages 10-13, 61-63.
23. John Cole, "Noah's Ark on CBS," *National Center for Science Education Reports,* vol. 13, no. 1 (1993), pages 4, 6.
24. Bret A. Corum, "Dan Quayle on Noah's Ark?" *National Center for Science Education Reports,* vol. 13, no. 3 (1993), page 6.
25. Paul Kurtz, "Exploring the Television Wasteland," *Skeptical Inquirer,* vol. 17, no. 4 (1993), page 354.
26. Alexander Heidel, *The Babylonian Genesis* (Chicago: University of Chicago Press, 1951), pages 1-140.
27. Cunningham Geikie, *Hours with the Bible, vol. 1* (New York: James Pott, 1905), pages 174-181.
28. Ellen van Wolde, *Stories of the Beginning: Genesis 1–11 and Other Creation Stories,* translated by John Bowden (Ridgefield, CT: Morehouse Publishing, 1996), pages 116-118.

Twenty: The Origin of Nations and Races—Genesis 9–11

1. Hana Unlauf Lane, ed., *The World Almanac & Book of Facts 1982* (New York: Newspaper Enterprise Association, 1981), pages 737, 740.
2. Carroll Quigley, *The World Since 1939: A History* (New York: Collier, 1968), page 167.
3. Pete du Pont, "When Nations Snuff Out Their Own Citizens," *Insight,* October 27, 1997, page 30.
4. Isaiah 57:20-21.
5. Isaiah 59:6-8.
6. Daniel 2:28-45; 7:2-18; 8:2-22; 10:13,20; 11:2-35.
7. Luke 12:51.
8. Luke 2:14.
9. John 14:27.
10. Genesis 10:8-12.
11. Genesis 11:1-6.
12. Genesis 11:4.
13. Genesis 1:28; 9:1.
14. Genesis 11:6.

15. Genesis 11:7,9.
16. B. Aschenback, R. Egger, and J. Trümper, "Discovery of Explosion Fragments Outside the Vela Supernova Remnant Shock-Wave Boundary," *Nature* 373 (1995), page 588.
17. A. G. Lyne, R. S. Pritchard, F. Graham-Smith, and F. Camilo, "Very Low Braking Index for the Vela Pulsar," *Nature* 381 (1996), pages 497-498.
18. Scott A. Elias, Susan K. Short, C. Hans Nelson, and Hilary H. Birks, "Life and Times of the Bering Land Bridge," *Nature* 382 (1996), pages 61-63.
19. Elias, Short, Nelson, and Birks, "Bering Land Bridge," page 63.
20. Heiner Josenhans, Daryl Fedje, Reinhard Pienitz, and John Southon, "Early Humans and Rapidly Changing Holocene Sea Levels in the Queen Charlotte Islands—Hecate Strait, British Columbia, Canada," *Science* 277 (1997), page 71.
21. Josenhans, Fedje, Pienitz, and Southon, "Early Humans," pages 71, 73.
22. Josenhans, Fedje, Pienitz, and Southon, "Early Humans," page 73.
23. Josenhans, Fedje, Pienitz, and Southon, "Early Humans," page 71.
24. Josenhans, Fedje, Pienitz, and Southon, "Early Humans," page 74.
25. Josenhans, Fedje, Pienitz, and Southon, "Early Humans," pages 71, 73.
26. Josenhans, Fedje, Pienitz, and Southon, "Early Humans," page 73.
27. Josenhans, Fedje, Pienitz, and Southon, "Early Humans," page 74.
28. Genesis 10:25.
29. Josenhans, Fedje, Pienitz, and Southon, "Early Humans," page 73.
30. Numbers 12:1.
31. Jeremiah 13:23.
32. Genesis 9:25-27.
33. K. A. Kitchen, "Canaan, Canaanites," in *New Bible Dictionary*, 2d ed., eds. J. D. Douglas, et al. (Wheaton, IL: Tyndale House, 1982), page 165.
34. Henry M. Morris, *The Genesis Record* (Grand Rapids, MI: Baker, 1976), page 234.
35. John 2:1-10.
36. 1 Timothy 5:23.
37. Manfred Heun, et al., "Site of Einkorn Wheat Domestication Identified by DNA Fingerprinting," *Science* 278 (1997), pages 1312-1314.
38. Jared Diamond, "Location, Location, Location: The First Farmers," *Science* 278 (1997), pages 1243-1244.
39. Melinda A. Zeder and Brian Hesse, "The Initial Domestication of Goats (Capra hircus) in the Zagros Mountains 10,000 Years Ago," *Science* 287 (2000), pages 2254-2257.

Twenty-One: Dispelling Myth About Genesis

1. David B. Gurallnik, ed. in chief, *Webster's New World Dictionary of the American Language*, 2d college ed. (New York: William Collins + World Publishing, 1978), page 942.
2. Van Wolde, *Stories of the Beginning: Genesis 1–11 and Other Creation Stories*, trans. John Bowden (Ridgefield, CT: Morehouse Publishing, 1997), page 1.
3. Roger Penrose, *Shadows of the Mind* (New York: Oxford University Press, 1994), pages 64-116.
4. 1 Thessalonians 5:21.
5. Romans 1:18-20.

Appendix A: Biblical Origins of the Scientific Method

1. 1 Chronicles 16:30.
2. Psalm 93:1.
3. Psalm 96:10.
4. Psalm 104:5.
5. James Broderick, *Galileo: The Man, His Work, His Misfortunes* (New York: Harper and Row, 1964), pages 75-78.
6. 1 Thessalonians 5:21.
7. 1 John 4:1.
8. Acts 17:11.
9. Revelation 2:2.
10. Romans 12:2.
11. Job 34:4.
12. R. Laird Harris, Gleason L. Archer, and Bruce K. Waltke, *Theological Wordbook of the Old Testament*, vol. 1 (Chicago: Moody, 1980), pages 51-52.
13. Joseph H. Thayer, *Thayer's Greek-English Lexicon of the New Testament* (Grand Rapids, MI: Baker, 1977), pages 512-513.
14. James 2:18.
15. Thomas F. Torrance, *Theology in Reconstruction* (Grand Rapids, MI: Eerdmans, 1965).
16. Thomas F. Torrance, *Reality and Scientific Theology* (Edinburgh, U.K.: Scottish Academic Press, 1985).
17. Thomas F. Torrance, "Ultimate and Penultimate Beliefs in Science," in *Facets of Faith & Science, Volume I: Historiography and Modes of Interaction*, ed. Jitse M. van der Meer (New York: University Press of America, 1996), pages 151-176.

Appendix B: Word Studies in Genesis 1

1. R. Laird Harris, Gleason L. Archer, and Bruce K. Waltke, *Theological Wordbook of the Old Testament*, vols. 1 & 2 (Chicago: Moody, 1980).
2. William Gesenius, *Gesenius' Hebrew-Chaldee Lexicon to the Old Testament* (Grand Rapids, MI: Baker, 1979).
3. Francis Brown, S. R. Driver, and Charles A. Briggs, *A Hebrew and English Lexicon of the Old Testament* (Oxford, UK: Clarendon Press, 1968).
4. James Strong, "A Concise Dictionary of the Words in the Hebrew Bible," in *Strong's Exhaustive Concordance of the Bible* (McLean, VA: MacDonald Publishing).

INDEX

ABOUT THE AUTHOR

HUGH ROSS earned a B.Sc. in physics from the University of British Columbia and an M.Sc. and Ph.D. in astronomy from the University of Toronto. For several years he continued his research on quasars and galaxies as a post-doctoral fellow at the California Institute of Technology. For eleven years he served as minister of evangelism at Sierra Madre Congregational Church.

Today he directs the efforts of Reasons to Believe, an institute founded to research and proclaim the factual basis for faith in God and His Word, the Bible. He also hosts a weekly television program called "Reasons to Believe" on the Trinity Broadcasting Network and a weekly live call-in radio program on several stations throughout the United States. Over the years Dr. Ross has given hundreds of lectures, seminars, and courses, both in the United States and abroad, on Christian apologetics. He is the author of *The Fingerprint of God, The Creator and the Cosmos, Creation and Time,* and *Beyond the Cosmos.* He lives in southern California with his wife, Kathy, and sons, Joel and David.

ABOUT REASONS TO BELIEVE

REASONS TO BELIEVE is a nonprofit organization, without denominational affiliation, adhering to the doctrinal statements of the National Association of Evangelicals and of the International Council on Biblical Inerrancy. It provides research and teaching on the harmony of God's revelation in the words of the Bible and in the facts of nature. Speakers are available for churches, business clubs, university outreaches, and so on. A hotline for those with questions or a desire to dialogue on issues pertaining to faith, science, and the Bible operates at (626) 335-5282, seven days a week, 5:00-7:00 P.M. Pacific Time.

A news magazine or a catalog of materials may be obtained by phoning (800) 482-7836 or by writing to: Reasons to Believe, P.O. Box 5978, Pasadena, CA 91117.

The e-mail address is reasons@reasons.org.
The Web site is http://www.reasons.org.

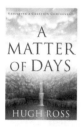